Forgotten Heroes of
WORLD WAR II

Forgotten Heroes of

WORLD WAR II

Personal Accounts
of Ordinary Soldiers—
Land, Sea, and Air

Second Edition

Thomas E. Simmons

TAYLOR TRADE PUBLISHING
Lanham • Boulder • New York • London

Published by Taylor Trade Publishing
An imprint of The Rowman & Littlefield Publishing Group, Inc.
4501 Forbes Boulevard, Suite 200, Lanham, Maryland 20706
www.rowman.com

Unit A, Whitacre Mews, 26–34 Stannery Street, London SE11 4AB, United Kingdom

Distributed by NATIONAL BOOK NETWORK

British Library Cataloguing in Publication Information Available

Library of Congress Cataloging-in-Publication Data Available

ISBN 978-1-58979-963-9 (pbk. : alk. paper)
ISBN 978-1-58979-964-6 (electronic)

∞ ™ The paper used in this publication meets the minimum requirements of
American National Standard for Information Sciences—Permanence of Paper for Printed
Library Materials, ANSI/NISO Z39.48-1992.

Printed in the United States of America

There is not a man, woman, or child today whose life has not been affected by the residue of World War II. Nor has any armed conflict since then not been related in some way to the greatest war of the twentieth century. Without vivid, up-close, and personal stories from the men and women who fought that war, the history of the war becomes a lifeless chronology. What follows is a fleeting glimpse of this very personal side. Even after more than half a century, it was not easy for the individuals whose stories are recounted here to share those stories. I thank each of them for doing so. This work is dedicated to them.

Contents

Prologue

WORLD WAR II was a time of thunder and flash, confusion and fear, and destruction and death on a scale never seen before or since. Although historians seem to focus on great generals, pivotal battles, unit histories, and the grand scheme of campaigns, wars are fought in bits and pieces by the combined efforts of individuals who, in the aftermath, are often forgotten. War correspondent Martha Gellhorn wrote of them, "There are those who received brief, poor or no recognition, all those history leaves unmentioned, not because they are lesser, but because they are too many." Those young men and women of whom she spoke, those who survived, those who know what the struggle was really like on an individual basis, are fading away. As a person I wanted to find some way to thank them. As a writer, I began a quest several years ago to preserve at least the stories of the few I knew, the ones I thought might trust me to record some small measure of what they did, what they gave, and the cost.

What follows is a collection of their unique stories of war, up close and personal, told without pretense or apology by those who lived them. At first they were reluctant to lay themselves bare, to unburden the memories they had been unable to confide even to their families. Each man thought himself no different from those around him, especially those who never came home. That was true insofar as they were all young, scared, miserable, and entangled in the sweeping current, chaos, and carnage of a world war. Yet they did their duty. They were the ordinary, the extraordinary . . . the now forgotten.

At first, without exception, these men refused to talk about the war when I first approached them. All made similar statements: There's really not much to tell. I was just there like everyone else. All

I wanted to do was get home. Each was uncomfortable at being singled out to speak of experiences he felt were common to so many others. Each professed, "It was so long ago I don't remember much."

I was gently persistent, beginning with simple questions. In each case a strange thing happened. Speaking quietly, shyly, honestly, and often painfully, vivid experiences began to flood from bottled-up memories that had been locked away decades ago, locked away because they were painful and because those who were not there, including loved ones, could surely never understand. Once memory's gate was opened, each man spoke with clear recall in remarkable detail.

None of them could ever be made to believe that they are heroes. To even mention the word would embarrass them. Yet for these men, and millions like them who faced mortal danger, and who in spite of fear, often terror, stood their watch and did their duty, what other word is there?

Each story handed to me was both a gift and a burden of trust. I have tried to present them truthfully, respectfully, and without embellishment. My hope is that the reader will be informed of a time when ordinary men sacrificed their innocence and youth, and somehow found their courage in a sea of fear, at a time when the world teetered between enslavement and freedom. At the time, Gellhorn said of them, "You wonder what happens to divisions of brave men after the war. And you wonder who is going to thank them and how and will it be enough?" The young Americans of whom she spoke then are now leaving us. It will soon be too late to thank them. It will never be too late to remember what they did.

ACKNOWLEDGMENTS

In writing acknowledgments, an author is ever fearful someone deserving credit will be left out. If that happens here, please forgive me. All of the following talented people helped make this book possible.

At Cumberland House for the first edition: Ron Pitkin, Ed Curtis, Julie Jayne, Stacie Bauerle (who had her first baby in the middle of it all), and Gabby Benson. At Taylor Trade for this

expanded second edition: Flannery Scott, Rick Rinehart, Karie Simpson, Laurie Kenney, Alden Perkins, and proofreader Susan Barnett. And I am ever grateful to my agent, Jeanie Loiacono.

Above all, I give my sincerest gratitude to the men who reluctantly, often painfully, revealed experiences kept so deep inside that they had never shared them even with their families. Told for the first time in the pages of this book, the reader will be taken on a personal, up-close journey through World War II. Through words, which never seem enough, I tried to show that victory was won by the individual efforts of hundreds of thousands of ordinary yet extraordinarily dedicated young men and women, just like the ones within the following pages. I am deeply honored to have known each contributor, those present and those now absent, and to have been privileged to call them by that most cherished word, friend.

Author's Note

Each of the stories presented herein originated with the memories of the men who lived them. Some might think that memories of events that took place fifty or more years in the past may be flawed—details lost, jumbled, or confused. For that very reason the memories of the men given herein were verified in terms of events, place, time, and context. These men remembered their training, units, friends, missions, and combat—often confined to what was going on fifty or a hundred yards to either side, or aboard ship, or in the formations and fighting of their squadrons in the air. What they did not and could not know or understand at the time was the "big picture." In order to ensure accuracy of the stories presented in these pages, I researched historical records, including official unit histories, action reports, battle plans, their execution and results, corresponding weather, geography, maps, location details, enemy reports, weapons, uniforms, rations, individual issued equipment, weapons, vehicles, boats, ships, and aircraft. Untold hours of research verified each man's story. It was/is astonishing to discover that their memories, so starkly imprinted during horrendous events and locked away in the closets of their minds unrevealed to anyone including family members, proved accurate right down to the smallest details. If that proved not the case, an individual's story could not be included herein.

The work necessary to confirm and authenticate the chapters contained in this work was both exhaustive and, for me, exhausting. There is not room here to list every source of information reviewed during the verification of stories presented herein; such a list would take up pages and pages. Having said that, I must at least present, with thanks and gratitude, a small sample of resources available, or made available, to me as follows: the National Archives;

U.S. Naval History and Heritage Command; the American Merchant Marine Museum records; U.S. Army Center of Military History; U.S. Army Vessel Lists; history of the Mississippi Air National Guard including that of the 153rd Reconnaissance Squadron; Task Force 38 and Pacific Typhoon of December 18, 1944, Department of the Navy; *The Army Air Forces in World War II*, edited by W. E. Craven and J. L. Cate; the history of Ninety-fourth Bomb Group, Fourth Air Wing; Eighth Air Force; unit history, 87th Armored Field Artillery Battalion; records of Operation Overlord, D-Day, June 6, 1944; Records of Operation Neptune, D-Day, June 6, 1944; history of the Twenty-fourth and Twenty-fifth Combat Regimental Teams, Fourth Marine Division; unit history of VMF 323 Death Rattlers Squadron; NavSource.com; Ron Swanson, historian of LCT Flotillas WWII Veterans Group; records of Operation Iceberg (the Battle of Okinawa); and the National Association of USS LCS (L) Veterans Group.

These and the vast amount of additional sources of historical information served to verify and confirm the remarkable memories of the men whose stories of combat, personal hardship, fear, courage, and duty fulfilled are presented in these pages.

T. E. Simmons

CHAPTER 1

BRUCE CREEKMUR

NO BREAKFAST FOR THE CHIEF

I T WAS SUPPOSED TO be a lazy Sunday for Chief Creekmur. He was off duty, his time his own. He slept late (7:30), dressed for shore leave, and headed for the chief's mess. The passageway smelled of coffee, ham, frying bacon. As he neared the source of those inviting aromas he heard an odd, muffled whomp! Once. Twice. He entered the chief's mess and was a few steps from the serving line when the klaxon sounded.

AARRRRROOGAA!

"Damn! Why do they have to pull a drill on Sunday?"

The country's chief concern during the 1930s was the great economic depression. Young men across the nation were desperate for jobs. Many, including Bruce Creekmur, tried to enlist in the navy. There one was promised clothing, housing, food, and a real paycheck— thirty-six dollars a month. Few men, however, were accepted. Those who were found the duty to be routine, often boring. Promotions came so slowly that many junior officers and noncoms were gray-beards. Thus in 1931 eighteen-year-old Bruce Creekmur felt lucky when the navy accepted him.

Ten long years later, in early 1941, he was awarded the rate of chief electricians mate. Chief Creekmur—Bruce liked the sound of that as well as the raise in pay and the privileges that went along with his new rating.

With the promotion came orders to report to USS *Camden,* a World War I German war prize permanently moored at the Brooklyn Navy Yard to house personnel awaiting the arrival of their various ships to which they had been newly assigned. I was twenty-nine at the time, but when I arrived aboard *Camden* I found the oldest bunch of non-commissioned officers I had ever seen. The navy had just recalled them to active duty. These old sea dogs showed up wearing World War I peaked caps and slept in nightshirts. Most of them were not the least amused at being called up. For the first time I realized neutral America was nervous about the war in Europe.

My ship, USS *Pelias,* arrived in New York on time. She was formerly the old Moore-McCormack passenger vessel SS *York,* but the ship had recently been converted into a submarine tender with repair shops and storage areas for tons of food, spare parts, torpedoes, ammunition, and fuel—everything needed to repair, refurbish, and supply submarines. I was proud to be given charge of her new electrical repair shop. *Pelias* sailed out of New York Harbor, down the East Coast and into the Caribbean, through the Panama Canal and into the Pacific to arrive at a naval station most Americans had never heard of: Pearl Harbor. When we arrived in late November 1941 nothing much was going on. It looked like an easy duty station to me.

AARRRRROOGAA! AARRRRROOGAA! Bruce was within a few feet of his ham and eggs when the ear-shattering alarm sounded for general quarters.

None of the chiefs were very excited. Those who were eating figured it was just another training exercise, plenty of time for one last sip of coffee or a last bite of biscuit as they slowly rose from their seats.

Then an incredible announcement blared out from the ship's public address system: "Battle stations! Battle stations! Man your battle stations! We are under attack. This is no drill. I say again, this is no drill."

For a moment every man in the chief's mess was frozen in place, a stunned expression on his face. Suddenly dishes and cups clattered over tabletops and trays of food were dropped to the deck as we all rushed to the doors at once.

Pelias's skipper, Comdr. William Wakefield, ran a tight ship, even in peacetime. Every man aboard knew his ship and his duty. I checked my shop first. Most of the repairmen were standing by. Then I ran up to the main deck to check my topside fire-and-damage-control team. They got to the assigned station about the same time as I arrived. Explosions echoed across the harbor, and we could see smoke rising in the sky.

"Christ!" someone yelled, and every man on deck ducked simultaneously. I can close my eyes and still see the flash of wings, red-ball insignias, long black torpedoes, roaring engines, flashing propellers crossing over our heads. The flight of planes seemed so low we could reach up and touch them.

They were making a run straight for Battleship Row across the harbor from us. We watched the planes release their ordnance and zoom skyward. Seconds later *Oklahoma* and *Nevada* were both hit. Fountains of water and flame shot up the sides of their hulls.

It was a Sunday morning in a home port. Many ships' officers were ashore. Sailors on their own initiative broke open locked magazines and struggled to get ammunition to the antiaircraft guns. Feeble at first, defensive gunfire grew in volume. An attacking enemy plane turned out over the harbor trailing heavy black smoke.

"My God!" someone nearby said. I looked up to see the battleship *Arizona* completely enveloped in a huge fireball. Seconds later we felt the shock wave of the explosion.

It had only been a few minutes since the alarm had sounded aboard *Pelias,* and already clouds of smoke had erupted all across the harbor—great black clouds punctured by flashes of exploding bombs, torpedoes, and ships' ammunition. Thousands of barrels of heavy bunker fuel oozed thickly across the water from ruptured tanks, then ignited. The oily flames surrounded ships and torched docks, blocking any hope of escape from the conflagration or rescue. Fires raged ashore as well. Ford Island's main water lines ran directly beneath the *Arizona's* berth. When she settled to the bottom heavily, she severed the island's primary source of water. Firefighters stood helplessly watching hangars, aircraft, fuel tanks, buildings, everything burn out of control.

Pelias was a front-row seat from which her men and officers watched the entire attack. For a few seconds, maybe minutes, I felt completely isolated. Everything was happening across the harbor. It was as if we were in a surrealistic dream colored by chaos. I remember having no feelings of fear or anger, in fact, no feelings at all. I stood there . . . numb.

This kind of shock descends on the safe and uninjured when they witness terrible destruction "just over there." The men on *Pelias* were close enough to see the flames, hear the thunder, the terrible rending screech of steel, yet too far away to see the dying or hear their screams. Time was compressed, expanded, or frozen in the minds of those who watched.

Breaking the spell was another flight of Japanese planes roaring low over *Pelias,* so low that those on deck ducked once again. The sky was full of enemy aircraft. When those planes were free of their bombs and torpedoes, they joined the fighters in strafing targets of opportunity. There was already blood on their feathers—now from all quadrants they screamed down to peck and claw for more.

I do not remember how long it took for *Pelias's* gun crews to break out their ammunition and open fire with the only defensive weapons the ship had: two obsolete single-shot 3-inch guns. The ship was directly under the flight path of Japanese planes attacking Battleship Row, although the vessel was not designated a target. Our old gunnery officer (he had been a young sailor aboard the Great White Fleet during its world cruise in 1905) was as tough as sun-cured rawhide. He knew his stuff and had seen to it that his gun crews knew theirs. "Forget the harbor. Turn the guns to shore and catch 'em coming in over us."

Out of the 432 attacking Japanese planes, 29 were shot down. *Pelias* was credited with one of them. "Flew down the —ing gun barrel!" the old salt later said in explanation.

In the middle of the attack, one skipper got his sub under way and came alongside *Pelias.* I can't remember the sub's name, but Commander Wakefield was on the bridge at the railing. The sub's skipper yelled up, "Sir, I need fuel, torpedoes, ammunition, food, and spare parts. We plan to go after those bastards." Commander Wakefield then yelled to us, "You heard the man. Let's get to work!" We did.

Shortly after 9 A.M., less than an hour after they had arrived, the enemy planes departed. Left in their wake was more wreckage, horror, and death than any other single attack in the history of naval warfare. The roar of planes dissipated into silence, but great, foul clouds of putrid smoke, roiled by the fury of fires beyond control, spoiled the bright, empty, blue sky.

Confusion ruled at every level. Trained fire and rescue teams, hopelessly overwhelmed, were joined by spontaneously organized groups of volunteers—sailors, soldiers, cooks, clerks, civilians. Damage control teams fought to save their ships. Military and civilian hospitals overflowed with the injured. Temporary morgues were set up. Unit commanders aboard ship and onshore were trying desperately to reach their duty stations, find their men, and determine the extent of casualties and damage.

In the midst of the chaos, the paramount concern pressing heavily on the command staff was Will there be another attack? Or, God forbid, an invasion? There was little left in Hawaii to prevent either.

By early afternoon the initial damage reports reached Washington over the navy's new rapid communication system. The magnitude of the situation became shockingly clear to the War Department and the president. Following the attack at Pearl Harbor, the Japanese navy was undisputedly the mightiest in the world. Of most concern was the status of American naval forces in the Pacific. At the time, all that stood between Japan and America were a few subs, wooden PT boats, a handful of old destroyers, a cruiser or two, and hopefully still afloat somewhere at sea, three aircraft carriers.

Darkness provided no relief from the scenes of destruction. Pearl Harbor was illuminated by flames.

We were all afraid the Japs would return after dark and try to finish the job by firelight. We had nothing but a few antiaircraft guns. Sometime well after dark, I was standing on deck when I heard the distinctive sound of approaching aircraft. A few seconds later searchlights from all quarters of the harbor blazed on, lacing the sky with blinding shafts of light. I looked up to see a formation of planes caught, ghostlike, in the stark white beams. Then all hell broke loose. Every serviceable antiaircraft gun in the harbor opened up. The planes, illuminated in a sky filled with tracers, frantically scattered in every direction, weaving, diving, climbing, all desperate to escape. No bombs dropped—nothing. The guns suddenly stopped, and the searchlights were shut off. We didn't know exactly what had happened, only that something had gone badly wrong.

Fortunately, when the Japanese attack occurred, the U.S. carrier group was at sea on a training exercise. Immediately upon receiving word of the raid, the carriers steamed for Pearl Harbor at flank speed. When barely within range, *Enterprise* launched her planes for Pearl under orders to maintain radio silence. They were sent as the only air defense available to Hawaii following the attack. Aircraft from the other carriers could not be spared, because they were the only protection the carriers had. And at that moment, the carriers were the only major operational U.S. naval task force in the Pacific.

The reception given the arriving navy planes by the frightened sailors below scared the hell out of the unsuspecting pilots above. Worse, the planes had no choice but to doggedly continue inbound for landing. Launched at maximum range, they were all but out of fuel. Shot at, shot up, furious that some of their fellow pilots were casualties of friendly fire, the surviving pilots landed their planes on dark and damaged runways strewn with debris. (Rumor has it that later that night the officers' club was raided of a fair sum of "medicinal alcohol" by a very annoyed group of naval aviators, some sporting bandages, who had sweated themselves into a state of dehydration sometime between leaving *Enterprise* and entering the bar.)

The friendly fire fiasco had been caused by the second major communications foul-up in less than twenty-four hours. (The first had happened that morning. For reasons never satisfactorily explained, Army Gen. George C. Marshall insisted on sending a coded general warning to Pearl Harbor from Washington by Western Union telegram rather than use the navy's rapid communication system, which was made available to him. As a result, the message that could have arrived in time to warn Pearl Harbor before the attack was not received and decoded until hours after the attack.) Word of the incoming friendly planes, their course, and estimated time of arrival failed to reach the antiaircraft gunners in time to prevent their firing on the American aircraft.

The next morning, December 8, *Pelias* was called upon for a rescue mission. The captain called me to the bridge and told me to take a team with flame-cutting tools to the *Oklahoma*. She had "turned turtle," rolled on her back during the attack. Many claimed to hear banging coming from inside her, near the stern.

When we reached her, we climbed onto the exposed bottom. I tapped a hammer a few times and immediately had a response: Someone was alive down there. I tapped a few more times, using the answering taps to determine as best we could their position. First, we cut a small hole with the torch then stuck a hose through and started pumping in fresh air. If we had just started cutting a large hole, the torch might have burned up all the remaining oxygen or started a fire that would have suffocated whoever was down there before we could free them. (That reportedly happened during a similar rescue attempt where such precautions were not taken.)

The men aboard ship had already been down there for more than twenty-four hours and probably didn't have much oxygen left. It took a while to burn a hole through the thick bottom plates and framing below. We finally cut our way through into the aft steering engine room.

I peered into the dark hole and saw a couple of anxious faces looking back. A moment later there was a whole chorus of voices shouting up at us. We hauled eight men out of that hole. How they survived the overturning of the ship and found their way to a compartment with trapped air, I don't know. They were too happy at being alive and out of there to talk about it, but it must have been hell.

The same thought occurred to all of us—God help any men trapped in air pockets deep inside a ship. Hard-helmet divers were already surveying the damaged ships, but it was unlikely they could get to anyone trapped inside one of them.

On the third day, December 9, the captain asked me to take a salvage team aboard the battleship *Arizona*. We were to conduct a survey of any recoverable electrical components we could find: controls, switches, cable, communication gear, motors, light fixtures, electrical cabinets, junction boxes, anything that might still be of use. Repair of

U.S. NAVAL HISTORICAL CENTER

Three days after the bombing of Pearl Harbor, the wreck of the *Arizona* was cool enough to allow men like Bruce Creekmur to begin salvage operations.

the least damaged ships, the ones that could be returned to service quickest, had already begun, but parts, especially electrical parts, were in short supply.

We had to wait until the third day because it took that long for *Arizona's* hull and superstructure to cool down and allow anyone to board her. We didn't know it at the time, but my team would be the first to set foot on her since the fiery explosions that put her on the bottom. We crossed the harbor in a motor lifeboat. The water was foul with oil, charred debris, and bloated bodies. I tried not to look as we passed boat crews pulling bodies and pieces of bodies from the harbor. I thought our job was going to be easier than theirs. I was wrong.

Arizona was sitting on the bottom with most of her main deck and superstructure still above water. All we had to do to board that once mighty ship was to come alongside and step from our little boat directly onto her deck. Her plates were twisted and buckled, her teak decks burned to charcoal. Every inch of steel superstructure from the deck to the top of the mast was corroded from fire. And she was still radiating heat; all the metal structure was warm to the touch.

The forward half of the ship was twisted and buckled where she had taken direct bomb hits on her superstructure and forward gun turrets. There just wasn't much left up there.

A few yards toward the stern we came upon the first of many anti-aircraft gun tubs. *Arizona* had tried to defend herself. The crews had gotten to the guns, loaded them, returned fire. We knew that because they were still at their posts. A pair of charred earphones remained fitted to the blackened skull of the first gunner I saw. I wondered if the man's ears might still be in them. If so, they would be the only flesh left. From the earphones down, there was nothing but charred bones all the way to what had been a pair of shoes. As horrible as that was, other remains were worse. We came upon some that still had chunks of charred flesh and muscle hanging raggedly from bones. The worst were the bodies that still had facial skin, black, sometimes with streaks of pink, drawn into grotesquely twisted, eyeless expressions, the nose and ears burned away, the lips melted to expose teeth in a grim grin. The smell was terrible, unforgettable. Burned ship, burned oil, burned flesh. You never forget that odor.

I climbed up the tall observation tower to the observation and control center. It was leaning about thirty degrees and was awkward to climb. High up in the cab I found two bodies, the only ones we found not completely burned. They were more cooked than charred; their uniforms hadn't been burned away. A pair of binoculars was lying near one of them. They must have seen it all. Seen the dive bombers and torpedo planes coming at them, felt the concussion of the explosions, maybe lived long enough to see the flames come up all around them. I hope not. If the explosions didn't kill them or knock them unconscious, they died terribly hard.

We didn't disturb the dead. God pity those who later had to collect them. We just did our job, listing anything that might be usable. There wasn't much.

On my way down the deck back to our boat, I noticed a blown skylight above the ship's galley and looked in. It wasn't completely flooded. Sitting on counters and tables were rows of blackened turkeys. They were to have been Sunday dinner for *Arizona's* crew.

I've never been able to forget what we saw that day. It's still so vivid in my memory that I have to turn away from charred meat. I can't do a backyard barbecue, can't look at steaks or roast beef that are charred on the outside. I just can't. I don't dream about it much any-more . . . but sometimes . . .

About the only items salvaged from *Arizona* were the big guns from her aft turrets. Her superstructure was cut away for scrap, and her massive hull left sitting on the bottom with a few ragged steel plates breaching the surface to mark her grave. Someone raised a mast with an American flag on her, and warships returning to Pearl initiated the custom of saluting her and her crew, the twelve hundred or so of them that remain aboard her to this day. There, down below, far from the battle's flame, they are cooled by clear tropical water only slightly soiled by threads of oil that, after more than half a century, still seep slowly up to mark the shimmering surface with rainbow-colored tears.

BRUCE CREEKMUR came home in 1945, a lieutenant commander, and married his long-time sweetheart, Edith.

CHAPTER 2

EDWARD HAWKINS ANDERSON

A Bizarre Tale of April Fools

A WEEK INTO THE FIRST patrol, a lookout spotted two aircraft, the first they had seen. One of the boat's jobs was to rescue downed pilots. Maybe one of the approaching planes was in trouble and planned to ditch beside the boat. The crew watched curiously as the aircraft made a slow, graceful, descending turn astern and lined up behind L-430. Suddenly the water on either side of the vessel erupted into small geysers of water, and her deck crackled and sparked as the aircraft opened fire. When the planes flashed by overhead, the nineteen-year-old lieutenant looked up in time to glimpse red-meatball insignias on the gray underside of their wings. Then they were gone, disdaining to make a second run on so unworthy a target. Or maybe they were low on fuel. The Japanese fighters disappeared over the horizon toward some Pacific island home.

Spring is a season when young men's thoughts turn to adventure. So it was on April Fools' Day 1942 (three months after Pearl Harbor). At five that morning, Edward Hawkins Anderson, freshman engineering student at Mississippi State College, and three classmates took off from the campus bound for New Orleans in Ed's 1930 Ford roadster.

11

After driving nearly eight hours on mostly gravel highways, the dusty foursome found themselves cruising Canal Street and primed for a good time. A few blocks shy of Bourbon Street, Ed's roommate, Sumrall, called attention to a large poster of Uncle Sam in front of a recruiting center.

"STOP!" Sumrall insisted. "Lets go in and tell 'em we're signing up."

"Are you crazy? We have a college deferment."

"Yeah, dummy. We're in ROTC. We'll be on active duty soon enough."

"Remember what day this is?" Sumrall insisted. "Come on. I'll yell 'April Fools,' and we'll run like hell. Park this thing, Ed. Anybody doesn't follow me in is a chicken. Just don't trip on the way out."

They walked in as a group, ready for the cue to run, but each man quickly found himself sitting in a booth separated from the others with a no-nonsense recruiting sergeant for company. Twenty minutes later the good-time boys had a discussion on the street.

"Sumrall, you dumb bastard, why the hell didn't you yell 'April Fools'?"

"When we all got separated by those guys," he explained, "I couldn't figure out when to say it."

"Well the damn joke's on us, you dimwit. We couldn't just get up and run out like a bunch of cowards. We're all in the army."

"Not me," Sumrall replied.

They looked as though they might kill him, then he grinned and said, "I'm in the marines."

Following the recruiters' instructions, Sumrall went in one direction while I drove the three of us army recruits to Jackson Barracks, where we filled out a stack of papers, passed physical examinations, and reported to a distinctly humorless sergeant. He told us it was too late in the day to draw uniforms from supply and assigned each of us to a bunk. I told him I left my car out front and asked where I was supposed to park it.

"You won't be needing it," he said. "Better get rid of it while you have a chance."

I hadn't been in the army two hours, and I hated it already. Doggedly I drove my roadster back to Canal Street. It was old, the ragtop leaked, and the paint job wasn't too good (I had painted it with a brush), but I sure hated to part with it. I sold it for twenty-five dollars and caught a bus back to the barracks and felt pretty low.

The next morning, several names were called out at breakfast, mine among them. This small group reported to some captain who said he had reviewed our enlistment papers and knew that each of us had had some college ROTC. Then he asked if any of us would like a commission.

Someone inquired about the difference in pay. He said, "Thirty dollars a month as a private, or $125 a month as a second lieutenant." I think all but one of the group went for it. He might have been smarter than the rest of us.

The captain told those of us who had accepted the offer to follow him down the hall. He led us into the office of a brigadier general who swore us in as second lieutenants right then and there.

After the brief ceremony, the captain asked, "All right, how many of you lieutenants have had some experience with boats?"

Like a fool, I raised my hand. He asked me a few questions, and I told him that I had occasionally run my dad's thirty-foot cabin cruiser to Ship Island and back. The captain wrote down the information and instructed all of us to report back to the medical clinic.

I guess they hadn't looked too closely at our teeth the first time around, because they sat me down and gave me eleven fillings. I squeezed the arms of that chair so hard my handprints are still there. Immediately afterward I was sent to a line of inductees where I received thirteen immunization shots.

From the clinic, we all reported to the finance office where we were each given a $120 clothing allowance and a list of articles to buy from the downtown stores. (Officers weren't issued uniforms from army supply; they had to buy their own.)

It was nearly four in the afternoon before we started downtown to make our purchases. We got as far as Mack's Bar on Canal Street, where a sign in the window proclaimed: Oysters on the half shell—40¢ a dozen, Beer—5¢ a glass. None of us had eaten a thing since breakfast. Someone made up a contest—the fellow who ate and drank the least paid the bill for all. By the time we staggered out the front door of Mack's, most of the uniform shops were closed. I managed to buy an overseas cap and an army shirt from a combination army-navy store and pawn shop. No sweat. As a group, we figured we would get our uniforms the next morning.

We were a happy bunch until we returned to base to find a very unhappy sergeant. He snapped at us like a bulldog, "You were supposed to report back here at 1730 hours." Someone mumbled, "What the hell time is that?" The sergeant ignored the question. "Here are your assignments, gentlemen," and handed a mimeographed sheet to each man.

At the top of the list I saw my name: Anderson, E. W., 2nd Lt. Alongside it was the notation: "is hereby ordered to proceed immediately to Poland Street Wharf, New Orleans, Louisiana, and report to vessel LT-430."

I said something like, "Damn, Sarge, what's going on?" He said he didn't know, but that I better get a move on. (You might think I'm making all this up, but I promise it's all just the way it happened!)

I tried to call my parents, but no one was home. Then the sergeant saw me in the phone booth and told me to get going. I packed what little I had into an overnight bag: a shaving kit, two changes of underwear, socks, two shirts, an extra pair of pants—the clothes I had brought from Mississippi State for what was supposed to be a "fun" weekend—and the regulation army overseas cap and khaki shirt I had purchased earlier. I had a military identification card but no dog tag and no insignia of rank. The little amount of money I'd brought with me from State, the twenty-five dollars I'd gotten for my car, and the uniform money the army had given me was in my pocket. That was all I had.

While other recruits were heading for bus and train stations en route to training camps, I was left wondering where I was going. Things were moving faster than I could comprehend. I was a nineteen-year-old kid suddenly caught up in a situation I couldn't have imagined. Feeling about as alone and scared as I ever had, I went out on the street to flag a taxi.

By the time I reached the Poland Street Wharf it was dark. Wearing civilian clothes and clutching my small canvas bag with Mississippi State College printed across it, I walked out onto a deserted wharf. There wasn't a ship or anything I could see, just old warehouses.

An armed guard stepped out of the shadows and yelled, "Hey, buddy, this is a restricted area. What are you doing here?"

I told him I was supposed to report to a ship and gave him my orders. He took out a flashlight and examined them then pointed down the dock to a white light twelve or so feet above the dock. "That light down there," was all he said.

The river was about twenty-two feet below the dock, and the light was at the top of a boat's masthead. I looked down at a 125-foot U.S. Army seagoing tugboat, the LT-430. The only other person around was an older man sitting on the cabin top aft of the pilothouse. He was dressed in khaki pants but wore no shirt. He was barefooted and busy shining the shoes he probably wore regularly.

I climbed down a ladder tied to the dock and said something like, "Hey, bub, who do you report to around here?"

"To the captain," he said with a heavy Norse accent.

"Well, where can I find him?" I asked.

"You're talking to him," he replied.

The captain was Norwegian. I didn't know it, but when Germany invaded Norway, most of Norway's merchant ships at sea put in to Allied ports where their crews volunteered for Allied service. The captain of LT-430 was one of them. I told him my name and added "sir" to try and make up for calling him "bub."

He looked over my orders. "Anderson. That's a good Nordic name. What do you know about navigation, Lieutenant?"

I answered, "Nothing!"

"How are you at math?" he asked.

I told him that math was my best subject, that I was studying engineering at college.

"Excellent," he said and went into the wheelhouse. When he returned he handed me three small leatherbound books and a sextant and told me to study them. I had never seen a sextant.

With hardly another word the captain showed me to one of the tiny officers staterooms below. I placed the books and the instrument on a small desk.

He pointed to them. "You need to learn how to use the tables in those books and the sextant to find your position." As he was leaving, he turned and said, "I almost forgot. Congratulations, Lieutenant. You are our new navigator." I was stunned, but before I could say anything, he added, "You have the watch at 0800 in the morning," and walked out of the cabin.

Late that night I was reading up on navigating when the rest of the crew began to drift back aboard. Some looked like gangsters, some like kids. A few were even sober. One came in and introduced himself as Jack White and said that he was first mate and would be sharing my cabin. Talking to Jack, I discovered that the only army personnel aboard was a buck sergeant, who would be the radio operator, and me. The other twenty-two men of the crew, including the captain, were merchant seamen.

So far the army wasn't anything like what I thought it would be. I went to sleep with the hope that some bureaucratic mistake had been made and that it would all be straightened out in a day or two.

I awoke the next morning, April 3, to the rumbling sound of two twelve-hundred-horsepower diesel engines. The boat was under way. After a 6 A.M. breakfast, the captain took everyone not on watch for a tour of the vessel, emphasizing machinery, equipment, and operating and emergency procedures.

At the end of the tour he informed us that we were going downriver to be degaussed, explaining that was a process to demagnetize the steel hull with electric current to protect it from magnetic mines. With that happy thought, I went to the pilothouse to take up my "watch." I wasn't sure what having the watch meant other than standing in the wheelhouse out of everyone's way.

After we degaussed somewhere below New Orleans, the Department of Agriculture marched aboard and sprayed the boat and each crewman from stem to stern with enough DDT to kill an elephant. We then untied and proceeded farther downriver. I had never been on the river and stayed on deck to watch the land fade into marsh.

Right after dark, the captain called me out on deck in private and asked, "How well have you memorized the books?" I told him the truth, that I had not had time to do more than glance through them. "Lieutenant," he said, "as I explained when you came aboard, you are our navigator." Then he told me to look back astern. In the moonlight I was startled to count a string of eight other tugs following us. The captain continued, "We are fortunate to have you in the crew. That's why we are leading those other boats, Lieutenant. Not one of them even has a navigator."

He motioned me to followed him back into the wheelhouse where he pointed to the chart table. "I want you to set a course for Panama."

"Panama City, Florida?" I asked.

"No, Lieutenant, Colón, Panama," was his reply.

PANAMA! I had no military training other than a little college ROTC. I had been made an officer and assigned duty as navigator on an army boat on its way to Panama. I had been in the army all of three days.

The captain stood in the wheelhouse waiting. I had never set a course in my life. Never used a chart. At home I just followed buoys to get to Ship Island and back.

I bent over the chart table, put a few charts together, took a long straight edge, and simply drew a line from the mouth of the Mississippi river across the charts to the one that had Panama on it. Then I figured out how to use parallel rulers and came up with a magnetic course. I didn't know what magnetic variation and deviation were, didn't know how to figure true course, or that you had to calculate drift from tide and current tables, or which end of a sextant to look through. I gave the captain my course, and he ordered the helmsman to follow it. I had never felt so lost, lonely, and inept.

Soon, in the moonlight, we left the river and entered the Gulf of Mexico. That's when the skipper announced to the crew, "We are under orders to maintain radio silence. German U-boats have been reported in the Gulf. I expect every man to stay alert." With warnings of mines and U-boats, the captain had definitely gotten the crew's attention, at least the young ones like me who had not gone to sea before.

Fourteen hours later, April 4, I was on watch. In the dim gray before dawn I thought I saw something in the water. I looked through a pair of binoculars for the first time in my life and picked up a periscope cutting the water several hundred yards off the port bow. I yelled "Submarine!" as loud as I could.

Wearing nothing but undershorts, the captain rushed into the wheelhouse and saw the sub surface a few hundred yards away. It signaled us by blinker light. He, the mate, and the army sergeant were the only ones aboard who knew Morse code. We complied with their signal to come alongside.

Someone on the sub yelled, "Just where the hell are y'all going? We received orders to report your position if we saw you. You're lucky we found you. You're WAY OFF COURSE."

The captain acknowledged that he knew that but said he was conducting navigation training. No one had told him about a sub escort.

An officer on the sub yelled, "We'll see you in Panama—if you can find your way there!"

After the sub submerged, the captain motioned me over to the chart table. He pointed out our position and told me to give him a new course to Colón. I drew a new course line and gave it to him.

He looked at it. "Lieutenant, you and I are going to make a deal. I could do your job for you and get us to Panama in three days, but you are the navigator. The deal is that I'm going to give you the honor of navigating all nine of these tugs there if it takes you three months. Now go below and read your books, practice using that sextant, and start recording our daily positions. I'll help you learn, but I won't do it for you. By the way, we have only thirty days' supply of fuel and food."

The next night while I was on watch, a brilliant white light appeared directly ahead. All ships were running blacked out. I hadn't seen a light the whole way. I thought it must be the spotlight of a warship and woke up the captain. As we steamed toward the light, it began to separate into smaller lights. I was more than a little embarrassed as we got a few miles closer and could clearly see that the lights formed the words Havana Hotel. I don't know why the sign was turned on—the rest of the coast was blacked out—but if it hadn't appeared, I would have run the boat straight into Cuba.

The captain didn't say a word. He just shook his head and went back to bed.

This young navigator was very proud when on April 9 LT-430 and the eight tugs following it steamed into the Panama Canal. I made it in six days. Miles up the canal when the string of tugs entered the first lock, we found our submarine, the crew of which gleefully expressed in very colorful language what they thought of "those damn army boats."

When LT-430 reached the Pacific end of the Panama Canal at Balboa, the crew was allowed ashore for the first time since leaving New Orleans. I found that I couldn't walk straight. Twice I fell down.

I had been seasick most of the way and was unable to stop rocking when I stepped on dry land. It took me about three hours to get my land legs back. We went to what old hands called the Club House. It had a large comfortable lounge area, a snack bar with a jukebox, hamburgers, ice cream, milkshakes, and a PX-type store. I bought two khaki shirts, two pairs of pants, and shoes, all they had that would fit me at the time, but they were out of second lieutenant insignia.

At the cigarette counter, I ran into Jack Farmer, a friend from Gulfport High. It turned out that he was a merchant seaman homeward bound. I asked him to call my folks when he got home, explaining that they thought I was still at State College.

Anderson's story to this point seems either like a fantasy or the comical result of some bureaucratic foul-up. It was neither. His one-day promotion to lieutenant and immediate dispatch to war was neither accidental nor uncommon during the months following the attack on Pearl Harbor. The U.S. Navy was badly crippled from that attack. The army air corps and land-based naval air units in Hawaii and the Philippines had been virtually annihilated. The U.S., Philippine, and British armies in the Pacific were being wiped out or taken prisoner at Bataan, Corregidor, Luzon, Hong Kong, Singapore, and Wake Island. Much of China was occupied. Burma and New Guinea were under siege, and Australia was threatened. By April 1942 the effective Allied naval and land force presence in the Pacific essentially ceased to exist. The entire western Pacific had become a "Sea of Japan."

General MacArthur, ordered to escape the Philippines, barely made it aboard an eighty-five-foot PT boat, the only type of vessel then available in which to make the attempt. His job was to get to Australia and somehow build a new army for the Pacific campaign. In the meantime, a cruiser or two, a few destroyers, PT boats, submarines, unarmed utility craft, and three aircraft carriers were all that was available to face the entire Japanese onslaught.

Without seriously preparing the country for war, the U.S. president and Congress had watched the evolution of war spread from

China to the Pacific to Europe to Africa to the North Atlantic and to the Mediterranean. By January 1942 the United States found itself losing wars on two fronts. All of Western Europe had fallen, England was on her knees, a vast amount of Russia was in German hands, and almost the entire Pacific and much of the mainland of Asia was controlled by Japan. Confronted with the terrible and frightening possibility of a world dominated by the combined military dictatorships of the Axis powers, the United States was desperate.

Ed Anderson's story serves as an illustration of that desperation and of the American resolve to defend democracy by whatever means available.

The next morning the crew of LT-430 was introduced to the huge rolling swells of the Pacific Ocean. I was already seasick when the captain called the crew together to open our sealed orders:

> LT-430 is to Proceed South West Pacific to Good Enough Bay, vicinity New Guinea. Its mission is to seek and salvage allied ships in distress, and search for and rescue shipwrecked seamen and downed allied pilots.

I was proud but as surprised as the rest of the crew to discover that, without further aid from the captain, I had navigated this slow tug (speed nine knots) and the string of tugs with us over six thousand miles across the Pacific to New Guinea and up the coast to Good Enough Bay.

After spending a week at anchor looking for someone to tell us what to do, we discovered that there was no army command group on shore to claim us. On his own, the captain drew fuel and supplies from the navy, registered our radio call sign and the area we would be searching with the local naval headquarters, and cast off on our first search-and-rescue patrol.

There are countless islands around the mainland of New Guinea, especially in a sweeping arc running from north to east to southeast. There the islands of the Carolines, Marshalls, Territory of New Guinea, and the Solomons are scattered like steppingstones. Besides places with names like Guadalcanal, Bougainville, New Georgia,

Rabaul, New Britain, and Kwajalein Atoll, there are thousands of nameless small islands, channels, and bays. The Japanese held most of the islands, the United States was preparing to invade many of them, and over and among them, the navies and air arms of both sides hunted each other.

Over the months that followed—alone, unarmed, and boasting thin quarter-inch steel plates—tugboat LT-430 carried out her own hunt while maintaining radio silence. (We received messages—weather reports, SOS/mayday distress calls, special orders—but never once used our transmitter. To do so would risk giving our position away to the Japanese.) With unreliable charts, we threaded our way among the many small islands off New Guinea. At night we anchored in hidden bays and lagoons, any place that seemed deserted . . . so we didn't come under fire. Daily we searched for distressed ships and boats that could be towed in for repair or for the crews of those that couldn't.

A week into our first patrol, two Japanese planes made the strafing attack recounted at the beginning of the chapter. Machine gun bullets walked up the vessel's wake and the entire length of our deck. The crew took cover as best we could. Four seconds of terror later, and L-430 was once again alone.

I got up from the deck and looked around. Somehow no one had been injured, but there were holes in the deck and cabin top. It suddenly dawned on me that I was in the middle of a real war!

Many long patrols later, I had worn out the few military and civilian clothes I had brought aboard in my Mississippi State overnight bag. I had put away one new pair of khaki pants, shoes, a shirt, and my overseas cap to wear ashore. After a while all my other clothes just wore out. I finally had to fashion clothing out of pillow cases and mattress covers. I cut holes for my head and arms in the pillow cases and wore part of a mattress cover as a sort of sarong tied around my waist with a piece of rope. It looked a little weird, I guess, but it was that or go naked. I got a few laughs, but the civilian crew didn't spend much time on military spit and polish anyway. I later got some dungarees and shirts from the navy. At the time, army uniforms were pretty scarce around Good Enough Bay.

We continued our patrols, staying out several weeks at a time. One night, we were anchored off a small nameless island when, by accident or design, an incendiary device of some sort dropped directly on top of the wheelhouse. We heard a thud, and the whole boat lit up like a star. It may have been an aerial flare whose parachute failed; they were constantly dropped by both sides. We were sure we would be under attack the next second, but I guess if there were any Japs on shore, they didn't know what was happening either.

Whatever the damn thing was, it blinded anyone who looked directly at it. We couldn't put it out. We used up all our fire extinguishers and tried buckets of seawater. That thing burned a hole through the wheelhouse roof, the deck, the deck down below, the bottom of the boat and lit up the sea below us before it burned out. We were lucky it didn't get anything vital—like the fuel tanks. We had an eight-inch hole in our bottom, though. Even with the pumps going all out, we were up to our knees and more in water before we got the hole plugged with part of a mattress shored up with timber. It was the best we could do with what we had. With the pumps running full blast, we slowly made it back to Good Enough Bay.

While we were under repair, the first supply ship we had seen steamed into the bay. They had ice cream! I can still remember how good it tasted. They also had orders for us from MacArthur to proceed to Australia. Someone knew we were out there after all.

Our new mission was to put coast watchers onto certain islands to observe and report Japanese air and naval movements; we took them off or resupplied them as the situation warranted. The watchers had to move a lot, because after they broadcast a few times, the Japs could pinpoint their signal. When it got hot for them, they had to be picked up. In a lot of movies, you always see subs doing that job, never army tugs. I guess our tugs weren't macho enough for Hollywood. Sometimes we carried an Australian or two who were familiar with a certain island, but mostly we transported U.S. Navy teams. I gained great respect for those unsung heroes we put off on enemy-held islands.

The job for us was to get them as close to the beach as possible. We put them ashore and picked them up only late at night. Sometimes we had to search most of the night to find a passage through the reefs that surrounded many of the islands. Our charts weren't too accurate on things like that. We didn't just drop off these men; we had to launch the teams in shallow water so as to keep their bulky radio gear dry.

Sometimes we backed the tugs in, letting our big screws dig a channel in the sandy bottom so the team didn't have so far to go in the water. They were very vulnerable until they got across the beach into the bush. If they got caught in the water, well, they didn't have much of a chance. I think they were more afraid of being captured than of getting killed.

Working against us was the noise of our boats and our limited speed. If the hull was clean, the vessel was capable of a "blistering" nine knots. Many times the mission didn't go quite as planned.

On one occasion we were ordered to an island that had a small mountain, which was perfect for coast watchers. Naval intelligence had reported the island was deserted. There was a little moonlight when we arrived; we didn't like moonlight. Based on the naval information we had been given, we decided to ease in to a quiet stretch of beach. The coast watchers were gathering their gear on the stern when all hell broke lose.

The Japs walked light mortar fire right up to us while rifle fire opened up from the tree line behind the beach. The tug took a couple of mortar hits and sank quickly in the shallows.

We got into the water with our wounded, one radio, and as much of the watchers' supplies as everyone could carry. The Japs did not have a boat to come out after us, but they continued shooting at the tug. We hoped their muzzle flashes would blind them as we let the tide take us parallel to the shore.

After we had gone a good distance, a sergeant crawled onto the beach to reconnoiter. It was a mistake. He was captured by a patrol. He shouted his name and serial number to his captors loud enough to warn us off.

Some men carried supplies; some carried our wounded. We drifted for several more miles before trying to drag ourselves across the beach into the bush. We made it, though, rested about twenty minutes, then as carefully as we could, used the rest of the night to move inshore.

By dawn we had walked a good way up the mountain where we hid in the bush to wait for night to move again. Several days later a miracle happened. The navy team "captured" our sergeant. They had watched him stumbling around in the mountain bush for more than

Army tugs such as Ed Anderson's played a vital role in placing, supplying, and extracting the coast watchers (such as these in New Guinea) who gathered vital information on Japanese movements.

an hour to make sure he hadn't been followed before they grabbed him. He wasn't in the best of shape. His captors had beaten him pretty good, and he hadn't eaten or had any water for three days. He told us the Japs had tied him up that first night, screamed at him, and beaten him unconscious. He didn't remember what he told them, but he didn't think they understood English. They were into a little rice wine or something and made the mistake of leaving him bound up alone in a tent. He was really scared, scared enough to work himself loose and escape before dawn.

It took a couple of days to dry out the radio and get it working. Nearly a month later a night rendezvous was set up with another tug to take us off. The Japs never stopped looking all over the island for us. We moved every night. Even with severe rationing, by the time we were taken off the island we had exhausted all the navy team's food and water we had managed to carry off the tug. And we had used all the medical supplies on our wounded. We didn't lose anybody, but it was close. We were gone long enough for our families to receive missing-in-action telegrams.

Back in Melbourne, Australia, without a boat, I was temporarily assigned to captain a stripped-down PT boat that was used to rescue downed airmen off the coast. That damn thing would go about fifty miles an hour!

After a month or so I was assigned a space on a C-47 cargo plane bound for San Francisco. My orders stated I was to report to a new tug. It took about three days of flying time, not counting layovers for fuel and rest, to get across the Pacific. I had to sit on the floor between the extra ferry tanks in the cargo bay the whole way. By the time we landed in San Francisco it felt like my body had been welded to the airframe.

From San Francisco I traveled by train and bus to a shipyard at Orange, Texas, to report as first mate aboard a new seagoing tug with an army crew. The captain was named Zek Brandon; he was Jewish, twenty-four years old, and a lieutenant colonel.

Our first stop after negotiating the Panama Canal was San Pedro, California, where two 20-millimeter antiaircraft guns were installed atop the wheelhouse. We never hit anything with them, but the sight of them made us feel better. Zek had never been to sea but immediately became an excellent seaman. He did everything expertly. He was the most able and brilliant man I ever met, had a true photographic memory. Yet he was a regular guy and became my best friend.

Back in the old hunting grounds, we settled into the routine of putting ashore, supplying, and picking up coast-watcher teams. I taught Zek everything I had learned about the business. He caught on quick then taught me a thing or two.

Truth was, when we weren't being shot at, we had fun. Like the time we put into a tiny bay at sundown to hide overnight. We cautiously eased up to a small pier.

A path led to a village on top of a hill overlooking the bay. We had no sooner secured the boat than down the path came a tall black man dressed in a derby hat, a necktie, and absolutely not one other stitch of clothing. He introduced himself as King Edward, the village chief, and invited us up. He spoke the king's English better than we did. The whole village did. As a result, we made that little bay our home port. The people welcomed us, fed us, talked with us, sang to us, made us feel at home. I'll always remember King Edward as a good man with great dignity.

On a mission one night to another island we were told was unoccupied, we were close in to the beach when we came under intense small-arms fire. We immediately turned back, but before we could get out of range, the tug foundered. It took a lot of rifle and light machine-gun fire at the waterline to sink us, but they did it. The tug settled on the bottom with just the wheelhouse above the surface.

We had casualties, but somehow no one was killed in the initial attack. We got the wounded off and hovered in the water on the sea side of the wheelhouse. After the boat settled, the shooting gradually died down. I guess the Japs were trying to decide what to do. Apparently they didn't have a boat. So we sat there trying to figure out just what we were going to do. The water was calm, and there wasn't any tide to carry us away. We would probably be seen if we tried to swim out from behind the wheelhouse.

After thirty or forty minutes the Japs started shooting again, but not at us. We looked around to see that they were shooting at a friendly tug almost on top of us. The boat had been returning to some other island when they saw the firefight in the dark. They risked taking hits to ease in behind our wheelhouse and pick us up.

We were damn lucky that night. We got home with every man alive, although some were shot up pretty good.

Once more without a boat, I was again sent back to the States to pick up a new tug, LT-530, this time as her captain. My former captain and friend, Zek Brandon, had been reassigned to England. (Considering his young age, intelligence, and high rank, especially for assignment as skipper of a tug, I guessed that Zek may have been sent to the Pacific for firsthand knowledge in placing and retrieving special teams on enemy shores in preparation for the invasion of Europe. I suspect he may have been in the OSS, although he never said so.) I took my new boat with a fresh crew on the now familiar route to New Guinea.

After more of the same duty as before, LT-530 was assigned a task that became my strangest and most memorable mission. We received orders to pick up a tow and deliver it to an island where a Jap airstrip was supposed to have been captured. It was the first time any tug I was aboard actually towed anything. The object was a little unusual—a big wooden barge filled with thousands of gallons of aviation gasoline. In addition, it had eight navy planes lashed to its deck. The planes' wings were folded and covered in some kind of waterproof wrapping. I'm not sure what kind of single-engine planes they were. We had pulled pilots out of the water, but most of the planes we had seen in the Pacific up to then had been Japanese. I do recall that they carried a crew of two, a pilot and a gunner. So they were possibly Douglas SBD dive bombers.

Towing the cumbersome barge, I figured we were racing along at a speed approximating four knots. We felt more vulnerable than at any time since we first arrived in the area. One enemy plane or patrol boat could fry us. Late one afternoon we finally arrived at the designated island—the one that was supposed to have been captured. What we found was one hell of a battle raging just inland from the beach.

The island was divided lengthwise by a low mountain ridge. Not wanting to lose my tow (or be blown up with it), we stayed well off-shore and rounded to the other side of the island where we found everything quiet. As night fell we nudged the barge into the beach, held it there with a little power, and stood by. When the noise of the fighting persisted after sunrise the next day, I knew I had a dilemma. If we towed the barge back around the island and tried to deliver it, chances were good that the Jap guns on the far side of the ridge would blow it to bits. On the other hand, my boat, crew, and cargo were at risk if I stayed where I was in broad daylight. Our destruction would be easy work for a Jap plane or patrol boat.

About midmorning I decided to check out the situation on the other side of the island without risking it all. I pushed the bow of the barge onto the beach. I know the crew believed their captain had gone crazy, but they followed my instructions to unlash the aircraft-loading ramp, manhandle it into position, and by brute strength got one of the planes onto the beach.

I used to hang around the airport at home and bum rides, and the summer before going to college, I had taken flying lessons from the airport manager but had never soloed. I had looked at those navy planes and figured, Why not? What the hell?

You have to remember that I was twenty years old and didn't know any better. We stripped off the covering, fueled the tanks from the barge, and by trial and error, our engine mechanic figured out how to get the thing started using homemade jumper cables and batteries from the tug.

I put my first mate in charge of the boat, climbed into the plane, strapped in, studied the controls, and figured out how to unfold and lock the wings in place. Looking around from the cockpit, especially down at my crew, I was suddenly struck by how large that plane seemed. The crew were all looking up, waiting for me to do something.

I gingerly taxied the plane up and down the long stretch of hard-packed beach, increasing speed with each run. I noticed it took a lot of right rudder to taxi straight. The plane was considerably larger than the Waco biplane trainer in which I had taken lessons. It occurred to me that maybe my plan was a little too ambitious, but by that time the crew were all up on the barge and watching. I figured they had no doubts that their captain was fixing to kill himself.

The machine was really powerful. I thought it just might eat my lunch, but twenty-year-olds think they will live forever. At the end of one last fast run up the beach, I turned the thing around, took a deep breath, and poured the coals to it. I had no helmet, and the roar of the engine was like nothing I had ever heard before. It had a hold on me, but I sure didn't have control of it. I had never been in anything as powerful and was doing everything I could just to keep it rolling straight.

When the tail lifted off the ground, the thing started walking sideways toward the water on my left. I held right rudder against the powerful engine torque, but my leg was too short to get full rudder. (At the time, I didn't know the rudder pedals were adjustable.) It looked like I might run off the beach into the water. Just as the thing got right to the edge, I did the only thing I could do: I pulled back on the stick. Suddenly, there I was, on my first solo flight.

Looking back, it was a dumb thing to do. I was just a kid with more ego than sense—but there was a war on.

Once I got into the air and my heart slowed down a little, I decided that plane flew pretty much the same way as that old Waco. Hell, it was fun. I just wished I had taken a few more lessons.

I followed the shoreline around the island to the other side. To stay out of enemy range, I flew parallel to the beach a mile or so off-shore. That's when I saw an American flag flying from a pole beside a dirt landing strip. It looked like the fighting had moved inland and up the ridge.

I turned in and flew over the field. A couple of guys waved at me. It looked okay, so I brought the plane around and lined it up for a landing. That's the part that was really exciting. I made five low passes at that runway before I worked up enough courage to try and put down. Three tries after that, I was actually down. I figure the handful of navy pilots who had come ashore with the marines witnessed the worst landing they had seen since their flight-training days at Pensacola. I bounced about a dozen times, used up all the strip, and nearly ran into the flight shack by the flagpole at the bitter end.

The commander of the captured field was incredulous. "You're telling me that a brand-new navy plane shows up out of nowhere? That this son of a bitch who just nearly killed us all is an army officer who's not even a pilot? And that he got it off a barge full of gasoline?"

"That's what he says, Commander. Says he's got seven more planes for us. You want us to shoot him or check out his story?"

The navy pilots there were an advance party to set up the airstrip. One of them checked the plane all over at least twice. He pointed me to the back seat, climbed in the front, checked everything in the cockpit, ran the engine up, turned the plane around, took off, and flew back around the island to have a look.

That guy couldn't believe what he saw. He spent the rest of the day flying one pilot at a time back to the beach to ferry each plane to the airstrip. When the last one was gone, my crew was damn near dead from getting those things off the barge, unwrapping them, fueling them, and getting them started. After the last one lifted off the beach, we unlashed the tug and got the hell out of there. I never heard what happened to the fuel barge. I signed it over to one of the pilots before we left.

LT-530 returned to dropping off and picking up coast watchers. A few weeks later we quietly approached a small island to anchor for the night.

We eased the boat quietly into a small lagoon and were preparing to drop anchor when a single shell blew the side out of the boat. She started sinking fast. The Japs obviously knew our position, so I ordered the radioman to break our silence and send out an SOS. We left the sinking boat and carried our wounded into the water with us. There was a little chop and a strong tide that swept us down the beach.

In the meantime the Japs amused themselves by blasting away at the tug's pilothouse, all that was left above water. Their target practice and the darkness allowed us to avoid capture. We came ashore about three or four miles down from where our tug sank and kept wading for a few miles farther to avoid leaving footprints, wading as far as we could carry the wounded before giving out. I took inventory. We had a little water, one flashlight, a pistol, and pocket knives, but no food and no medicine.

We crossed into the bush, erasing our footprints as best we could. By morning the Japs began patrolling the beach looking for us. We remained hidden well back from the beach but couldn't risk moving around to forage for food. At night we would send two men to keep watch near the beach. Our water ran out the third day. We were doing the best we could for the wounded, but things began to look a little grim.

The third night was pitch black with no moon and an overcast sky. I couldn't see my hand in front of my face. About two that morning, the crew on watch picked up a faint red light at sea and answered it with the one flashlight we had. We got everyone down to the beach, and a short while later one of our sister tugs eased into shore and took us off the island.

For the third time I had a boat shot out from under me. When I finally showed up at Melbourne, again without a boat, I was assigned temporary duty as skipper of a long, narrow yacht that had been painted battleship gray and re-engined with two powerful gasoline engines. She was about ninety feet long and could cruise at better than thirty knots.

By the caliber of the passenger we carried, I must have had a decent reputation as a boat skipper. The souped-up yacht was Gen. Douglas MacArthur's personal transport.

We traveled only at night, rendezvousing with navy ships or meeting with commanders on one island or another. I remember one occasion very vividly. I was to take the general to a rendezvous with some troop commanders about six hours' cruising distance away. Just after dark, MacArthur came aboard without a word to me or anyone, sat down on the couch in the salon just behind the helm, put his elbows on his knees and his head in his hands. He stayed like that for hours. Things were still pretty touch-and-go out there, and that night you could see he was carrying a heavy load on his shoulders.

During the spring of 1944 I was sent stateside once again to pick up another tug, this time from a yard at Decatur, Alabama. When I got there I found that it was a fifty-foot harbor tug. My orders were to sail to New York, load the tug on a ship, and take it to England.

After coming downriver to Mobile and into the Gulf of Mexico, we encountered the Great Hurricane of '44 somewhere between Dry Tortugas and Key West. In all my time in the Pacific, I had never lost a crewman, not even from among the wounded. For the first time during the war, I lost a man sometime during the night of that hurricane. Long before I knew I had lost anyone, I thought I might lose the boat. The tug was so damaged by the time we limped into Key West that it had to be pulled out of the water at the naval station and repaired.

With my boat under repair, I walked around Key West. Somewhere on the main street there, two sailors jumped me from behind. I swung around to defend himself and saw a smiling Slick Orr and Buck Cospalich, high school classmates. They took me to a navy NCO club where we had one of those wartime, old-home-week celebrations that you nearly die from the next morning.

By the time we docked the tug at the Fifty-ninth Street Wharf in New York, it was late September 1944. A colonel met me at the dock and said that that things were looking good in Europe. "Can't last more than six or eight months," he said. "Fact is, Captain Anderson, they really no longer need your tug over there." Then he asked a silly question: "How would you like to go home?"

I had been at war on small boats for three years, had sailed almost forty thousand nautical miles, had three vessels shot out from under me, and had survived a hurricane. Not much later I heard that Sumrall, my college roommate who started everything that April Fools' Day, had been killed in action on some Pacific island. (I never heard what happened to the other two who had also signed up with me.) Then I learned that my best wartime friend, Zek Brandon, had been killed early on D-Day at Normandy. I was not quite twenty-two years old, but I was mentally and physically exhausted.

The first and only time during the entire war that I wore a complete officer's class A uniform with proper insignia was the day I was relieved from active duty.

ED ANDERSON finished his engineering degree, got a pilot's license (has owned several planes), and occasionally will even go out on a boat. He still follows the buoys to Ship Island. He came home from his wars (World War II and Korea) highly decorated, but he won't talk about the medals. "I used to have a few in a cigar box, but I don't know where they are now. I think maybe they washed away with my house during Hurricane Camille."

CHAPTER 3

MILTON TALLY EVANS

OTHER THAN THAT, LIEUTENANT, HOW WAS THE FLIGHT?

THERE'S A DIFFERENT STORY for every flyer, but most begin the same way: the unforgettable first airplane ride. It had been that way for a young lieutenant named Evans who found himself flying a stripped-down, unarmed British Spitfire over France in October 1942.

Eleven years earlier, in 1931, Meridian, Mississippi, had honored its world-renowned pioneer aviators, Al and Fred Key, by dedicating its new airport to them. Boy Scouts were assigned to protect visiting aircraft from onlookers, and young Mitt Evans took the job seriously. He stood all day by the shiny new plane flown by a Capt. Vernon Omlie and slept under its wing all night to protect it from the curious. Impressed, the good captain, as the boy had hoped, gave the scout his first ride aloft, and the sky captured the soul of another fledgling. Mitt spent weekends washing planes, cleaning hangars, anything that would get him a ride, sometimes a lesson. In 1934 he was at Mississippi State College. It took money to go to school and money to fly, and money was hard to get during the Great Depression. Determined, Evans found a way.

I couldn't play any musical instrument well enough to be in a dance band, but I had enough business sense to manage one. That band put me through school. I convinced the head of the aeronautics department at State to give me flying lessons before I transferred to Ole Miss for a little law and as much flying as I could earn the money to pay for.

At the little grass airfield in Oxford, I met an older fellow who liked to hang around, sit in the shade of an oak, chew on a straw, and talk flying. I had heard of him, but what impressed me most was the fact that he owned a hot little low-wing monoplane. On weekends he would come out to the field and sit around and talk most of the afternoon. Finally he'd roll that beautiful little plane out, crank it up, and fly off. After a while he would zoom overhead, come back for a landing, and walk over to sit down in the shade again. On one occasion he grinned at me and said, "That son of a bitch tries to kill me every time, but I beat it again." Bill Faulkner liked to get away to the airport like that. Nobody talked about books.

I graduated from law school in 1937 only to find there was no market for young lawyers. Four years of college ROTC had gotten me a commission as a second lieutenant in the infantry reserve, but the impoverished peacetime army didn't have an active position either.

I couldn't find a job. Then I noticed that as hard as times were, guys still managed to scrape up enough change to take girls out Saturday nights. I formed another band, went down to the Gulf Coast, and auditioned at the Markham Hotel.

Mitt Evans and His Orchestra became a hit at the Top of the Markham. While there, a very pretty girl at the hotel swimming pool caught my eye. I asked her for a date on the spot. When she said okay, I was so excited I forgot to get her name. Determined, I finally found her and gave her a new name I couldn't forget: Mrs. Milton Tally Evans. A short time later, however, in 1940, a nervous America called this reserve lieutenant to active duty. Hitler had crushed Poland and France and was bombing England.

The first thing I did was insist on meeting my very busy commanding officer. "I'd like a transfer to the air corps," I said. "You can see on my record there, I'm already a pilot."

"Denied. In spite of what Roosevelt is saying, we're going to war. You're assigned to this outfit, and that's that, Lieutenant. Besides, your pilot's license isn't enough. You have to have two hundred hours in at least a two-hundred-horsepower aeroplane to qualify for a transfer."

Determined, I bought an old 225-horsepower Stinson and flew it in my free time. It held together for a year, long enough to give me the requisite hours and a commercial pilot's license. In the summer of 1941, with my newly earned pilot qualifications in hand, I again requested a transfer to the army air corps. It was denied.

While building up my flying time, I had gotten to know a major in the 153d Army Air Corps Observation Squadron, the only military flying outfit in the state of Mississippi. The major flew with me on several occasions. When the Japanese attacked Pearl Harbor a few months later, I concocted a sneak attack of my own. Once again I went to my captain, this time with a form requesting a transfer to the 153d Observation Squadron.

"Dammit, Lieutenant, I told you not to bring another request in here."

"Yes sir, but I have the two hundred hours required and a commercial ticket, and this request is from the 153d Squadron all ready for your signature."

"Denied. We're in a war now, and I need every man and officer I've got."

"Captain, sir, even if you put 'denied' on the form, the major is going to override it." I was sweating, but I was too deep into the bluff to quit.

"You've gone over my head to see Major Holifield on this?"

"No sir, Captain. Major Holifield sent me the papers. He's asked for me. Pilots are in short supply, sir; you can court-martial me or you can let me fly."

"And Major Holifield is going to endorse this?"

"Yes sir. And sir, you'll be rid of me."

That last part did it. I reported to the 153d Observation Squadron commander and handed him a transfer form signed by my captain. Major Holifield looked up from the document. "How did you get the captain to sign this, Evans? He hates your guts, hates the air corps for that matter."

"I told him you would get it approved whether he did or not, sir." I held my breath. The major almost smiled. "You ever do anything like this again, I'll have your ass roasted over a slow fire. Do you hear me, Lieutenant?"

"Yes sir!" I replied but couldn't keep the grin off my face.

"You have a hell of a lot to learn and damn little time to do it. Mitt, this outfit is probably headed for combat within sixty days. You're one of the best natural pilots I've seen, and we're going to check you out in every plane we have, teach you tactics, but it's just to give you a head start. I'm sending you to Randolph Field for regular flight training."

I started to complain, but the major cut me off. "If I take you with us now, you'll be the youngest, most inexperienced, and deadest combat pilot in the outfit. Starting today we are going to work your tail off to give you what you'll need to get through pilot training. Now get down to the flight line." The major picked up his telephone. "See you around, Lieutenant."

I graduated from Randolph Field in August (Class of '42) and was immediately checked out in a new single-engine dive bomber, the A-36.* Then a new assignment came. It was to an outfit equipped with twin-engine A-20 Havoc light bombers.

When I reported to my new commander, he did not appear happy.

"Evans, I need twin-engine bomber pilots. You're a single-engine pilot."

"Yes sir, but I have civilian twin time. I can fly 'em."

"Not in this outfit. You won't fly my bombers if you haven't been through multi-engine flight school. Besides, I need a maintenance officer and you're it."

"But look at my flight experience." (At the time, I had more flying hours and more formation flying time than the commanding officer.)

"I'll want an inventory list of spare parts on my desk tomorrow morning. Dismissed, Lieutenant."

Miserable, my only joy was the bootleg hours I got in the A-20 on weekends, thanks to a couple of pilots in the outfit I had befriended. (This flying time, logged into my record, inevitably led to the most memorable flight of my life.)

Once again the Mississippi 153d Observation Squadron came to my rescue. Delayed months from going overseas to perform instead

---

*Equipped with an Allison engine and dive brakes, the A-36 Apache was an early production model of what later became the famed P-51 Mustang.

desperately needed U-boat patrols off the East Coast, the 153d found itself short a pilot when orders arrived sending it to England. Holifield remembered me and called at six in the morning: "Mitt, we're cutting your orders as I speak. Pack your bag and be on your base flight line at three this afternoon."

I packed a bag, kissed my wife, Nellie, good-bye, and left the apartment for the base. It was the last time I would see her for three long years.

Holifield hung up the phone, flew to Atlanta where he received staff approval for my transfer, then flew to my base where he literally stole me from my enraged C.O.

"Don't grin at me, Evans," Holifield greeted me. "You're not out of the woods by a long shot. Before we ship out, you have to log fifty hours in every type of plane the unit has. And you have just thirty days to do it."

"That's plenty of time to get fifty hours," I replied.

"Dammit, Mitt, you're not hearing me," he explained. "I didn't say fifty hours. I said fifty in every type of aircraft we have."

"Yes sir!"

I started flying twelve hours a day, seven days a week. Just days before we were to leave for New York, someone asked for my inoculation card.

"It's in my file," I responded nonchalantly.

The flight surgeon's nurse just stared at me. "It is not."

I had had all of the sixteen shots that were required, but those records had not caught up with my file. The army solution was simple. I was given all sixteen shots again—on the spot, in one afternoon. I was sick for three days, during which time I had to keep flying. I barely qualified in time to ship out with the unit to New York.

We were going through processing when the company clerk discovered that my new shot record hadn't caught up with me. Holifield called me in.

"Evans, we've tracked down your shot records but they won't arrive before we ship out tomorrow. I've talked to transportation, but they say you can't board ship unless you have proof you've had the shots."

For the third time, twice in less than a week, I was administered the required shots. One bureaucracy satisfied; one lieutenant very sick.

The 153d Reconnaissance Squadron was one of the first American air corps units to reach England. The Brits were more than glad to see us, but we were more than disappointed when we learned that, due to a bureaucratic foul-up, the 153d was not going to receive the new aircraft that had been promised. Worse, we were told it would be months before we would have access to any aircraft at all. What does an air reconnaissance outfit do without aircraft?

The Royal Air Force, desperate for any assistance, quickly came up with a solution. British Fighter Command was replacing the older Mark II Spitfires in one of their fighter squadrons with Mark V Spitfires. As a result, the newly arrived American reconnaissance squadron flew its first reconnaissance missions over France in castoff Mark IIs still bearing British rondel insignia. As time permitted between missions, the rondels were painted over with the American insignia, plane by plane, until all were finally identifiable as American.

I found myself flying solo photo reconnaissance missions in stripped-down, unarmed Spitfires deep into German-occupied France. It was a lonely job. Many of the missions had to be performed at low level to photograph the defenses, staging areas, rail yards, sometimes buildings suspected of housing enemy headquarters or communications systems far behind the lines. (Such targets would be hit by daring low-level attacks from special RAF units flying very fast Mosquito light bombers.)

On such missions I would cross the English Channel just above the waves to avoid enemy radar, fly at minimum altitude across France, and flash low over a specific target to get detailed photographs for Allied intelligence. Flying so low, I was vulnerable to ground fire from small arms and light antiaircraft (AA) guns. And I couldn't fly directly to the target, because spotters would send the information on my headings to the area air defense network. If they guessed my photo target, they would be waiting for me with plenty of AA.

Just navigating the long distances at such a low level was a challenge. Our Spitfires had been stripped of guns, ammunition, gun-belt trays, anything nonessential in order to lighten them. This gave the already fast planes added speed, but that increase in speed was the only defense we had. Low and fast meant the light AA gunners would have very little time to get their sights on us. Additionally, when we were low to the ground, the camouflage paint scheme of our planes made it extremely difficult for enemy aircraft above to see us. Flying low and fast, we zigzagged to throw off the spotters and AA gunners and kept a sharp lookout for enemy fighters behind or above us.

We flew high-altitude missions to gather photographs of large industrial complexes, harbors, road and railroad networks, bridges and tunnels, airfields, coastal defenses, and damage assessment of the same sites after they had been hit by a bombing raid. After taking off on such a mission, I would spiral up over England to gain altitude then head for the target. Bombing missions and invasion plans depended on photographs like the ones we delivered.

High-altitude missions could not avoid radar detection, which made us open game to enemy fighters . . . if they could catch us. Our modified Spitfires could outrun the heavily armed German fighters if they were behind us. If the fighters were waiting somewhere between us and the English Channel, only our flying skills could save us.

We had one other advantage. With sufficient time, fuel, and oxygen, the stripped-down Spit could climb to a higher altitude than

Unlike these Spitfires flown by the French later in the war, the Spitfires used by Mitt Evans's reconnaissance squadron were armed only with cameras and were lighter in order to exploit the aircraft's speed, ceiling, and maneuverability.

U.S. ARMY

the heavier German fighters. And at such high altitudes, it was harder for AA gunners to see us, but they would still throw up some flak from time to time. We often returned with a few bullet holes and more than a few times with a lot of them.

After several months of flying the Spitfires, I got a call from my C.O. "Mitt," he said, "good news. We're getting A-20 light bombers stripped down for photo-recon. They're being assembled over here, and the first one is ready. You were with an A-20 outfit stateside, so I'm sending you to pick up the first one. We need that plane to start checking out all our pilots so they'll be ready to go as soon as we get the rest of the new planes."

I acknowledged the order but decided not to explain to the "old man" that I had only been assigned to staff duty with the stateside A-20 outfit. I had clocked some time in an A-20, a grand total of fifteen and a half bootlegged hours, all with an experienced A-20 pilot behind me.

On the other hand, the C.O. didn't bother to tell me that the aircraft we were getting had originally been ordered by the French before they surrendered. When I arrived to pick up the plane, I discovered that the flight manual and every instrument, control, and instruction placard in the aircraft was in French. Worse, the fuel mixture controls worked backward from what I had flown in the States.

The A-20 was a sleek single-pilot, twin-engine light attack bomber that normally carried a crew of three. There was no second set of controls for a check pilot. Either you crawled in and flew it, or you didn't. I delivered the plane to the base without incident.

Regulations, however, required that any new plane had to get the chief mechanic's approval and a thorough test flight before it could be assigned to a squadron for operational use. The C.O. was so anxious to get this A-20 into service that he had the mechanics work all night to perform their inspection. The next morning he called me in.

"There's a low overcast and a little fog in today's forecast, Mitt, but see if you can't make the test flight. Here's the checklist—shouldn't take long. We need to get that bird signed off so everyone can fly it."

Weather conditions that day were indeed a little foggy, but the commander was willing to authorize the flight in order to get the plane into service as soon as possible.

I did the preflight inspection, cranked the engines, and took it up. After punching through a thin, low overcast, I ran into a second overcast a couple of thousand feet higher. There was enough clear airspace between the layers to conduct the test, so I went by the book and checked off every item.

The plane was fine, and I thought the hard part was done when I took a heading back to our field. I descending through the lower cloud layer and kept getting lower and lower. The altimeter unwound to the point that there wasn't much air left between me and the ground when I broke out at about six hundred feet with scattered "scud" below. That wasn't too bad until the patchy scud turned into England's infamous fog—thick, dark, and ugly.

I got on the radio telephone and heard the bad news. My home field and every other field within range reported fog with zero visibility. To make matters worse, the already low overcast was getting lower. It looked like Henny Penny was right: The sky was falling.

All I had was a dead-reckoning course for my field. I was thankful that the terrain was fairly flat, mostly cleared farmland. Feeling reasonably safe, I eased the plane down to two hundred feet so I could occasionally see a familiar landmark, but I was too low to get reliable radio signals.

Quickly I knew I was in serious trouble. I decided to swap my airfield for any field, a road, a pasture—anywhere wide and long enough to set the plane down. But all I saw, when I could see the ground at all, were small farm patches surrounded by stone walls and narrow, single-lane roads.

Then a familiar landmark, a farmhouse and a barn, flashed by beneath me. I knew it was just a little southeast of my field and immediately corrected my heading for home. I figured it was only a couple of minutes away. Patting the dash, I told the plane to stay with me. "We're almost home, baby." That sounds funny, but most pilots talk to their aircraft.

I couldn't see much out in front, but I could see the ground by looking out my side window. I concentrated on holding my altitude steady at two hundred feet while I glanced at the ground through the side window every few seconds. I never saw the little wooded hill, hardly more than a rise in the ground, but I sure heard and felt the treetops beating the leading edge of the wings. I pulled up just as the right engine quit.

The right wing started to drop a little, and the plane began yawing toward the dead engine. I was losing speed fast. Simultaneously I leveled out, kicked in a lot of left rudder, feathered the right propeller, and began to ease slightly back on the stick to get a few more feet of altitude. The battering from the treetops stopped and wings were coming back to level when WHAM! there was one really big bang and the plane yawed hard to the right again and tried to roll on its back.

I thought I had lost it. Already holding left rudder, I jammed it full against the stop and racked in all the left aileron there was. I was clear of the trees, but the plane was shaking and bucking violently. If I eased off even a slight bit of aileron, the left wing would start rising. With full left rudder, the plane was still crabbing slightly. I thought maybe I was carrying too much power on the left engine, but my airspeed was marginal. I didn't dare pull back on the throttle.

My left leg was shaking. It was all I could do to stretch my leg far enough to keep the left rudder pedal against the stop. The plane was on the ragged edge of control, maybe a little over the edge. It was shaking so badly I could barely read the instruments. I only needed three of them anyway: compass, altimeter, and airspeed. The rest were irrelevant. If anything else went wrong there wouldn't be a thing I could do about it.

I had pulled up too high to see the ground, so I eased back down to two hundred feet. I had no choice. I still couldn't see much straight ahead, but again I could see the ground by looking down to the side. It took all my concentration to fly the aircraft.

I needed a miracle, and I got one. A fence flashed beneath me, and I saw lots of tire marks on the grass below. I hit the gear switch, pulled off a little power, and eased back on the stick. If it wasn't my field, it had to be somebody's airfield. I thanked heaven the Brits had big square grass airfields at that time. There was no way I could have lined up my approach on a narrow paved runway. Still holding full left rudder and aileron, I eased the throttle back and forgot to breathe. The plane quit flying almost immediately and touched down hard about a half-second after the gear locked in place.

I didn't know what might be on the field out in front or how much more landing area there was. I shut everything down, all the switches, fuel valves, everything, eased on the brakes, and held on. The plane rolled to a stop and was enveloped by fog.

My left leg was shaking uncontrollably from holding hard left rudder. The rest of me was shaking on general principle. I didn't have enough spit in my mouth to lick a stamp. It must have taken several minutes for me to get out of my seat and weakly climb down to the ground. When I did, I had to sit on one of the main tires for a moment. The plane was wet with water droplets. I was wet with sweat. In a couple of minutes I could stand up and walk around the A-20. It was a shock.

I sat back down on the tire, wrapped my arms around the landing gear strut, and thanked God and that tough little bomber for bringing me down in one piece.

The chief mechanic, Major Holifield, and a few others had been anxiously awaiting word. They had heard Mitt on the radio trying to find an open field after they had told him they were socked in, but they hadn't heard a word since.

Someone burst into the flight shack and yelled, "I think I hear a plane!" The major and everyone else piled out on the flight line. At first they didn't hear anything. Then someone said, "That's a single engine. Can't be the A-20." The anxious group picked up the fog-muffled sound of an aircraft approaching the field. They couldn't see the landing because of the fog, but they definitely heard an aircraft engine shut down somewhere on the field. They piled into a Jeep and went looking for it, expecting to find a fighter or liaison plane of some sort.

When they finally found the plane, Mitt was sitting on one of its wheels. He didn't wave or say a word. They were a little speechless themselves. There were evergreen needles, leaves, bark, and a branch or two pasted across the deformed leading edge of the left wing. On the right side, the splintered stub of a moderate size tree limb was jammed deep into the right engine cowling. The tips of the propeller blades on both engines were curled back. And oh, yes, the outer four feet of the right wing and aileron were missing.

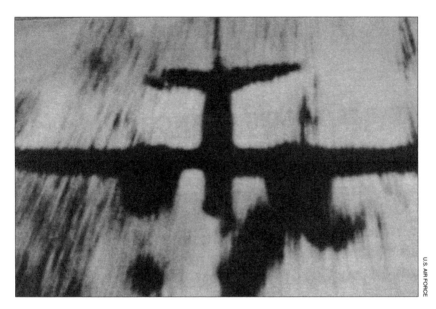

The shadow of a lone Douglas A-20 Havoc, presumably on a reconnaissance mission, was captured in this photo somewhere over France.

While the rest of the party stood gaping at the jagged metal at the end of the right wing, the chief mechanic walked silently around the aircraft . . . twice. Mitt, now standing alone on the plane's left side, still hadn't said a word. Finally the sergeant walked up to him, spat a wad of tobacco juice, nodded toward the right wing, and asked, "Other than that, Lieutenant, how was the flight?"

As I stood watching the plane being towed away to the flight line, I felt all the tension melt away. Suddenly I felt very calm. I got the strangest feeling that God must not mean for me to die in an airplane. I never worried about it again—just flew the hell out of anything they gave me.

The Spits were fun to fly. I loved them, but you were way out there, over occupied France, all by your lonesome—one plane, unarmed, with only one engine, maintaining radio silence.

I liked the A-20. I think that's my favorite plane. It flew like a fighter but had two engines—and I knew firsthand how tough they were built. It was also nice to have someone to talk to; the planes usually carried two other crewmen, a gunner in back and a guy to handle the cameras.

Later the 153d's mission was changed. The A-20s were rearmed and the bomb racks reinstalled. We were merged into a mixed light bomber outfit. We'd go out on missions with twelve aircraft in flights of four. At first we took turns leading: Brits one day, Free French the next, and our flight of four the next.

We flew the missions right down on the deck. We would pull up to fifteen hundred feet for the bomb drop so we wouldn't blow ourselves up, then take them right back down, so low we'd have to pull up to miss houses, trees, and wires, sometimes fences. We would flash by ground gunners before they could get their sights on us, and if we stayed down there, the AA guns in the tall flak towers couldn't be depressed low enough to hit us. The Brits told us if a horse or cow got in the way to fly under or around it, never over it. That would put you high enough to get hit. We sometimes came back with oats and barley in the air intakes. It was the kind of flying that kept your attention. You didn't take your eyes off the terrain ahead. Lose your concentration for a split second, even sneeze, and the earth could rise up and smite thee.

The Free French flyers were crazy. The Brits finally put out the order that the French couldn't lead anymore. Then we received orders that if any of the French started to drop out of formation, we were to shoot 'em down.

It was not a question of courage. They fought all right. The problem was the nature of Frenchmen.

Most of them flew wearing civilian clothes with French papers and money. If they went down, it was easy for them to melt into the French populace. They might also be shot as spies. The reason the British were upset was that the crazy bastards would sometimes fall out of formation on the way back from the target and land to see their girlfriends or to pick up a few cases of wine. If the plane was there when they got back, they flew it home and we all drank the wine. If the Germans had found the plane, the Frenchmen made their way to the coast and caught a fishing boat back to England. After the Brits put a few tracers across their noses, firing one across their bow, so to speak, the French got over the habit of stopping off for a quick visit. But we missed the wine.

Those are the things Mitt readily talked about: the flying, the fun, but the low-level missions weren't all fun and games. He received the French Croix de Guerre, the U.S. Air Medal, a couple of Bronze Stars—the list goes on. Mitt never mentioned them during his interviews, nor did he mention that after one bombing mission, his was the only plane of twelve to return.

The mixed light bomber outfit was broken up in early 1944, and Captain Evans found himself assigned to the Thirty-first Transport Group equipped with C-46 and C-47 aircraft. While the British measured pilots by their skills, the Americans were more regimented. When thirty-year-old Mitt requested assignment to a fighter squadron, he was rejected. The brass reasoned that since he had never flown with a fighter outfit, he was too old to make the transition to fighters. By that time, however, Evans was certified to fly almost every type of American single- or multi-engine aircraft, including P-51 and P-38 fighters, Spitfires, and several other British fighters.

He was promoted to major and given command of one of the transport group's squadrons then promoted to lieutenant colonel and given command of the entire group. Commander or not, Evans continued to fly missions, taking the lead ship into every new area of operations. He was the first to land a transport on the Normandy beachhead and set up a landing strip there (designated T-1). His outfit was the first to set transports down on German soil, flying in more tons of supplies and more wounded soldiers out than any other outfit of its size.

We cheated—a little. Things got very tough for the troops in the months following D-Day. The temporary supply port the engineers had set up off Normandy was destroyed in a huge storm. That slowed the supply line considerably. I decided we would carry as much as we could on every trip, even if it meant pushing the preassigned weight limits a little.

I had a C-47 loaded with sandbags to the allowable gross weight. Then I had the crew load an additional five hundred pounds and flew the thing with no problem. We kept adding more sandbags until the crew chief signaled for me to cut the engines. The tail wheel strut had bottomed out under the load. We unloaded about six hundred pounds, and the strut came up an inch or two.

That gave me an idea of how to gauge our loads. We put a man with a ruler back there to measure the height of the strut while the plane was being loaded. When the tail wheel strut was about six inches above the stop, we would stop loading. Test after test, we found the C-46s and C-47s would carry the loads, and the load was always carefully distributed to maintain a proper center of gravity. Granted, it took a little more runway to takeoff and the rate of climb was slower, but the planes flew without any problems in spite of the increased weight.

We never lost a plane due to load or control problems. A crew chief came up with the idea of building ramps so that the trucks could back up level with the cargo doors. That simple idea saved a lot of turnaround time and allowed us to make more round trips in a day.

Eventually our performance record got us in trouble. An inspection team paid us a visit. When they found that we were using the tail wheel strut as a load scale, they were not pleased. There wasn't much I could say except that the aircraft were capable of safely carrying heavier loads than the book said they could. The inspection team was not impressed. I was ordered to follow the book on weight and balance. And we did from that point on . . . most of the time. The inspectors, however, did like our loading ramps and soon the other outfits were using them.

As the fighting moved across France and into Germany, the Thirty-first Transport Group followed it and was always the first to land at hastily prepared forward landing strips. It was dangerous flying, and I recommended combat medals for my pilots and crews, but the brass wouldn't approve the recommendations on the theory that cargo outfits didn't fly combat!

Most of the time we didn't rate fighter escorts, so we delivered the goods without them. We were told that German fighters were only interested in stopping the bombers. Right! They wouldn't be interested in shooting down a fat, slow transport loaded to the gills with ammo, fuel, food, and vehicle parts. I lost thirty planes and crews to gunfire. Thirty! Some we lost on the ground to mortar and artillery fire, but most were lost in the air to the Luftwaffe that we had been told was finished before D-Day. If that wasn't flying combat, tell me what was.

Some of the planes we lost were full of the wounded we had picked up at the front to evacuate to hospitals. On flights sent directly in to evacuate wounded, there was always a flight nurse aboard. One of those lost crews included a nurse who had married one of my pilots a few weeks before. I put her in for a medal, too. Nurses and cargo planes weren't in combat, huh? I would like to have had the brass who kept turning down those recommendations to fly one or two frontline supply missions with us, then tell me my people didn't deserve metals.

WHEN THE war ended, Mitt Evans had not seen home or family for more than three years. Like the others who returned, he tried to put the war behind him. He was offered a good flying job, but Nellie put her foot down, "Don't even think about a flying job," she warned him. "You've used up every bit of your luck in the sky." Mitt couldn't find much to do on the ground, so he got himself elected mayor.

CHAPTER 4

OSWALD M. "JAC" SMITH

No Honors,
No Parades

AS A BOY, O. M. Smith so disliked his name that he gave himself a new one. Pronounced "Jack," he spelled it "Jac." Woe be any schoolmate who called him Oswald Marion! Jac was from an old and good family that was suffering hard times in 1938 with the rest of the country when he entered high school. A year later the second world conflict in less than twenty-one years was boiling up on the plains of Poland. By 1940 freedom was dying in Europe. Only the tiny British Isles and parts of the Soviet Union remained free from occupation by German or Italian fascist troops. While America remained neutral, U.S. industry was awakened from economic depression by orders for war materiel. Languishing for years, Ingalls Shipyard, twenty miles from Jac's home in Biloxi, was suddenly bustling with orders for new ships, three of which were to be aircraft carriers for England. British sailors were sent to Biloxi to man the new acquisitions to his majesty's Royal Navy, and many were invited to dinner by local families. Around the Smith table the sailors marveled at the abundance of food and told of the desperate battle for survival England was fighting. They said that Britain was totally dependent on merchant shipping for food, medicine, fuel, and materiel, but that German submarines, aircraft, and dreadnoughts were destroying their lifeline across the Atlantic. Merchant ships and their crews were being lost faster than they could be replaced. The sailors said that Britain was on her knees and only help from American merchant shipping could save them. Young Smith listened to every word.

In less than six months, America was at war on two fronts and losing badly. It was clear that there would be little chance of invading German-occupied Europe unless the British Isles could be used as a staging area. A free England had to be sustained at all cost. To do so would require the building of merchant ships at unprecedented rates as well as the training of vast numbers of American seamen to man them. Ships, however, could be built faster than crews could be trained to operate them. To meet the demand, training schools were opened, and the minimum age for merchant seamen was lowered to sixteen. No maximum age restriction was established. Every old salt who volunteered was accepted. Soon kids who had never seen an ocean were serving at sea alongside men old enough to be their grandfathers.

A few days after his high school graduation, Jac came home to tell his parents he had volunteered for the U.S. Merchant Marine. The day he left by train for the Merchant Marine Training School at Tampa, Florida, Jac's mother tearfully packed a lunch for him and gave him all the money she had in the house—five dollars. His father solemnly shook his hand at the Biloxi train station and waved good-bye.

Jac Smith had been around small boats all his life. He was good in math, in fact in every subject, and he was a natural leader. He did so well at Tampa that they kept him as an instructor. When a group of Russians arrived for training, Jac was put in charge of giving them lifeboat and gunnery training. The Russian sailors were virtually prisoners of their political officers. They were marched to and from their training sites by armed guards, never allowed off base, and were forbidden to fraternize with the Americans.

Smith repeatedly requested sea duty. Finally, the school reluctantly released him with orders to report to the Seaman's Union Hall in Chester, Pennsylvania.

This union affiliation caused much misunderstanding and undeserved resentment of the merchant marine by the armed services. The navy had no great fleet of cargo ships, so the government turned to American ship owners, private companies whose crews had been unionized for years. They were asked to volunteer their ships and operate new ships as they were built. Who else was there for the job? The result was that merchant seamen, who subsequently received union wages and bonus pay for service in battle zones, were never forgiven for making more money than their peers in the armed services. Yet the casualty rate of the merchant marine was greater than that of any of the armed services except for the Marine Corps, and then only by one-tenth of 1 percent. With the exception of the naval armed guards who manned the few guns that were aboard merchant ships, almost no one knew that statistic. The gun crews knew this because they fought alongside them, survived sinkings alongside them, died alongside them.

Merchant seamen had to buy their own seagoing clothing. Jac had never been out of the South and owned no warm clothing. He spent his second day in Chester and all his money buying warm clothes, foul weather gear, and a medicine kit. He was told by old hands that merchant ships rarely had any treatment for common illnesses but aspirin and castor oil. For minor injuries, up to and including broken arms and legs, there were only iodine and splints. The captain's medicine chest was reserved for grave illness and injury.

Jac bought a great sheepskin-lined coat, insulated gloves, heavy wool socks, a tough pair of work boots, and a wool watch cap. He chose wisely. There would come a time when, far from the ocean, those clothes would save his life.

It's a good thing he bought his supplies on the second day. On the third day he was hired on as boatswain mate (bosun) aboard the new T-2 tanker *Cedar Creek*, just completed at the Sun Shipyard. Jac was in charge of all deck equipment and had twelve able-bodied seamen under his command.

On a cold winter's day in early 1943, Jac Smith sailed into the North Atlantic bound for Scotland aboard a tanker loaded with ninety thousand barrels of high-octane aviation gasoline. He had never been so cold in all his life.

The huge storm-tossed, freezing waters of the North Atlantic took more lives than German torpedoes and bombs. Ships in convoys had orders not to stop to pick up survivors of sinking ships. To do so would make them excellent targets for the attacking U-boats. Jac saw ships go down around him and watched helplessly as *Cedar Creek* sailed past men freezing in the water or in lifeboats and rafts, all struggling to survive. Many were never seen again. Some were picked up by trailing tugs and small escort vessels assigned to the task. Some men spent weeks on the freezing sea in lifeboats or rafts before being rescued. Many died in frozen agony, and among the rescued a great many lost limbs to frostbite and gangrene.

Even in the summer the North Atlantic was deadly. On a rare day of calm seas on a return voyage from England, *Cedar Creek's* bow lookout spotted a chain of life vests. When they were close aboard, Jac looked down from the ship's rail. Eight men, hoping not to lose one another, had tied themselves together with rope. They were still together, what remained of them; patches of bleached bones and sundried hide drawn tightly to skulls. As *Cedar Creek* slipped by, Jac watched them fade silently away, bobbing on a lonely sea. And he wondered what it must have been like for the last man to die.

Of all Allied ships, tankers were the most important target for the U-boats. Stopping the flow of oil and gasoline to England was their primary task. One U-boat captain recorded the horror he witnessed when he surfaced after torpedoing a tanker at night: "The tanker and the sea around it was an inferno of flaming gasoline. I saw her lifeboats and crew burning with her. It was my job to torpedo them, but my God! To see them jumping from their flaming ship into the flaming sea! Any man who steps aboard a tanker crosses the threshold of hell!"

Jac and *Cedar Creek* were lucky, always surviving in spite of the ninety thousand barrels of highly flammable aviation gasoline aboard ship. Neither the tanker nor Jac Smith burned at sea, but fire was not the only kind of hell this sailor would face.

Cedar Creek put in to the Brooklyn Shipyard for an overhaul. While there Jac learned that she was to be turned over to the Russians as part of the Lend-Lease program. A Soviet captain came aboard to ask if the ship's engineer, bosun, and at least one able-bodied seaman would volunteer to help get the tanker to Russia. The ship and its systems were unfamiliar to the Soviets, and the captain needed help to train his crew during the voyage. He promised the Americans would be paid in U.S. dollars upon arrival at Murmansk. Jac had trained Russians before in Tampa. He agreed to go.

The run from Scotland up the Norwegian Sea to the northwest Russian port of Murmansk had become so costly (one convoy lost half its ships) that it had been closed. Desperate for materiel, Soviet premier Josef Stalin threatened to shut down the eastern front if the shipping lane wasn't reopened. Thus the convoys were renewed, and *Cedar Creek* was on its way to Murmansk.

Before leaving the United States, the tanker was loaded to capacity with aviation gasoline. That was not all *Cedar Creek* was planned to haul across the North Atlantic, however. Two massive railroad steam locomotives were welded to her tank tops, and several dismantled bombers were lashed aboard, the wings crated and the engines hung on the ship's midsuperstructure. No tanker ever had been designed to carry such a load.

Crossing the Atlantic was the easy part. Offshore from Iceland, winter storms pushed the North Atlantic into monstrous forty-foot seas and higher. *Cedar Creek*'s main deck was constantly awash; ice formed on the superstructure, rigging, piping, and deck cargo. Whenever the seas subsided enough to allow men on deck, Jac Smith had to take a group out to chip the ice away with axes. Even without the added weight of ice, he remembers how the ship groaned as her hull twisted and bowed under the weight of her extra deck cargo. "Each time she rolled to one side or the other," he recalled, "farther than I had ever seen her roll, she would hang shuddering there as if trying to make up her mind whether to give up and roll over or struggle upright once more."

As bad as the North Atlantic storm was, the worst of the voyage lay ahead. *Cedar Creek* rendezvoused with a new convoy off Scotland and steamed into the Norwegian Sea. Their course took them north of the Arctic Circle, around the convergent tips of Norway, Sweden, and Finland, into the Barents Sea, and the northwestern USSR port of Murmansk.

We stayed as far from occupied Norway as the Arctic ice fields would allow, but it wasn't far enough. This time of year was the season of the midnight sun. There was no darkness to hide us. German planes came out from Norway to bomb and torpedo us day and night. The convoy wasn't making more than ten knots. We were easy targets. The planes would scream down, and you could see the bombs release from their bellies. *Cedar Creek's* luck held. Shrapnel from near-misses lay on her decks, and some of the crew were wounded, but we steamed on while some of the ships around us died.

The captain feared the German minefields off Murmansk. He chanced the ice to enter the White Sea and dock at what I thought was Archangel. It turned out to be Molotovsk—now known as Severodvinsk.

Despite the promises made to us in New York, we were paid in worthless Russian currency. Our protests were to no avail. Later, that first night in Russia, after all we had been through, we were arrested on an unpaved street, ankle deep in muddy, snow-melt slush only a block from our small hotel. Taken by armed guard to a dimly lit office, we were charged with violating a curfew of which we had been told nothing. Thirty minutes later we were shackled in the back of a truck as it slogged down a rough, dirt highway into the freezing night. The guards refused to stop, even to let us relieve ourselves.

In the dim light of dawn the next morning the truck passed through a gate into a barbed-wire enclosure and stopped. The three of us were ordered down from the truck onto a yard of frozen, trampled snow and mud. Icicles hung from the eaves of the buildings in the compound. We were turned over to two Soviet soldiers. The truck turned around and drove out of the gate, its occupants wearing the wristwatches they had taken from us. We were led to a "supply building" and issued a blanket, a spoon, and a tin soup bowl. Frightened, in a state of shock, we were separated and marched away, each of us clutching the bare possessions we had just received.

I was taken to a large wooden building and roughly shoved inside. The smell was of filth, vomit, and unwashed bodies. By the dim illumination of a single bare light bulb hanging by a cord in the middle of the warehouselike building, I saw that the walls were lined with three tiers of crude wooden bunks. The guard pointed me to an empty one in the top tier. There was one small stove for the whole building. Sitting out in the middle of the floor was a single open slop jar, the community toilet for the hundred or so wretched men and women I saw being rousted out of their bunks by the guards to start a new day. There were even some children.

Less than twenty-four hours after arriving in Russia from a harrowing voyage, I was a prisoner in one of Stalin's labor camps somewhere above the Arctic Circle.

I had arrived just in time for breakfast. I put my blanket on the third-tier bunk and joined the desolate people moving toward the door. Each carried his spoon and soup bowl. We lined up in the snow and filed past an old rusty oil drum sitting over a wood fire. I held out my bowl like the rest. It was filled with weak potato soup, and I was handed a small piece of black bread. That was it. I learned that we were given only two meals a day, and it was always the same: one bowl of watery potato or cabbage soup and a piece of black bread. On rare occasions, for a treat, they would throw in a fish head or two.

At first my shipmates and I thought surely someone would find out about us, learn we were missing, search for us, and get us out— the merchant marine or the navy or maybe even the Soviets when they saw Americans had been taken to the camp. We were their allies. We had brought them a ship and gasoline and locomotives and bombers. We cheered each other with such talk.

As the weeks went by, a month, more, the truth began to sink in. We had been on a Russian ship. They had painted over *Cedar Creek's* name with a new one in Russian. Who knew we were even in Russia? So many seamen were lost and never seen again. No one would come for us. Every day was torture; every day was the same. We grew bone tired, hungry, cold, and hope slowly died. We quit talking of home or rescue, quit meeting. Sometimes I would see one or the other of them and nod or wave as they marched out of camp on some work detail.

Luckily, to ward off the Russian cold when I went ashore from *Cedar Creek*, I had worn long underwear, two pair of pants, two wool shirts, my great coat, boots, gloves, and my watch cap. One man in the barracks spoke English. He warned me never to take off any of my clothes or someone would steal them. Among many other things, I owe my life to those clothes. Later, when this man decided he could trust me, he would talk to me at night. He was the only person I could talk to.

He said that the people in the camp were from all over western Russia. Some were farmers who had tried to hold back enough food from the government to feed their families. There were teachers, professionals, educated people that the communists somehow believed to be a threat. Others were unlucky people who had simply been gathered up and sent to the camp. They were all part of the forced labor required to build a railroad into the northern wilderness as a means of getting the raw materials from there to the industrial centers of the country.

My friend claimed to be thirty years old, and he had been in the camp for almost two years. He was skin and bones and looked a hundred years old to me.

Sometimes at night the guards would come in and take a woman, sometimes a boy, for their own sport. If the women tried to resist, they were beaten with fists. Some had husbands with them. If they tried to defend their wives, they would be beaten with clubs. One man in our barracks had gone mad. Day or night he repeated the same prayer over and over without stopping.

At first I couldn't sleep. Moans, crying, and coughing filled the nights, but after a while one learned to shut things out.

I was given two jobs. One was mixing cement and making concrete blocks from dawn until dusk. The Russians wanted to build a locomotive maintenance shop. The labor foremen cussed us because the blocks kept freezing and breaking during the night. They finally moved the work into a semiheated wooden building. Most of the blocks froze anyway.

Everyone's hands had grown raw in the cold, even with gloves. The skin would dry and crack open and ooze. I was told to rub mine with urine. It was all we had. It seemed to help.

Mixing cement and stacking concrete blocks all day was hard work, but it was my other job that nearly broke me. I was probably given the job because I was not a model prisoner. I was young and foolish and defiant to the sons of bitches. Maybe I was just too scared to completely give up hope.

I dreaded the sound of the biweekly supply train. When I heard it coming I would get sick at my stomach. A guard would yell at me and motion for me to come forward. I had to leave my other work, get my cart, push it to the tracks, and stand waiting in the snow. Guards with dogs waited also.

The tree line around the camp grew farther and farther away as the trees were cut down to make crossties and firewood. Slowly the locomotive would come into view as it rounded out of the trees far down the track. It came relentlessly lumbering toward me like some evil black monster billowing clouds of smoke. Spitting steam and the heat of it all condensed in the air around the engine, turning it into fog. First the engine came clanking and wheezing past me, then flat cars loaded with rails, cement, and other supplies. Behind them came the boxcars. It was the boxcars I dreaded.

Each boxcar was packed with as many people as could stand shoulder to shoulder. Men, women, sometimes a child or two. They were the replacements for the slaves who had died in the camp from lack of food and brutal work. When the doors were unlocked and opened, a wave of stale, foul-smelling air rushed out. The living staggered down from the cars where they had been standing for three days without water, food, sanitary facilities, heat, without room to even sit down. The sunlight blinded them, and many fell, their muscles so cramped they couldn't walk at first. Off-duty guards would stand around to note if any young women were among the new arrivals.

After the new guests of Stalin were marched away, my work began. I was forced to climb into the cars and clean the filth out of them, the excrement and urine and vomit left by eighty or more people packed so tightly that they had to relieve themselves where they stood—but that was not the worst part.

There was almost always at least one dead person left in each car, more often several. People who had been sick when they started, or old, or had a bad heart and didn't last the trip. I had to drag the dead out and pile them on my crudely made handcart. Most of the bodies were stiff and in a sort of slumped position, ones who had died in cars too crowded to allow their body to sink to the floor. People who slept were held up the same way, slumped against those packed around them. I guess no one paid attention. Sleeping or dead—they were all too miserable to care.

Their frozen faces revealed the agony of their deaths. Many died with their eyes open. It was horrible. I remember the first time I took hold of the arms of a "soft" body. It was an awful feeling. The body was cold but soft to touch. You knew those kind had died only a short time before the train arrived. One time there was the body of a woman laid out with her hands folded and eyes closed. She must have been very special, placed like that by some caring people, friends or relatives. Somehow they had made room.

It is hard to think about the camp. I have never told anyone about it until now.

When my cart was full, I pushed it along the tracks to the pits. The ground was frozen too hard to dig in the winter. I was told that new pits were dug every summer and the old ones covered over. The cart wheels were crude rounds cut from the trunks of trees and fitted to wooden axles. As I pushed it over the rough ground, the bodies bounced and jiggled. Sometimes their open, lifeless eyes would stare at me. They wanted to know why. All I could do was ask their forgiveness.

When I reached the pit, I dumped the bodies in and shoveled lime over them. There was always lime dust on my clothes. I left it there hoping it would annoy some of the vermin that infested my body and the straw on which I slept.

Once I found the body of a little girl in one of the cars. She must have been just six or seven years old. I carried that little girl down into that awful pit in my arms and covered her eyes so the lime wouldn't get in them.

I knew I would go insane or die in the camp, maybe both. One day I arranged to meet my old shipmates after work. We had talked of escape before, but we had never planned anything concrete. I told them I had to get out and that I had been studying the camp security. It was not all that tight; the gate was left open all day until the last work gang came in from the rail line. We talked about it for a while.

In the end, the engineer said that he was too old to try it. Bob, the able-bodied seaman, reminded me that the reason security was lax was that there was no place to go. He said, "If you follow the railway or the road, you will be picked up quickly by the patrols. I've heard they beat you to death in front of the whole camp if they catch you. In my barracks I was told to shut up about it, that if you said anything there were people who would turn you in for extra food or a blanket. And what if you go into the forest? There is nothing but wilderness for two hundred or more miles. We saw that when they brought us here. You go out there and you'll die, Jac, freeze to death or starve."

Bob was scared, scared of getting caught, of not making it if he wasn't. I knew he was right. All of it. I was scared too, but I knew no one was ever let out of the camp. Inmates worked until they died. The trains brought their replacements.

I told Bob that I'd rather die out there a free man than die a slave in camp, and I meant it. I saved what little bread I could and waited for the right moment.

One evening it was snowing pretty hard. The guards and their dogs were by their stove in the gatehouse. I just walked out in the swirling snow and turned west. I don't remember a lot of those first three days and nights except the cold and walking in knee-deep snow and trying to eat pine needles. The pine needles were bitter and helped to keep me awake. Sometimes I slapped my face, anything to make me keep walking. I knew if I stopped, I would freeze to death. I was so cold, so tired. It was hard just to put one foot in front of the other one. I wanted to stop and sleep, but somehow I kept going. The weather finally cleared, and I remember the stars looked so bright and close. I thought they were decorations on the trees, thought I could just reach up and pick one off.

Then the stars were gone; it was daylight. I couldn't see very much, just a hazy glow. Maybe I was snow blind, I don't know. Suddenly I was surrounded by big furry animals, and they were talking, but I couldn't understand them. I couldn't remember what I was doing there. Then I made out the shape of a small man in front of me. He just appeared out of nowhere and said something in a strange language. I didn't know if all this was real or I was crazy or dying.

I woke up later in a warm tent. I was clean, and I was naked under a heavy fur blanket. There was some kind of salve on my frost-bitten face and hands and feet. I still couldn't see very well, but there were strange people there, small people in colorful clothes, and little children peeking out at me. I recognized my clothes hanging near a small fire in the center of the tent. I went back to sleep for a long time it seemed.

When I woke up again they fed me thick hot soup. I think it was the best meal I have ever had in my life. I tried to tell them with sign language that I was an American, but I was never sure they understood or believed me. I crossed my hands at the wrist and pretended they were tied, and I think they understood that I had been a prisoner. I had to use sign language to communicate with them. Now I know they were nomadic Laplanders. I had stumbled in among their reindeer herd and thought the animals were talking when it was the Laplanders whose voices I heard.

Those kind people took me in, nursed me back to health, and carried me with them as they migrated with their reindeer toward the grassy highlands of Norway, where their herd would spend the summer.

When we crossed into Finland, which was Germany's ally against the Russians, and later into occupied Norway, the Laplanders seemed to always know whenever a German patrol was near. Every time, before the Germans reached the camp, the nomads would take me to one of the pack reindeer, strap me by my arms and legs underneath it, and drape bundles of skins over the animal's back to hide me. Sometimes the Germans would walk along several hours with the Laps, and my hands and feet would go to sleep, but I never complained. The Laps risked death to take me with them across German-occupied territory.

One day the leader of the little band motioned to me and started walking away from the camp. I followed him for a mile or two. Suddenly, across a small hollow, a man with a rifle stepped out from behind a tree. My Lapland friend motioned for me to go to him. About halfway toward him, I looked back for my friend, but he was gone. I was really scared. I couldn't believe the Laps would turn me in or abandon me. They hadn't.

The man who took me in was a member of the Norwegian resistance. He passed me on to another who passed me to others in turn, each a member of a different cell and zone. Some of them spoke English and understood who I was, but I never knew their names or where we were. That way, if I was captured, I could not compromise a cell or the resistance group.

I learned to sleep covered with snow without freezing. We would burrow under at the base of trees where the low branches hid us. I only spent one night in a house. The homeowners allowed me to take a bath and sleep in a real bed. There were several women there. One cooked and fed my guide and me while the others loaded loose ammunition from a British army box into clips of some kind.

We traveled south, mostly in the high mountains. I was pretty good on snowshoes but never very good when it came to skis. My guides were patient, though, because I fell a lot. The one thing they would not tolerate was noise of any kind. We never spoke out loud, using only hand signals or whispers. Sound carries far in the mountains, and there were always German ski troops patrolling. The guides had I.D. papers identifying them as hunter-trappers or timber men in certain zones, but I had none. Had we been discovered, the Germans would have taken us prisoner.

I don't know how many months I was with the Laps, or how many with the Norwegians, or how many different Norwegians I was handed off to, or how many miles I had walked, but the season was changing. There was no longer snow in the valleys down below.

Then came a very special day. Just before dark, I smelled the ocean! The next morning I saw that we were high above a fjord. We began a long descent to a small fishing village, where I was hidden on a fishing trawler. The next day the fishing fleet put out to sea. One night the boat broke away from the little fleet and took me across the North Sea to Scotland.

Jac didn't realize until after the war what a terrible risk the Laplanders and Norwegians had taken in helping him. Later he learned that, when some Norwegians were caught helping two British SAS agents, an entire fishing village had been destroyed and all the men and boys fourteen and over were taken away to concentration camps. Nor did he know that the captain and little trawler that carried him to safety were part of what was known as the Shetland Bus. It was a network of courageous Norwegian fisherman who, time and time again, slipped away from their fishing fleets to brave the North Sea without charts or radios to smuggle out individuals wanted by the Nazis and to ferry back guns, ammunition, explosives, and British agents from Scotland and the Shetland Islands to aid the Norwegian resistance.

Determined to regain his freedom, Jac Smith had walked nine hundred miles across northwest Russia, Finland, Sweden, and more than halfway down the length of Norway in mostly brutal weather conditions, then crossed the North Sea. Yet he did not find his freedom when he landed in Scotland. The moment the little trawler docked at Aberdeen, Jac was taken into custody by British naval intelligence.

They said my story was preposterous. They were sure I was a German spy. It was shortly after the Normandy invasion, but I didn't know anything about that. I was afraid they might hang me before they had time to get my records, if anyone still had them. I had been missing for the better part of a year and hadn't seen a newspaper or heard a radio the whole time. Merchant seamen from the ships in our convoy that reached Murmansk reported that *Cedar Creek* never made it. They didn't know we had gone on to Molotovsk. Worse though was the fact that the Soviet captain had never filed a crew list with American authorities prior to leaving Brooklyn and joining the convoy. There was no official record of Jac Smith and the other two volunteers being aboard *Cedar Creek* with the Soviets.

Finally, at one of the many Royal Navy boards of inquiry I sat before, an officer said that if I was from Biloxi, Mississippi, I should know about a large shipyard nearby. I said that I did. He asked me to tell him where it was and about the coast. I answered that the ship-yard was in Pascagoula and that the name of the yard was Ingalls. Then I told him about the British aircraft carriers that had been built at Ingalls, their names, everything I knew. He believed me, knew I was telling the truth. In 1941 he had been there to man one of those ships for the journey to England.

I was released from custody and sent to another British navy compound. There an officer handed me an envelope: "Here is a train ticket and lunch card that will get you to the port of Millhaven. There is a ship scheduled to leave tonight for the U.S. You just have time to make it. Oh, by the way, I've checked, and I'm sad to report that nei-ther we nor your American navy is authorized to pay you any money, and the merchant service says if you sailed under Russian orders, then the Russians must pay you. I'm ever so sorry, Bosun Smith. I wish you luck."*

---

*Jac never received a penny for the voyage to the Soviet Union or the time he spent captive and escaping.

When I reached the designated port, a young woman in the Royal Navy Auxiliary greeted me. "Well, here you are," she said. "You play it pretty close, Yank. Better follow me quick march." She ran to the end of the dock to a harbor tug where she ordered me to cast off the lines as she entered the pilothouse. The harbor was blacked out. You could not see your hand in front of your face. I was surprised to find a pretty woman commanding a tug, and all by herself, too. She was good, too. I don't know how she found the right ship in the pitch-black harbor crowded with vessels, but she did. She took me directly to the tanker *White Horse*. The crew was weighing anchor. That's how close it was. They threw down a rope ladder as the ship began to get under way.

I had only the clothes on my back, the same I had worn since my ordeal in Russia had begun. They were clean but ragged. Fellow seamen aboard donated clothes to tide me over on the voyage to America.

There was just one more ordeal to weather on this long way home. Less than two hundred miles from our destination, we were overtaken by the Great Hurricane of '44 that wreaked havoc up the East Coast and went ashore near New York City. Although damaged, with all of her lifeboats smashed or missing, *White Horse* limped into port. I was all of nineteen years old.

The tanker's captain, a Norwegian, asked Jac to serve as his bosun once *White Horse* got out of dry dock. Rather than steaming the turbulent waters of the North Atlantic, the ship served in the Pacific. During the massive and devastating Japanese kamikaze attacks against the U.S. invasion fleet at Okinawa, twenty-six ships were sunk and more than two hundred were damaged. In the middle of that havoc, the tanker *White Horse* delivered vital aviation gasoline to the U.S. aircraft carriers, the main targets of the kamikaze strikes.

FOR JAC SMITH, World War II was only the beginning. After helping to deliver the goods to England and the Pacific, he worked on ships that supplied U.N. forces in Korea and U.S. needs in Vietnam.

During World War II, American merchant seamen were volunteers. They risked their lives to deliver vital materiel across the combat zones of the world's oceans. Yet when they came home from the war, those who made it home, there were no public honors for them, no parades, no monuments to commemorate their service, no G.I. Bill, no veterans hospital to care for the broken ones. Much of the public looked upon them as stereotyped waterfront bums.

It didn't come as a surprise to the merchant seaman. On leave between voyages, they weren't allowed to go to the USO clubs. They wore work clothes, not sharp uniforms. No one seemed to know or care what their job was. Many spent their time between voyages alone with a bottle trying to forget the horror of war in the North Atlantic, the Mediterranean, the South Atlantic, the Pacific, not to mention the severe losses to U-boats off the U.S. East and Gulf Coasts. Perilous by nature, seas are deadly in war. And yet the merchant seamen returned to duty time after time. Not a single merchant ship failed to sail for lack of a volunteer crew.

Almost every bullet, every gun and tank, every drop of fuel, every blanket, every ounce of medicine and food, and most of the aircraft and American combat troops were carried to the fight by merchant seamen. Thousands of Allied merchant ships were sunk; 948 of them were American. Some eight thousand American seaman lost their lives, and tens of thousands suffered terrible wounds, burns, and the loss of limbs.

By way of comparison, England lost thirty thousand merchant seamen killed; nearly one out of every three who went to sea. They were at war three years earlier than America, three years during which the English had virtually no effective antisubmarine warfare weapons.

Fifty years later, paid for by American merchant seamen's own donations, a monument was finally erected in remembrance of these sacrifices. The monument, a life-size bronze sculpture, stands at the verge of New York Harbor. It is simple, honest, and moving. The monument depicts a group of merchant seamen in a lifeboat reaching over the side to pull a fellow shipmate from the cruel sea.

Forty-five years after the war's end, Congress finally awarded veteran status to World War II merchant seamen who had served in combat zones. Of this belated act, Jac Smith said, "I suppose some may get a little medical help from a veterans hospital, but it comes too late for most."

CHAPTER 5

FRED RANDOLF KOVAL

No Foxholes in the Sky

Twenty thousand feet over Germany, twenty-one B-17 bombers of the Ninety-fourth Bomb Group, Fourth Air Wing, Eighth Air Force are alone deep in enemy territory. German Me-109 and FW-190 fighters knit through them, stitching wings and fuselages and flesh and bones with machine gun and cannon fire.

Long-range fighter escorts are not yet available in England. On each mission, when the friendly P-47 Thunderbolts reach their maximum range and turn for home, the bomber crews watch their "little friends" bank away and get a lonely feeling in the pits of their stomachs. Like a school of fish seeking safety in numbers, the bombers fly in a tight "box" formation, which is designed to allow the combined fire of all the guns in the formation to concentrate on attacking fighters. It is the only defense they have.

One . . . two bombers have lost engines to enemy fire. The stragglers drop behind. Enemy fighters wait like sharks to finish them. The formation cannot afford to slow down to protect crippled planes. They are on their own.

The fighters break off their attack.

One might think the bomber crews would be glad to see them go, and they are, except that it means the flak will soon be coming up to blotch the blue with black splotches and spew sky-shredding shards of steel. That's why the fighters have pulled back. They know what is coming and want no part of it.

Shortly into the flak zone, a bomber starts a slow slide down the sky and trails smoke. The crews above watch the stricken plane fall off on one wing and start a slow spin. Six tiny dots tumble into the air and randomly blossom into white parachutes, only six. The remaining four crewmen go down, all the way down, with their stricken aircraft. Of those who get out, some may bleed to death from wounds, pass out from lack of oxygen in the thin air, get frostbite from the intense cold, or break legs or backs or necks on landing. The lucky ones, the ones who aren't beaten by irate civilians who have been on the receiving end of their bombs, the ones German soldiers get to first, may live. The wounded will be taken to hospitals, the rest to prison camps.

The bombers turn onto the IP (Initial Point) for the bomb run. Bomb bay doors open. For the next few minutes the lead pilot turns his aircraft over to the bombardier who leans over his Norden bombsight in the naked Plexiglas nose of the plane. It is here that the aircraft, all the aircraft, are most vulnerable. The remarkable bombsight compensates for drift, speed, altitude, and bomb trajectory to determine the exact release point over the target. There is just one catch—there's always a catch. The entire procedure is dependent upon the plane flying an absolutely straight and level course from the IP until the bombs are released. All the other planes must do the same and release when the lead bomber does.

The German antiaircraft gunners below know all of this. It makes their job easier.

It all began with my first meeting with the C.O.

"Lieutenant Koval reporting for duty, sir."

"Koval, we're damn glad to see you. Ready to fly?"

"Yes sir."

"Good. I've already assembled your crew, all new men. Tomorrow you will fly second seat with one of our experienced pilots, and we'll scatter your crew among other veteran ships for the first mission so you can all see how things work. I'll see you at mission briefing at 0330. If all goes well, you and your crew will join the group the following day in your own ship."

I know what he means by "if all goes well." He means if we all make it back tomorrow. The flight the next morning was my down-and-dirty orientation to my new job. The Ninety-fourth group commander, Col. Frederick W. Castle, was losing planes and pilots faster than he could replace them. In the past six weeks the Ninety-fourth Bomb Group had lost twenty aircraft and crews. There wasn't time to ease new replacements into combat.

I had little time prior to this first mission to get to know my crew, all new to me except for my friend and copilot, Glenn Gordon Grant, who I had known during flight training in the States. I met my aircraft's ground crew and chief mechanic the night before this "orientation flight." There would be time to get to know them all in the days ahead . . . I hoped.

Awakened at 2:30 in the morning the day after that first flight, I dressed, ate breakfast (black oil-thick coffee, powdered eggs, and milk), and reported to the briefing at 3:30. Grant was already there. I took notes: my position in the formation, assembly point, bomb and fuel loads, route inbound to target, altitude, radio frequencies, checkpoints, times, weather, outbound route, what to expect from the enemy. The route in would take us across the English Channel and France then north into Germany to the target then out over part of Holland and across the North Sea for home—Rougham Air Base, Station 468, Bury St. Edmonds, East Anglia, England.

It took me a few minutes to be sure all my crewmen were present and to load us all into a truck for the half-mile ride out to our new ship. My crew chief had followed my request from the night before and painted a name on the nose of the new bomber. I got a little ribbing from the crew when they saw it, but the name suited me: *Erie Ferry*. I was from Erie, Pennsylvania, and figured I would be ferrying bombs to Germany.

New planes and crews got to bring up the rear, in my case, the outside lower corner of the formation—a slot particularly vulnerable to fighter attack. I had been scared before the mission began, but I wasn't now, didn't know enough to be scared, was too young to be scared, was too busy checking out my big bomber to be scared. The crew seemed okay. Most of them were eighteen- or nineteen-year-old kids. Hell, I was barely twenty-one. Only Sergeant Haggen, the flight engineer, was what you might call old. He was married and real old, almost thirty.

One thought lingered foremost in my mind that morning, and every morning to follow: *I'm responsible for the lives of every one of them.*

We met no fighters inbound. Maybe the Germans were concentrating on another group or down refueling. What looked to me like dirty puffs of cotton candy began to fill the sky ahead. At first it was all below the flight, but soon the antiaircraft gunners got it right. Now the puffs were all around us. The explosions of the close ones could be heard over the roar of the four big engines. We could also feel the concussion waves from them. The air became rough, and I fought to hold the plane steady.

Then the time came to open the bomb bay doors and maintain our position in the formation. Today the bombardier, Lt. Mike Wysacki, would release his bombs when he saw the plane in front release his. If the lead bombardier was on target, we would all be. If he wasn't, the mission would be wasted and some group would have to repeat it.

Each crew member—tail gunner, two waist gunners, ball-turret gunner, top gunner (flight engineer), navigator, radioman, all except the bombardier—had little to do now but huddle alone at his station in a drafty, freezing, rattling aircraft bouncing along in a sky full of exploding shells and shrapnel. There are no foxholes in the sky, just thin aluminum impersonating protection where there is none.

Bombs away. I grabbed the controls, closed the bomb bay, and prayed the flight leader would quickly rack the formation into a turn and get us all out of the flak-saturated target area.

WHAM! . . . HARRUMP! SHAKEEEEEEE! PING! THWAK!

Whatever happened had happened fast. A shell tore straight up through the left wing and exploded not more than ten feet above it.

To me it seemed the thing had blown up inches from my side window. Shrapnel ripped through the wing, fuselage, and cockpit glass sounding like some giant had thrown a handful of rocks against

U.S. AIR FORCE

The B-17 is an icon of the air war over Europe. With a crew of ten, the aircraft carried as many as ten .50-caliber machine guns. Such armament emboldened the American flyers to undertake a daylight bombing strategy.

the plane. The concussion slammed into the cockpit throwing Grant and me hard against our seats. We were momentarily stunned, deafened, but maintained control of the aircraft. We looked at each other, amazed we were unhurt.

I turned to stare out Grant's pockmarked side window. The skin of the wing around the large shell hole was peeled back in jagged strips. There were smaller ragged holes everywhere.

After testing the controls and checking the instruments, I asked the flight engineer in the top turret to check for damage and the ball turret gunner below to look for fuel leaks. Somehow nothing vital had been hit. Number-one engine was running a little rough, and the hole in the wing was adding drag to the left side of the plane, but everything else was holding together. The plane seemed all right, but there was trouble inside.

Woulff, the right waist gunner, was down. A piece of flak had hit him in the back and thrown him hard against the ball turret stanchion, knocking him out and ripping away his helmet and oxygen mask. Wirtz, the left waist gunner, was at first stunned by the flak explosion. He turned around as if in slow motion to see his buddy Woulff lying on the deck. There was blood but not a lot of it. Wirtz was quickly jerked back to full consciousness. His immediate concern was Woulff's naked face. Men could die at twenty thousand feet with no oxygen. Wirtz grabbed an emergency oxygen bottle and placed the mask on his crewmate then rolled him on his right side and applied a bandage over the wound in his back. Finally he hooked him up to the regular oxygen supply. That's about all he could do. Wirtz reported in and got back to his gun.

The bomber formation left the flak behind only to encounter a new wave of enemy fighters. The German pilots were brave and determined. They attacked from any angle but usually came from above and often from out of the sun, diving right through the formation. Their small fighters were almost twice as fast the bombers. Thus their main aiming point on the bombers were their engines. They knew if they knocked out just one engine, the loss of power would cause the bomber to lag behind the defensive formation and be an easy target to pick off. Like sharks swarming around a wounded whale, the fighters then ganged up on the crippled bombers and chewed them to pieces.

Other tactics were equally effective. Sometimes they came head-on at high speed and aimed at a bomber's nose and cockpit, trying to kill the pilots. In the early months of their deployment, B-17s were highly vulnerable to these head-on attacks. On days and at altitudes where atmospheric conditions caused billowing white condensation trails to form behind a bomber's engines, German fighters would sometimes come from behind, flying right up the white contrails like salmon swimming upstream, all but invisible to the targeted bomber until the fighters sprang on them.

Running fighter attacks lasted as long as an hour or until the fighters ran low on fuel or ammunition. They intercepted the bombers as they lumbered toward the target, then they broke off their attacks when the gunners on the ground opened with antiaircraft fire. While the bombers flew through the flak, the fighters landed, refueled, rearmed, then returned to the skies to intercept the outbound bombers.

As we headed for home, the Ninety-fourth began a descent so as to gain some speed as we fought our way toward the North Sea. *Erie*

Ferry took a lot of hits, but all four engines kept turning. The fighters pursued the formation almost to the middle of the North Sea. My gunners ran out of ammunition before we made it to the sea. We were all new, so the gunners were a little excited, fired a little wild, kept their fingers on the triggers a little too long. We would talk about conserving ammunition before the next flight.

One plane and its crew went down on the way home; two others were limping back in serious trouble. One called air-sea rescue to report it was ditching. The other crash-landed shortly after crossing the coast. Many, like *Erie Ferry*, had wounded aboard.

As we entered the traffic pattern for landing, I ordered the flight engineer to fire a red flare, the signal that we had wounded onboard. Planes with wounded crewmen were given landing priority.

I called for gear and flaps, and Glenn clicked the switches down. Langston was the ball-turret gunner. For takeoffs and landings, the men who manned the ball turret were seated in the fuselage. If the plane bellied in, the ball turret was usually crushed. As a prelude to landing, they stayed in the turret long enough to confirm that the flaps and landing gear were down.

As we descended from this first mission, Langston called up, "Flaps look okay, Skipper, but we got trouble. A big piece of the right tire is gone, and I think the left one is flat, too."

I ordered Langston up and the crew into crash positions.

Crippled planes landed in the grass. With a whole squadron returning and being low on fuel, the group couldn't afford a wreckage-blocked runway.

I turned into my final approach, lining up on the grassy area parallel to the runway. I was thankful we still had all four engines. Making a normal approach to within a few feet of the ground, I cut the switches and pulled the mixture controls back to idle cutoff.

As the big plane touched down, the right tire flew off its hub. The left tire was flat but stayed on, flopping wildly, shedding chunks of rubber. The right bare hub cut deeply into the dirt. Finally the gear strut collapsed, slamming the right wingtip on the ground and causing the plane to carve a large arc across the field, banging, protesting. The spinning propellers threw up clods of grass and dirt and clouds of dust.

After all the clatter, there was a sudden silence as the plane came to a stop. Every man was stunned for a moment. Then the same thought screamed through each mind: "Get Out! Everyone out!" Fire and an explosion from ruptured fuel tanks often follow a crash.

We all came alive. Moving as fast as they could, Wirtz and Haggen dragged Woulff out of the plane.

There was no fire. Not this time. *Erie Ferry* had brought her men home, all of them, but she was finished. Her right wing was torn and bent, fuselage twisted, landing gear torn away, propellers curled back, ball turret crushed, and 256 bullet, cannon, and flak holes in her skin and frame.

Woulff was taken away in a field ambulance. His wound wasn't so bad, he said, but his left ear was killing him, and he had a knot on his head the size of a golf ball. He had been lying on his right side since his helmet had been torn away at twenty thousand feet; his exposed left ear had frozen in the subzero temperature.

The crew piled onto a truck to join the other crews for the mission debriefing. It was a new and chaotic world for us, but just another routine mission to the old squadron hands who stood around drinking coffee, eating donuts, some lighting cigarettes with trembling fingers. No one liked the daylight missions. The British bombed at night. The young American flyers all had serious doubts about the wisdom of daylight bombing raids, not to mention the horrendous toll it took on men and machines. But it was our job. We would do it.

As so often happened in England, rain and fog swept in and grounded the squadron for almost a week. All of us had time to visit Woulff. He was doing okay. A couple of days later we all rode bicycles out to see the new B-17F assigned to us. (Ground transport around the base was scarce. There was even a shortage of bicycles.) It took us awhile to find it in the fog. The plane was parked in a dispersal bay on the far side of the field.

We climbed all over the new bird, inside and out, ran the engines up, checked the radio, talked to the ground crew, satisfied ourselves that it was a sound ship.

Bomber crews had to have a total of twenty-five missions before they could rotate back to the States. I was standing with Grant and Mike Wysacki, the bombardier, in the fog, looking up at the dripping

Plexiglas nose of the new plane. "Damn!" Mike said. "Only two missions, and we're already on our second plane. We don't stand a ghost of a chance of making twenty-five."

"Mike," I said, "you've just named this new bird." *Ghost of a Chance* was painted in big white letters on the olive-drab skin beneath the cockpit.

Soon the weather improved, and it was time for another mission. After the briefing we were just about to climb onto the truck that would take us out to *Ghost of a Chance*. It was the same crew, except we had a new man as right waist gunner.

Suddenly Woulff showed up in flight clothes with a huge bandage on the side of his head. "Skipper, I'm going," he announced.

"You're supposed to be in the hospital," I replied. "How's your wound?"

"It's fine, sir. All stitched up. Doesn't hurt a bit."

"How did you get out of the hospital? I'll bet they're looking for you right now."

A view of the bomb dump at an airfield in the English countryside. Fuses and fins were added just prior to loading them into the planes.

"Please, Lieutenant, I've got to go with you guys. I don't want to be assigned to a new crew. If I don't go with you guys, I'll never last, never get twenty-five missions. I won't survive, Skipper."

"Hell, Fred," Grant spoke up. "Let him come along. You know, one for all and all for one."

"I'll probably get in trouble for this," I answered. "Besides, he can't even get a helmet on."

"I'll fix him up with one," Sergeant Haggen offered.

I looked at the pleading eyes of the boy and thought, *This kid would rather go back to hell with us than stay here alone.* "Okay, Haggen. Show me how you're going to get a helmet and oxygen mask on him."

The substitute gunner was relieved from his assignment and got off the truck.

Just before starting the plane's engines, I looked back in the waist and had to laugh. Woulff was loading a .50-caliber ammunition belt into his gun. Haggen had cut a huge hole in the left side of a flying helmet, strapped the helmet tightly on the waist gunner's head, buckled on the oxygen mask, and taped the whole thing up for added strength. Sticking out the side of Woulff's helmet where the left earphone used to be was a huge white rabbit's ear made up of layers of bandage and cotton wadding designed to keep the ear under it warm. Woulff must have felt my eyes on him. He looked up and grinned.

Three missions later, our fifth, the crew had become a close-knit team of veterans. Although we grew to trust and depend upon one another, we really had no choice. Individual survival depended on teamwork and professionalism. Each man worked to be the best at what he did out of a deep determination not to let the others down.

The tower never used the radio to launch a flight. German listeners would pick up the signals, know the time of departure, and have the fighters waiting for us. Instead signal flares were used; one color meant start engines. Another meant taxi, and a third signified cleared for takeoff.

The bombers lined up behind the group leader and took off in turn at thirty-second intervals. On this day there was a low ceiling and solid cloud cover up to fifteen thousand feet. After the planes left the ground, the pilots had to fly by instruments, circling in a prearranged pattern until we topped the cloud layer. Then we formed up in the clear and proceeded to the target.

It was a nerve-racking procedure. Other flights were doing the same at nearby airfields. Anyone making a mistake, getting disoriented, vertigo, not maintaining a constant climb rate, or wandering out of the established pattern could cause a midair collision. It happened, and when it happened, full gasoline and bomb loads exploded, vaporizing planes and crews. The flash would momentarily light up the surrounding gray mass with an enormous orange glow and send shock waves out to buffet nearby aircraft obscured by the overcast.

Returning from missions could be just as bad, sometimes worse. Bone-tired pilots had to let down through cloud and fog for a runway that had to be somewhere in the mist below, had to be there because there was no place else to land. Because they were low on fuel. Because they had wounded aboard. Because they were flying a crippled aircraft, fighting to keep it in the air a few minutes longer. They came down with only primitive instruments by which to keep the planes aloft: compass, altimeter, air speed, gyro artificial horizon, and maybe a radio beam to follow.

Pilots came down sweating, even when the temperature in the cockpit was freezing. They came down knowing the whole crew was depending on them to get them all down in one piece. Came down knowing they would need all the skill and concentration they had. Came down hoping the clouds and fog didn't reach all the way to the ground. Weather took its toll same as the enemy.

On this day there were no accidents during the climb out. *Ghost of a Chance* broke into bright sunlight at 15,600 feet and took her position in the formation that circled above the cloud tops until all the aircraft had joined up.

The flight turned on course and continued climbing to twenty-one thousand. We met little fighter interference on the way in, but their absence was more than made up for by the intense antiaircraft barrage over the target. We saw a solid wall of black flak bursts fill the sky. The crew put on their flak vests and helmets while flying steadily into hell.

Bombs away! The formation went into its prearranged escape mode to clear the target. We had almost gotten used to the rattle of shrapnel against our plane . . . almost. Sure, it could maim or kill you

A B-17F could carry a twenty-four-hundred-pound bomb load. The aircraft's weakness was a lack of forward guns, which allowed German fighters to attack head-on with deadly results.

or sever a fuel or hydraulic line or start a fire or stop an engine or tear a wing off, but every man tried to ignore it, had to ignore it to keep on doing his job . . . until . . .

The plane was bucking from the concussion waves created by the AA shells exploding all over the sky. Grant and I were both on the controls trying to hold the ship steady. Below and to the front a bomber suddenly lost a wing, rolled over, and began to cartwheel toward earth. There were no parachutes to count. The centrifugal force created by the violent gyrations of the falling aircraft pinned the hapless crew inside the plane. Their wide-eyed, conscious terror lasted all the way down.

We didn't have time to think about that. A tremendous jolt rocked *Ghost of a Chance*. The flight engineer in the top turret called, "We got a fire on number one!"

I looked out at the left wing. Black smoke and flame were sweeping over the wing from the left outboard engine. I pulled the fire handle while Grant pulled the mixture control back to idle cutoff and feathered the prop. I added right rudder to compensate for the yaw caused by the drag of the dead engine.

We were losing speed, drifting back from the formation, but the fire slowly died away. I pushed the nose down to gain speed and change altitude to both clear the target area faster and hopefully throw off the gunners below.

A quick, sickening metal-to-metal ping and instantaneous explosion was followed by a sharp yaw to the left. I called to Grant to shut down engine number two, cut off the fuel flow to try to avoid fire, feather the prop. A river of oil from the broken engine streamed over the wing into the slipstream. Both of us jammed our right legs on the right rudder pedals with all our strength and fed in right aileron to prevent the plane from pivoting hard to the left and rolling on its back.

The drag of two dead engines on the left wing and related loss of lift, combined with the thrust of the good engines on the right wing, were creating powerful asymmetrical forces that threatened to throw the bomber out of control. By lifting the left wing with aileron and pushing the large rudder all the way to the right, we were barely able to hold a straight course.

Ghost of a Chance was still under control, just barely. We could not hold altitude, but at least we were flying.

"Everybody stay put, boys. Nobody jumps unless I give the signal," I ordered. The words provided momentary relief to an anxious crew. Nobody jumped, but everyone except the pilots groped for their chest chutes and snapped them to their harnesses.*

I called to the navigator, "The hell with the flight plan. Give me a heading for the shortest route to England."

We're now all dependent on his navigational skill to get us home. He must calculate a course, corrected for wind drift—and two engines out. The lack of power also means we'll be losing altitude all the way. There will be no margin for error.

As soon as he gives me the course, I follow it. In the meantime, Grant and I are fighting to keep the bomber in the air.

We calculate the best possible (and controllable) airspeed to give us the slowest rate of descent under these perilous conditions. Our plane is all alone now. The rest of the flight is long gone. Every crewman

---

*Parachutes couldn't be worn in the cramped bombers. Crews wore harnesses and kept chestpack chutes nearby. In an emergency, each grabbed his parachute and snapped it onto his harness. His greatest fear was that he might panic and jump without first snapping his chute on—it had been known to happen.

scours the sky for enemy fighters. We know we're dead if the fighters jump us; *Ghost of a Chance* is a slow cripple gradually descending over enemy territory.

"Once we make the Channel, alert sea rescue and give them our position," I instruct the radio operator. We don't do that yet, not at fifteen thousand feet over enemy territory. Some fighter might hear the transmission and come looking for us.

Copilot Grant works the fuel valves, shifting fuel from the left wing to feed the engines on the right. They are drinking gas at a high rate. I have the two remaining engines pushed up as high as I can and still control the aircraft. Number three is running a little rough, but I have to ignore it. I have no choice. If I back off on the power, our rate of descent will increase and we'll land in enemy territory. I pray the remaining two engines will hold together.

Twelve thousand feet. We're flying in and out of layered clouds as we descend. That's good. It may hide us from roving enemy fighters and AA guns on the ground.

Both Grant's and my right legs are aching from the constant pressure we have to apply to the right rudder pedals. We can't let up, not even a tiny bit. To do so is to lose control of the plane.

It takes forever, but we make the Channel. We radio our position and situation.

A crisp British voice comes back, "We hear you, *Ghost*. If you have to ditch, we'll come pluck you chaps up, never fear. Good luck Yanks." The Brit would alert the air-sea rescue boat in this sector and notify any nearby aircraft to look out for the crippled bomber.

It's raining now, but the air is smooth. The bombardier and navigator climb up from the plexiglass nose. It's early to take up their crash positions. I glance at them. They are both soaking wet, water is dripping off their noses.

"What the hell are you doing wet?" I shout.

"Don't you know?" they shout back. "There's a big hole in the nose."

No, I didn't know.

Through a break in the clouds we see water below. We have only eight thousand feet left.

"Throw everything you can rip lose overboard. Guns, ammo, oxygen tanks, everything goes but the radio and the dinghies."

I know that we may need the dinghies. I will have to decide soon whether to try for land or turn parallel to the shore and ditch. It's taking full right rudder now just to hold a straight course. I don't dare turn left into the dead engines with all their drag. If I have to ditch, the only way I can turn right is to pull power on the two remaining engines to reduce their asymmetrical thrust enough to make the turn, then ease the good engines back up to slow the rate of descent to the water.

Both Grant and I are in agony. Our right legs are cramped and shaking violently from fatigue, but we hold right rudder.

Five thousand . . . three thousand feet. We descend below the clouds. It's still raining, but we see ahead the famous cliffs of Dover. The white wall of chalk rises before us.

One thousand feet.

"What do you think, Skipper?" Grant asks.

I don't answer. I'm concentrating my whole being on flying the ship, keeping it in the air.

"We'll make it," I finally say, more to myself than to Grant. "That grassy flat dead ahead."

Grant calls to the crew, "Crash positions."

Ghost of a Chance is just that. She clears the white cliffs by less than 150 feet.

Gear up, no time for flaps, mixture controls off, cut the switches, ease back on the yoke . . . the ship settles onto the ground, sliding, bumping, tearing along on the wet grass.

I can't help pushing on the brake pedals hard even though I know the wheels are up. We slide for what seems a very long time and then, with a slight bobbing of the nose, the ship stops.

"Out! Everybody out!" Grant and I think we are moving fast, but by the time we make it, the whole crew is standing in the rain waiting for us.

"Hell of a job, Skipper." They are a happy bunch, joking and laughing, shedding the great tension that only moments before seemed too heavy to bear.

Not fifteen minutes later a British staff car comes into sight across the field. It pulls up, followed by a truck. An officer steps out. "You chaps look like you could use a lift."

Driving to his base, the British officer asks me, "You Yanks haven't been over here long. My men don't know what you're up to. Would you meet with a few of them, tell them what you are about?"

I didn't think that was too much to ask for picking us up, and agreed. While my men were taken off to a hot meal, I followed this officer, I think he was a major, to his office. He made a couple of calls, gave me a glass of brandy, and about thirty minutes later I followed him across the way to a large wooden building.

A few of his men? There must have been two hundred, maybe three hundred of them seated in a theater.

There I stood in soiled, wet flying gear on a stage in front of all these men while the major introduced me. I don't remember exactly what I said. I think I assured them that they were correct in assuming that we were "overpaid, oversexed, and over here." My girlfriend had told me that was what the Brits thought of all Yanks. Anyway, whatever I said got me a hot bath, a whiskey, a good meal, and a clean bed to sleep in.

When we got back to base the next day, we were assigned a new plane then given forty-eight-hour passes to London. It wasn't because we had been shot up and crash-landed twice during our first five missions. It was simply that everyone got a pass whenever they completed five missions.

Grant and I checked into the grand old Regent Palace Hotel in Piccadilly Circus then proceeded to hit every bar and club we could find. And in Piccadilly, that's all there was. A couple of hours into the evening we were in some basement cabaret when we faintly heard the wail of an air-raid warning over the loud music and conversation in the club. No one seemed to pay any attention, so we ordered another round of drinks. We felt a few dull thumps then the all-clear signal sounded. The jazz band never missed a beat. I guess the London revelers were used to bombing raids, and Grant and I were too drunk to care.

We finally got to the hotel at about four in the morning. I went up to my room and started to get undressed when it dawned on me I was freezing to death. I couldn't understand why it was so cold and called down to the desk to complain. The clerk apologized profusely but said he couldn't do anything about it, that they had cleaned up all the glass. That was all they could do for now except send up some more blankets.

Even though its right wing is on fire, this B-17 continued on course to deliver its bomb load to the target. Compared to other Allied bombers, the B-17 was capable of absorbing the most punishment and remaining airworthy.

"Cleaned up all the glass?" I asked. Yes, he said and explained that while Grant and I were in the basement club having a wonderful time, a German bomb had blown all the windows out on this side of the hotel. I slept like a baby under a pile of blankets but woke up with the worst hangover of my life.

Grant and I arrived back at base discussing what we would name our new plane. All we had was its serial number. We asked where it was parked and were told it was "somewhere in Germany." Turned out that while we were on leave, our new plane had been flown on a mission by another crew and never returned. We had lost our third plane by proxy. A few days later we were given another plane. I asked the crew what they wanted to name this one, and they decided to name it *Jeanne* after Sergeant Haggen's wife.

Several missions later, I was coming out of the morning briefing when Raymond Miller, our flight surgeon, showed up in flying gear. Miller and I had gotten to be good friends.

"What are you doing, Doc?" I asked.

He pulled me to the side and said, "Fred, I'm missing the war. I'm supposed to look after all these flight crews, and I don't know what's happening up there. I want you to take me with you."

I told him he was crazy, but he said that he had to go.

I took him up. He had to sit on a box of flares we kept just behind Grant and me.

When things got rough, he did the best he could to call the fighters to our attention or look for the ones our gunners were calling out. He was a hell of a guy, and after that mission, when the air crews talked to him when they came back from Germany, he was one doctor who knew firsthand the hell they had gone through.

Later I got a call from Colonel Castle, commander of the Ninety-fourth Bomb Group. He was a good man. I had gotten to know him, but when I reported to him this time, he kept me standing at attention.

"I heard you took Doctor Miller on a mission. Is that correct?"

There was no use denying it. "Yes sir," I admitted.

"Goddammit, Koval, we need doctors in the hospital, not risking getting shot up on missions. How the hell would I explain something like that? You haven't taken him up again, have you?"

"Yes sir."

The colonel was incredulous. "How many times have you taken him with you?"

I was a little afraid to answer that one. "Five," I reported.

"Goddammit, Koval! If he has five missions, I'll have to give him the Air Medal. He's earned it. How the hell am I going to explain a flight surgeon with an Air Medal?"

"He's a hell of a doctor, sir."

"Captain, you will not take Miller or any other unauthorized personnel on any mission. Is that clear? . . . And you will not smuggle any more of your crew out of the hospital before they are declared fit to return to duty. Oh, yes, I heard about that, too."

I had just made captain and figured I was about to be made a lieutenant again, or maybe a private, but I wasn't prepared for what Colonel Castle said next.

"Fred, stand at ease. Now that we've gotten all that out of the way, I'm want you to take group lead starting with tomorrow's mission. I'll fly with you whenever I can get away from this desk. Any questions?"

"No sir."

When the colonel flew with us, which was usually on the missions he knew would be rough, he would sit on a little stool between and just behind Grant and me. You know, I was never sure if I got the assignment because he thought I was good, or just because of attrition; the number of experienced aircraft commanders was getting a little short.

Later, Colonel Castle was given command of the Fourth Air Wing, and Col. Charles B. Dougher became the new commanding officer of the Ninety-fourth. Dougher informed me that I would continue to fly group lead but said that, when he flew with me, he would fly the copilot's seat, not a stool. On those occasions, Grant could fly as command pilot on another ship. I agreed to this arrangement on the condition that Grant would fly on my wing. (Grant could have had his own ship anytime he wanted it, but he requested to continue flying copilot with me.)

When Dougher scheduled to fly his first mission with me, Grant picked up a spare crew and plane. The target was a rough one, but all except one plane got through to the target all right. Grant was flying just off and below my left wing. We left the target, and things quieted down. We were halfway across the North Sea, well on our way home, when someone screamed over the radio, "Bandits! Six o'clock high!"

It was unusual to be jumped that late in a mission so close to England. I don't know where the pair of fighters came from. Maybe they were returning from a raid on England, maybe they were a roving patrol, maybe they had been waiting for us. I've often wondered, if we had been a little more vigilant would we have seen them earlier? We had begun to relax too soon.

We were down to four thousand feet over the sea, not far off England, when they hit us. The two fighters made just one pass, diving from behind and above at tremendous speed. They dove right through us, rolled on their backs to reverse direction, and disappeared low over the water back toward Holland. The Me-109s came so fast and were gone so quick, I don't know if anyone got a shot off.

One of them raked Glenn's plane down the top of the fuselage, from tail to nose. Most of us kept our signal flares in an open box on the deck just behind the pilots, where the flight engineer could get to

German fighters and antiaircraft fire exacted a heavy toll from the American airmen, but there were scores of amazing stories about the reliability of the B-17s. Despite the severe damage above, this plane returned to base. The bombardier and navigator, however, were killed.

them easily. We think the German must have hit the box of flares. Glenn's cockpit exploded in bright-colored flashes and smoke, and in just seconds the plane dropped into a spin and never recovered.

I sat there and watched my best friend, the man I trusted most, the best damn man I ever knew—Lt. Glenn Gordon Grant—crash into the North Sea with his ship. There were no chutes. He was gone, his whole crew with him. They're all still down there in the North Sea. I think of him often.

A few missions later, *Jeanne* was the lead aircraft again. We took a beating on the way to the target, but no one was hit. I turned onto the IP for the bomb run and switched control over to Mike Wysacki, lead bombardier. All I could do was sit there and keep the needle centered on the PDI (pilot direction indicator), the ingenious device tied to the bombsight that directed the plane on the course set by the bombardier.

Jeanne's bomb bay doors opened, and the whole squadron opened theirs. At precisely the right moment, Wysacki pressed the bomb release. Bombs away! All the planes behind released their bombs as well.

Immediately I banked steeply to lead the flight on a turn away from the target. The sky was black with flak. A few seconds after I leveled the wings on course, a tremendous jolt shook the plane like a rat in a terrier's jaws. I knew we had taken a direct hit.

I checked the controls. The rudder and elevator felt more than a little sloppy, but the plane responded to the control input, and we still had four good engines. I called for a crew check. Everyone answered but the tail gunner. After several attempts there still was no answer. I asked waist-gunner Woulff to crawl back and check on the tail gunner.

Meanwhile, Sergeant Haggen, looking back from the top turret reported a lot of big holes in the rudder and horizontal stabilizer. That would account for the sloppy tail controls.

A few moments later Woulff's shaky voice came over the intercom. "Skipper, the tail cone is blown to hell. Most of it's missing, part of the rudder, too. The guns are gone, and . . . and, Skipper, there's not enough of a body left back there to bury."

There was none of the usual postmission, tension-relieving chatter on the plane's intercom as we reached the skies over England. It was bad enough that Glenn Grant had been lost while flying another bomber as his old crew watched. Now, for the first time, a crewman had been lost during a mission. The mood aboard *Jeanne* was somber.

I did not call for a red flare; I didn't have wounded aboard, just what little was left of the dead gunner. Except for a vibrating elevator, *Jeanne* felt solid enough, all four engines running in the green. I maintained a normal approach to Rougham Field and called for gear and flaps. My new copilot moved the gear and flap switches to the down position.

Langston, still in the ball turret, came on the intercom. "Skipper, the right gear is not down."

"Recycle the gear," I called to the copilot. The gear was cycled up then the switch placed in the down position again.

"Left gear is down, Skipper, but the right one hasn't moved," Langston reported.

Summoning the flight engineer, I said, "Haggen, try to crank it down manually."

A few moments later he reported, "No good, Skipper, I can't move it. It's jammed solid. Must have taken a hit."

"Out of the turret, Langston," I called. "Gear up. We'll belly the son of a bitch in. Pilot to crew: crash positions!"

The left gear retracted as I slipped the bomber to the right to clear the paved runway and land on the grass.

"Mixture idle cutoff. Switches off. Fuel off."

I eased the plane onto its belly. All four windmilling propellers kicked up great clumps of dirt as the blades bent backward and quickly ceased turning. *Jeanne* slid straight as an arrow to a stop at midfield.

The crew climbed out and walked in silence past the field ambulance and fire trucks and rescue personnel that had responded to the emergency. Usually the crew would hang around, look over the damage their ship had sustained, but not this time. No one walked back to the tail. No one wanted to see the torn and splattered horror that had been their fellow crewman and friend.

"That was a nice landing, Captain," my copilot said as we walked away from the wreck.

"I've had a lot of practice," was all I could say.

I survived twenty-five missions then let a fellow pilot talk me into signing up for a second tour. My friend was very persuasive, said he was coming back, talked of the need for experienced bomber pilots like me and him to help the "new kids" coming over. I took a mandatory thirty days leave in the States then reported back to my base in England.

On my first tour I had arrived fresh, green, enthusiastic, ready to fight the good fight. When I began my second tour, I was angry: angry at the Germans, angry at the war, angry at myself for returning when I didn't have to, angry enough to want the job done, the whole thing finished once and for all.

After I arrived in Bury St. Edmonds to begin my second tour, I was assigned to the very same sagging bunk in the same drafty, leaky hut I had left. I threw down my gear and reported to Colonel Dougher.

"Fred," he said, "I'm glad to see you, but I have to tell you, your friend decided not to come back after all." This wasn't really news to me. I already knew that he had decided not to come back. "I know he talked you into this," the colonel continued. "I asked him to, so this is what I'll do. If you say the word, I'll cut orders to send you home. They need good instructors back there."

I thanked him and started to leave. "Okay," Colonel Dougher said, "I'll cut the orders today, but it will take a few days to get them approved. In the meantime, we're a little shorthanded. If you could fly a couple of missions while you wait, I would appreciate it."

I accepted his offer then left the office. Outside, I got so damn mad I nearly split a gut. I knew, and I figured he knew, that if I shipped back home now, in my own mind I would be a coward the rest of my life. I walked back in and told him to give me a plane, told him I was staying. He gave me the group lead again.

Taking a Jeep, I drove out to look over the plane assigned to me. It was a brand new B-17, all silver aluminum. Someone had figured out that it didn't matter what color daylight bombers were painted, so they quit painting them. It saved weight, and that made the unpainted planes a little faster than the painted ones.

I got hold of my new copilot and took the plane up for a check. It was a beautiful ship, all shiny and new, but it was the noisiest B-17 I had ever flown. To me it sounded as if the valves were rattling. I asked the crew chief about it, but he said the engines checked out all right. I still don't know why it was so loud, but I decided to name it *Lucy Valves*.

Throughout the first several missions I led, *Lucy Valves* behaved well and hardly got scratched, just a few holes here and there. Things were looking up a little. The flak was as thick as ever, but we had finally gotten enough belly tanks for the P-47 fighters to allow good fighter protection all the way to the target and back on most missions. That didn't stop the German fighter attacks, but fewer got through to the bombers. On the other hand, it only took a few to chop up a bomber formation.

Following D-Day in June '44, we began to bomb more targets in France in support of the invasion. The Allied armies were having a hard time breaking out of the hedgerow country in Normandy. We hit rail yards, fuel depots, factories, everything that would interfere with the Germans' efforts to reinforce their frontlines.

On one mission into central France, the flak was extremely heavy. Whatever was down there, the Germans were desperate to protect.

My number-four engine began running rough and steadily dropping revolutions. I glanced at it and decided, as long as it was producing power, I'd keep it running. A minute or two later we dropped our bombs, and I was concentrating on leading my group away from the heavy flak zone.

Wirtz, one of the waist gunners, called up and calmly asked, "Skipper, do you know number four is on fire?"

I didn't. I glanced at the gauges that indicated the engine had lost about 30 percent power. I looked out at number four, the right outboard engine, and things appeared normal until I looked back behind the trailing edge of the wing. A blow torch was streaming out from under the wing behind it. My copilot pulled the fire handle for number four while I shut down the engine and called the ship off my left wing to take over the lead. The fire gradually died down, but not before burning a crescent out of the trailing edge of the wing.

With the bomb load gone, we could hold altitude on the remaining three engines, but our speed was reduced and we began dropping back through the formation. For a while everything seemed all right. We were alone, but the sky was clear of enemy fighters.

A strange thing happened as we reached the Channel at about ten thousand feet. All three of the remaining engines began to lose power gradually. To this day, I don't know why this happened. I had never heard of such a thing. Maybe the air intakes of all three engines had sucked in debris from damaged aircraft above us. Direct hits and midair explosions blew junk all over the sky, and you had no choice but to fly through it. Maybe the new engines had some defect, faulty valves or rings or fuel pumps that were wearing out prematurely.

Whatever the cause, the instruments confirmed we were slowly losing power, not exactly at the same rate, but the engines were all definitely sick. They acted like they weren't getting enough fuel or air. We couldn't figure it out. We tried auxiliary fuel pumps, switching tanks, shoving the throttles all the way forward, moving the mixture controls to rich then to lean, checked the magnetos, checked for air induction icing. Nothing we did helped.

We began to slowly lose speed and altitude, but because we were over the French coast I felt certain we could make it back to Bury St. Edmonds as long as the three remaining engines did not quit altogether.

U.S. AIR FORCE

The B-17G carried a heavier bomb load than the B-17F, as much as six thousand pounds. More than eight thousand B-17Gs were built before the end of the war.

We got pretty close. The engines were still producing partial power when I lined up on the runway. I waited as long as possible before lowering the landing gear. It takes awhile for the gear of a B-17 to lower and lock. And hanging out there, the descending landing gear produces drag. I didn't use flaps, couldn't afford the drag or loss of speed.

We touched down maybe a hundred yards short of the runway. I thought if I held her straight, the roll out would be okay. The runway was close enough to touch when she tilted slightly to the right. A wheel must have sunk into a hole or soft spot. The plane jerked hard, swerved to the right, and the right gear strut collapsed. We skidded around on the wing and came to rest well clear of the runway threshold.

There hadn't been time to cut the switches and kill the engines. Three of them were hot and running when we lost the gear and hit the ground. We could have gone up in a ball of fire. We didn't.

As we walked away, I couldn't think badly of ol' *Lucy Valves.* Up to that day she had been a good ship. She had lasted ten missions. Any ship that got us home in one piece was a good one.

I was very lucky. I survived when so many air crews did not. I don't know why. I still think about all the friends who were lost. I suppose I could have stayed in the air force; flying was all I knew at the time. I tried, stayed for a while, but I never considered myself the military type.

LIKE SO many of his generation, Fred Koval came home feeling very old and tired. He was twenty-three. His bomb group, the Ninety-fourth, had been deployed from Smoky Hill Army Airfield, Salina, Kansas, to England with an original aircraft strength of thirty-six B-17 bombers manned by 360 crewmen. After arriving in England in April 1943, the group lost nearly 75 percent of its original force, including twenty-nine first-pilots during the first six weeks of daylight bombing operations. At the end of its operational tour, March 1945, the group's losses totaled 163 aircraft and 1,453 airmen missing, wounded, or killed. Col. Frederick W. Castle, the former commander of the Ninety-fourth, was promoted to general on 14 December 1944. Ten days later, on Christmas Eve, General Castle, leading the Fourth Air Wing on a raid over Babenhouser, Germany, rode his burning bomber to his death, victim of a German fighter attack.

CHAPTER 6

FERD MOYSE

An Artilleryman's Short, Happy Flight

For a time no one around him knew exactly where they were, what was going on, where the rest of their outfit was, or which way lay their objective. One thing was certain, however: The Germans sure as hell knew where they were and exhibited a damn unfriendly attitude. With a bum knee, he had run across the field to the only available cover, a sunken road lined with trees. Capt. Ferd Moyse was on French soil, under fire, with a bunch of lost airborne troops. It was no place for an armored field artilleryman to be.

After graduating from Louisiana State University with four years of ROTC training, Ferd found himself commissioned a second lieutenant in the U.S. Army in the middle of World War II. His name was thrown into the ever increasing pile of fresh young officers being processed by a chaotic bureaucracy responsible for assigning them to duty. At first he was sent to Fort McClellan, Alabama, then to Fort Bragg, North Carolina, then he was shipped out to Panama only to be shipped back to Fort Knox, Kentucky, where he was assigned to the Eighty-seventh Armored Field Artillery for training on the new self-propelled 105-mm howitzer designated the M-7. From Fort Knox, Moyse and the Eighty-seventh traveled by train to the East Coast with orders to board a ship bound for the British Isles on Christmas Eve.

Barely settled aboard by Christmas Day, they were ordered off the ship then ordered a week later aboard another ship on New Year's Eve. It was as if some bureaucratic nincompoop was determined that the Eighty-seventh was to have no celebrations before leaving home.

With no Christmas, no New Year's dance, no booze, no girls to kiss them farewell, the Eighty-seventh unceremoniously sailed for England and into the invasion of Nazi-held Europe. By this time, Moyse was a captain and the Eighty-seventh Division's liaison officer. Liaison to what? He wasn't sure.

One fine foggy day after months of training near Banbury, Oxford-shire, England, I was called in by my commanding officer, Lieutenant Colonel Barber.

"Moyse, we need a volunteer for a damn important mission."

"You want me to get a volunteer, sir?"

"I don't want you to get one, Captain," he replied. "I want you to be one. We have an urgent request for an artillery liaison officer for D-Day. You're the most qualified man I have."

"What outfit will I be with, Colonel?"

"One of the best," he assured me. "You won't have to worry about them knowing their job. They already have some combat experience."

"Who are they?"

"The Eighty-second Airborne."

That surprised me. "Airborne! You did say this was a volunteer assignment?"

"That's right. I can't order you to go. Every man with the airborne is a volunteer."

"I'm familiar with the airborne from Fort Bragg, saw a lot of jump demonstrations," I said. "They're all a little crazy. If it's all the same, sir, I would rather not."

"Well, Ferd, like I said, I can't order you to go, but there is one thing I want you to think hard about before you turn it down. If I have to find another volunteer for this job, and he goes in your place and gets killed, you will have to bear the burden of his death for the rest of your life."

I ordered up my driver to take me to Leicester where the Eighty-second Airborne "All American" Division was bivouacked. The orders were simple and direct: You are to immediately report to the Eighty-second Airborne Division artillery commander. I was told to take only my shaving kit and the uniform on my back. My personal gear would be packed and looked after until I returned to the Eighty-seventh.

A lieutenant met me upon arrival. "Hell yeah, we have airborne artillery—75-mm pack howitzers. They aren't too big, but we can sure poop out a few rounds if we can find them after we land."

"That's encouraging," I answered. "In the meantime, what's my assignment?"

"The colonel will explain. He wants you to meet him here at 1630 hours. That will give you time to draw all your gear. The sergeant here will show you to your tent and take you down to supply."

"Draw what gear?" I asked.

The lieutenant managed to keep a straight face as he explained, but I was sure I detected a smile on the sergeant's face.

"You need to draw your jump boots, uniform, helmet, combat pack, weapon, radio, all the stuff you will need, and of course, your parachute."

As I drew my equipment, I realized that unlike the armored field artillery where there was room in trucks, Jeeps, and tracked vehicles for a soldier to carry a fair amount of gear, the airborne had room for only what each man could carry on his back and in his pockets, and what he carried would have to see him through several days without resupply. There was no room for such niceties as spare uniforms, heavy rain gear, and other extras. Except for airdrops, weather permitting, there would be no resupply for the Eighty-second unless and until they linked up with the Allied invasion forces.

The woolen combat uniform I was issued was heavily treated with some sort of paraffin that made it almost nonporous. I figured it was to make the uniforms waterproof since it would be the only uniform any of us had. (Only later did I learn that the treatment was a precaution against gas attack.)

The airborne uniform had a lot more pockets than my old one and with good reason. With a parachute, a combat pack, weapon, ammunition, rations, hand grenades, and special weapons such as machine guns, mortars, mortar shells, mines, and explosives, all the "cargo" pockets provided places to stuff what wouldn't fit anywhere else.

Things like extra socks, underwear, matches, maps, extra ammo, grenades, compass, flashlight, and a few personal items like a razor, bar of soap, toothbrush, and maybe a pack of cigarettes and a candy bar.

Most paratroopers boarded their planes carrying upward of a hundred pounds strapped to their bodies, some with even more gear in packs that would be unsnapped and let out on long tethers, dangling below the troopers to land just before them, thus lightening the parachute a little to lesson the man's own landing shock.

There were a couple of things that distinguished my uniform from the rest of the airborne troops. One was the Eighty-seventh Armored Artillery shoulder patch sewn just below the Eighty-second Airborne insignia. The second was a little more unusual, although it wouldn't show. Supply had issued me a recycled web weapons belt that turned out to have the name "General Maxwell Taylor" stenciled in large letters on the inside. In addition to all my other gear, I would carry a radio capable of communicating on Allied artillery frequencies. Like all airborne troops and the pilots who would fly them to their destination, I was also issued an escape kit.

Good planning, I thought. *We haven't taken off yet, and they are preparing us to escape when captured.* I wasn't supposed to, but I opened my kit out of curiosity. I found several interesting doodads. There was a gossamer-thin silk map (easy to conceal), four gold coins (Hide me from the Germans and I'll make you rich), and a tiny compass the size and shape of a button. The compass was smooth and rounded so it could be hidden from one's captors in a very private place.*

At exactly 1630 hours I reported to Col. Andy March, commander of artillery, Eighty-second Airborne Division. After the usual amenities, he told me, "Your job will be to keep friendly fire off our heads."

"I'll do my best, Colonel."

"I know you will, Moyse, 'cause it will be your head, too." Then he invited me to join him for a sendoff banquet.

The banquet was to be a dress affair. When Colonel March learned that I didn't have a class A uniform with me, he loaned me his jacket. It was a generous offer, but there was one small problem: The

---

*Officers called it the button compass, but the G.I.'s had a more descriptive term for it. They referred to it succinctly as the asshole compass.

colonel was at least two sizes larger than me. At the banquet every other airborne officer wore a crisp, tailored uniform that fit him perfectly, but I walked in looking like "Goofey Goes to War," wearing a jacket with sleeves so long they hung down to my fingertips.

During the dinner the colonel asked me if I had a preference between jumping with the paratroops or riding in on a glider. I had heard many say that the word *glider* was a synonym for *suicide*. So I told Colonel March that I'd prefer to jump, trying unsuccessfully to sound enthusiastic at the prospect.

"Good choice," March commented. "Don't repeat this, but that glider business is the only thing that bothers me about this whole operation. Landing in the dark in a parachute is one thing; landing a glider in the dark is another."

The very next day I was assigned to a glider. Reluctantly I turned in my parachute since glider troops didn't wear them. The supply sergeant explained, "In the first place they would make the gilder too heavy. Besides, y'all gonna be so crowded in that thing, there won't be room fer 'em anyway."

Later I was briefed on my "volunteer" mission. As I understood it, the Eighty-second Airborne was to drop behind the shore defenses to capture some key road junctions, which would block German reinforcements and also squeeze the coastal defenders between the airborne troops and the men landing on the beaches. All the airborne had to do was fight off the Germans who would be advancing toward the beaches as well as any other Germans who might be retreating from the coast.

While the Eighty-second was fighting all these Germans on both sides, my job was to keep friendly field artillery and naval gunfire from shelling us. Nothing like being farther out in front of your own artillery than the enemy. If our artillery overshot the German defenders between us and the beach, or if the big guns undershot the Germans advancing to reinforce the beach defenders, they would hit us and I would get the blame. I think that was the real reason I was there—to take the blame.

Then I had another happy thought. Who had worked out the problem of preventing the airborne troops from firing on the Allied troops coming up from the beach, especially if the two groups encountered one another in the dark? I also wondered about the air force. Would the pilots mistake us for Germans?*

In the meantime, we were moved to the village of Honiton near Exeter in Cornwall. I stepped out of the truck bug-eyed! There were Waco gliders and C-47 transport planes all over the place. It was the first time I had seen a glider, much less gotten close to one. The things were made out of plywood, canvas, and Plexiglas. It suddenly dawned on me that these aircraft were designed for a one-way trip. I hoped the same wouldn't be true for the occupants.

Also worth pondering was the weather, and there was plenty of it and all of it bad. We set up camp believing that we weren't going anywhere until the weather got better. We were wrong.

At midnight on June 5, 1944, the order was issued to load the gliders. I was glad to find that my glider was to carry only troops, about fourteen men. Some guys had to ride along with things like Jeeps or 75-millimeter howitzers. I could just imagine what those things would do if they broke loose during a crash-landing. Of course, we were assured that was the only kind of landing a glider would make. Later, as it turned out, we learned that not every glider suffered serious damage on landing—only three out of four did.

As I waited to board my glider, my least comforting thought was that the only guys more stupid than those of us who had volunteered to ride in the damn things were the guys who volunteered to fly them. They had to sit up front in the hinged Plexiglas nose and, naturally, had to arrive ahead of the rest of us.

The glider's nose section included the pilots' seats and flight controls. This assembly was hinged at the top, and opened straight up about ninety degrees to allow loading and unloading through the front of the fuselage. The pilots, of course, were not supposed to be in the seats when the nose opened.

Later we heard about one glider's hinged nose flying open while the aircraft was being towed across the English Channel. Both pilot

---

*These concerns unfortunately proved justified, and not just during the first few days of the invasion. Friendly artillery fire and aircraft mistakenly struck friendly troops—and just as tragic, friendly aircraft were mistaken as German and shot down by Allied ground and naval forces.

and copilot, strapped to their seats, suddenly found themselves facing up instead of forward. The air rushing past them and into the gaping mouth of the glider was almost forceful enough to blow out the sides of the kitelike plane.

The pilots of the C-47 towing the aircraft immediately knew something was wrong when the drag on the towline increased dramatically, almost stalling their plane. They turned back rather than release the damaged glider over the Channel. By the time they reached England, the glider troops had somehow managed to pull the nose partially down and tie it off without anyone's falling out. The glider pilots miraculously managed to hang on, maintain some control over the craft, and land the thing. For their efforts they got to refasten the nose properly, reconnect the glider to their C-47, and once more be towed out over the Channel to their drop zone.

While my group was waiting to load up, we watched other gliders being attached to the C-47s, sometimes two gliders to one transport. I was still trying to come to terms with the fact that I was actually going to get in one, get jerked off the ground, towed across the English Channel, and cut loose God only knew where over German-occupied France. About that time a sergeant came around and distributed three or four pills per man, telling us the pills were for airsickness. I had seen a couple of gung-ho troopers throw up already.

I didn't want to lose my lunch and let everyone see how scared I was, so I swallowed the pills. By the time I crawled into our glider, I was a party boy. The only thing I can remember about the flight that followed was how short and happy it was. Everyone else was rightfully scared, serious as a hanging, while I sat there smiling like some half-wit. I felt wonderful. I don't remember how high we flew—allegedly five hundred feet over the Channel, fifteen hundred feet over the French coastline, and eight hundred feet to release altitude—nor do I remember how long we flew. I vaguely recollect antiaircraft fire coming up past us; it struck me as being pretty, like fireworks.

I found out later that I was only supposed to take one pill before boarding the glider and keep the others in case I needed them during the flight. I had taken all four at one time.

As happy as I felt, I have a clear memory of the landing. I was suddenly shaken wide alert by the hard bounces the glider made, pounding across the ground, shedding parts—like both wings. That got my attention. The Germans had the forethought to plant six- to eight-foot-high posts in all the fields. They tore up a lot of gliders, but not ours. We had a good pilot. He missed the posts. Trees tore our wings off. I'm not sure if we lost them just before or just after we touched down. What was left of the glider bounced along until it hit a ditch—hard.

The fuselage stood up on its nose, hung there a moment, and fell back to a semi-upright position. The pilot and copilot were killed. An overdose of airsick pills or not, I was out of that thing in a shot. We had landed in the middle of some Germans and were immediately under fire. Other troops around us were hightailing it toward a sunken road about seventy-five yards away, so we followed them.

I ran about two steps and fell. When I started to get up, I felt a sharp pain in my knee. I thought maybe I had been shot, but it was no time to stop to see. I kept going until I got close enough to the sunken road to dive in. Taking a moment, I rolled up my pants leg and examined my bum knee. It was bleeding, but I could see I hadn't been shot.

Gliders lie discarded in these Normandy fields while the C-47 tow planes circle over the landing zone en route back to England. These particular ships brought reinforcements and supplies on the day after the invasion.

I must have cut it on a rock or a jagged piece of wreckage from one of the gliders.

Naturally, with bullets flying, I ignored the knee. Hurt was nothing compared to dead, and there were enough dead in the field in front of me to justify that opinion.

Tactically, the idea was that the Germans would be the defenders and we would be the attackers. For those of us in the sunken road it was the other way around.

Soon airborne troops were defending both sides of the roadway. At first the position gave us a certain sense of security. The banks of the road were deep enough to provide cover, and the trees and thickets lining both sides offered concealment.

In the dim light of the dawning day we found it difficult to distinguish the friendly troops running toward us from the attacking Germans. We had passwords and metallic "cricket" clickers to identify ourselves to one another, but neither was audible over the noise of battle. It was inevitable that some friendly troops would be shot.

I saw two Germans shot down while trying to surrender. This was the first combat experience for most of us, and men new to combat mostly shot first and asked questions later.

Then the German artillery opened on us. Although they overshot the sunken road, many rounds that might otherwise have landed well beyond us instead hit the tops of the trees lining the roadside. The result was an air burst directly overhead. Casualties mounted.

Someone with a map finally figured out we were just outside the little town of Campienville, about three kilometers from our objective, Sainte-Mère-Eglise. It was time to leave. The plan was to fight our way toward Mère-Eglise with the hope that, along the way, we would eventually link up with the rest of the Eighty-second. What we didn't know was that the rest of the Eighty-second was scattered all over the countryside, doing exactly the same thing as we were.

Although the scattering of the airborne troops was anything but intended, it confused the Germans. There were so many reports of parachutists over such a wide area that the Germans were convinced the airborne assault force was many times larger than it was. As a result their commanders wasted critical time trying to decide where best to commit their considerable reserve forces.

The airborne troops didn't wait to sort things out. Squads found other squads in the dark and formed mixed platoons and eventually companies on their way to Mère-Eglise. Some like to say that the Eighty-second Airborne secured Sainte-Mère-Eglise four hours before the armies landed on the beaches of Normandy. "Secured" may be a stretch.

We finally got to the edge of the town and fought our way in— several times. The Germans didn't politely give it up. We would take a little area; they would counterattack and drive us out. I really couldn't say just when we felt we had "secured" our little piece of Mère-Eglise, but it was near dawn.

After a very long day, June 6, we spent a long, wakeful night waiting for the Germans to come at us again. I could see hazy movements at the maximum of my vision, but in the darkness there was no way to determine if the shadowy figures were friend or foe. No one yelled the password across the open space for fear of giving it away or drawing fire, and the distance was too great for the cricket to be of use.

Dawn on D-Day Plus One was just beginning to nudge the darkness when I heard the unmistakable clanking of approaching tanks. The rumble grew louder, and we all held our breath. We had nothing that would stop a tank. And we didn't know if these were our tanks coming up from the beachhead or the German tanks retreating from the invasion.

When the first one crawled into our dim, shadowy view, we still couldn't determine if it was theirs or ours. That question dried the spit from everyone's mouth. The lead tank kept coming while we hid behind a stone wall. Finally we could see . . . a white star painted on the front. Everyone cheered.

During the celebration that followed, someone had the sense to light off an orange smoke grenade, the prearranged recognition signal. Otherwise, the tankers, just as nervous as we were, might have fired first and asked questions later. If it was hard for us to identify something as large as a tank in the dimness of dawn, it was even harder for them to identify friendly troops.

With the linkup of the airborne and the invading armies accomplished, I sought out Colonel March and asked permission to make my way back to my armored artillery outfit. When the colonel

U.S. ARMY

On D-Day, three out of four gliders were destroyed on landing. Surrounding the wreck of this glider are the posts known as "Rommel's Asparagus," which were designed to cause maximum damage to gliders attempting to land.

remarked that I had done my job and that no friendly fire had fallen on us, I was compelled to say that I didn't deserve credit for that.

"Colonel," I explained, "my radio was knocked out in the landing. I've been unable to contact a single artillery outfit, much less the navy. The best I could do was relay our position through the command net when I finally had access to an Eighty-second radio. Anyway, they know where we are now, and you'll soon have several forward observers up here with you. I'd be a hell of a lot more useful to the Eighty-seventh, if I can find them."

In truth, I really didn't do anything; I just happened to be along with the airborne. The worse thing that happened to me was that I shot at a German coming over a wall at me that first night at Mère-Eglise. I knew I had hit him, because I heard him groaning for what seemed like hours. The next day I found him sitting against his side of the wall. He died hard. I had hit him in the stomach. I searched him for papers, maps, anything that might be of value to intelligence. The first thing that spilled out were pictures of his wife and little children. I've never quite been able to forget that German. I did what I had to do after that, but I never touched another one, never again.

My long walk to the beach carried me through several landing zones. Seen in daylight, I began to realize the high cost of the glider assault. There were broken gliders scattered across the landscape on both sides of the road, and in one place I saw the burned hulk of a C-47 shot down by AA fire. The wounded had been removed, but there hadn't been time to collect the dead. Some were still tangled in the wreckage of their gliders, some lying where they had fallen to enemy fire. On down the road, graves registration units were just arriving to clear away the bodies.

There were bits and pieces of equipment strewn everywhere, and the fields were covered with paper from the ammo and supply packing cases. Death was so common it seemed a natural part of the landscape. I found out later that the landings cost 11 percent of the glider force.

Behind me I could hear the muffled sound of small-arms fire, but in the landing fields there was such a stillness that, as I walked along, I felt detached from reality. Occasionally the quiet was disturbed by the whoosh of an artillery shell passing overhead, or the sharp HAR-UMPH of one landing a few hundred yards away.

Ferd Moyse's hike from the hedgerow country to the beach brought him to a scene similar to the one below. As more men and materiel were landed, the gains made by the landings on D-Day were consolidated and secured.

U.S. COAST GUARD

Only after nearing the beach was my attention drawn to a hazard that had been completely absent from my mind: land mines. Now I saw engineers posting warning signs and marking safe lanes with white tape. I wondered how many times I had stepped near a German mine.

The closer to the beach I got, the more mixed were the dead: German and Allied lying together in the ditches. Finally I could see the beach. Already crowded with men, vehicles, equipment, and materiel of every description, more of everything was coming from landing craft of every size and type.

I think I was about the only man moving toward the beach. That evidently gained the attention of a huddled group of officers at the side of the road. One of them motioned me over. He was Gen. Matthew Ridgeway, commander of the Eighty-second Airborne Division.

The general pointed at the two shoulder patches on my sleeve. "What the hell outfit do you represent with an armored artillery insignia and an Eighty-second Airborne patch?" he barked.

I explained that I had landed with the airborne and that I was trying to find my outfit.

Ridgeway laughed. "Hell, Captain, you might be worth more to me if the Germans had taken you prisoner. They would have had a hell of a time trying to figure out just how we dropped the whole Eighty-seventh Armored Artillery."

I told him there was something else they might have trouble figuring out. I took off my web belt and showed him that the name of the commander of the 101st Airborne, Gen. Maxwell Taylor, was stenciled on it.

"Damn, Captain!" he said, "I don't suppose I could talk you into surrendering."

Several years after the war, by happenstance, I encountered Ridgeway again. I reintroduced myself as "that captain you wanted to surrender to the Germans." The general remembered and remarked, "You confused *me*. Just think what you would have done to German intelligence."

On June 9, D-Day Plus Three, the Eighty-seventh Armored Artillery Division spent the entire night unloading their equipment from a ship. Their landing had been delayed in part due to some confusion (some of our people had been on a ship sunk by a mine) as well as the fact that there was more materiel awaiting de-embarkation than there was room on the beach to put it.

The next morning, while I still proudly wore my jump boots, I moved again toward Sainte-Mère-Eglise, this time with the Eighty-seventh Armored. We had hardly gotten under way when we received our first fire mission and pulled off the road to "lay a few rounds on Fritz." For the next thirty days, the Eighty-seventh was almost constantly tasked with fire missions in support of the 82d and 101st Airborne and the 4th Cavalry.

It was not until thirty-three days after my D-Day landing that I finally got a field shower and a fresh uniform. It was the same for most of the invasion troops.

It wasn't easy breaking out of Normandy, but eventually we got on a road that allowed us to make good time beyond the hedgerow country. What I especially remember about that road is an encounter with a little old woman.

We had been told that the road we were traveling was clear for several miles ahead. I was scouting out in front of my unit in a Jeep, and we approached what looked to be a deserted village. The only sign of life was the old woman with a small suitcase walking our way down the side of the road.

My driver slowed down, and I nodded my head toward her. Silently she looked me in the eyes, subtly turned her head from side to side, then glanced back over her shoulder toward the village. I turned around right then and went back to bring up my lead units.

It turned out that she not only saved my life but the lives of my driver and machine gunner and probably a whole hell of a lot of our troops. The village was packed with well-concealed, dug-in Germans waiting in ambush. We had one hell of a fight taking the town, bringing up our armored artillery and firing directly at them. If it hadn't been for that little lady, God bless her, we would have rolled right into that trap.

The Eighty-seventh fought from Normandy across Europe until the final surrender of Germany, rarely passing a day out of combat. Infantry units were eventually relieved and pulled off the line to rest, but the armored artillery was constantly needed to provide close support to each relieving unit coming on line as the battle front pushed forward.

I served all the way, eventually becoming the Eighty-seventh's executive officer. Still, my single most vivid memory of the war is the airborne assault on D-Day, the one that began with a "short, happy flight."

SOME THIRTY-SEVEN years after the war, Ferd Moyse and his wife were in France. He was drawn toward visiting his D-Day landing site. They rented a car in Paris, and he had the agent write out a message in French explaining who he was and that he was looking for the place where his glider landed, the field with the sunken road near Campienville. They set out across the countryside toward the village.

As they neared the town, he got the strangest feeling, a funny feeling like the hair on the back of his neck was standing up. He told his wife they had to be near the place and turned in at the next farm down the road.

Moyse went up to the house and knocked. An elderly woman came to the door. He handed the note to her and hoped she could give him directions. She read it and suddenly looked up wide-eyed at him. Then she hugged and kissed him. She called to her husband and got Ferd's wife out of the car. The French couple could speak a little English and took them through the house and out beyond a barn. "There," she said and pointed.

It was the very field. He could see the sunken road from where they stood. His wife and the French couple stayed back while he walked alone out into the field and toward that road. The closer he got, the greater a feeling of anxiety gripped him.

"Once I was on the road," he recounted, "I had an unreasonable and uncontrollable fear that I might find the bones of the dead we had to leave there that day. It was silly, but I was afraid to glance in the ditches by the side of the road or under the bushes growing alongside. I was alone, but I was not alone. I could almost see the field the way it was that morning—scattered, broken gliders, men on both sides of the road, the living, the dead, the wounded, the confusion . . . I could see it all, but there was no sound of battle . . . only silence in a peaceful country field."

He doesn't know how long he stayed out there.

When he returned, the French couple took Ferd and his wife into their home. They broke out a bottle of wine and treated the Americans to a happy little celebration. The little French woman told them that she had been caught in her house, as surprised as the Germans by the landings. Alone, she hid in the cellar all during the fighting. She was by herself at the time because her husband was a prisoner of the Germans.

After the little celebration Moyse visited an American cemetery not far away . . . row upon row of white crosses. "I was one of the lucky ones," he said.

CHAPTER 7

OSCAR L. RUSSELL

THE AMPHIB SAILOR

A wartime ocean voyage across the North Atlantic in winter gives a man pause to think how he came to join seven thousand other American service men bound for England and the invasion of Europe. Twenty-year-old Oscar L. Russell, navy gunner's mate second class (GM2c), was one such man.

I was a teenager when Japan bombed Pearl Harbor and Germany declared war on America. I lived in Natchez, Mississippi, and my family, like most others, was just beginning to recover from the Great Depression. I wasn't old enough to sign up for war duty so I joined a National Youth Administration school and was trained in sheet metal work. This led to a job with the United States Aluminum Company where I helped make aircraft engine cores. The plant workers donated enough money to buy a complete military airplane. Sadly we learned it was lost on the first mission it flew. America was in trouble and there was little good news.

I felt I was not doing enough working at a defense job. On May 5, 1943, I enlisted in the navy and was sent to Bainbridge, Maryland, for boot camp. There we did a lot of marching, but no boating. We

Twenty-year-old Gunner's Mate Oscar Russell.

spent most of our off time washing our white uniforms which got dirty every day. I was getting tired of that when I saw a bunch of guys wearing dungarees (blue jeans) instead of whites and asked who they were. I was told they were different from the regular navy. They were in the Naval Amphibious Force, sailed on smaller boats where things were a little more relaxed. I took that to mean not so much spit and polish so I applied for and became an "Amphib" sailor without knowing exactly what they did. I should have known better.

Next thing I knew I was in Pontiac, Michigan, where it was cold as the devil, to train in gunnery at the Pontiac General Motors plant where 20-millimeter and 40-millimeter antiaircraft guns were man-ufactured under license, the former from the Swiss company Oberlikon, and the latter from the Swedish company Bofors. There, as part of U.S. Navy Amphib Group 9, I learned everything about the feeding and care of small arms, machine guns, and 20-millimeter automatic cannons. We later trained on the 40-millimeter antiaircraft cannon.

When we finished that training on December 18, 1943, an officer said anyone who volunteered for a special assignment would get five days' leave. That sounded good, so several of us found ourselves at a base near Washington, D.C., for a big surprise. We were told that the assignment was a test that was classified top secret. We all had to sign statements swearing never to speak of it to anyone. Then we found out we were to go through a test with mustard gas. They gave us various types of uniforms to wear during several exposures to the gas in a special Quonset hut. After exposure we had to wear the uniform all day. Everywhere that gas touched us it caused blisters, mostly on the backs of our hands and necks but other places when it got through the clothing; pretty horrible stuff. We went to a military hospital for treatment. After the effects of the test were cleared up, we got our five days' leave. Many years later, we got something else from those tests, but that story can wait a while.

Oscar's group reported to Norfolk, Virginia, where they were introduced to landing craft of various sizes from the Landing Craft Vehicle and Personnel (LCVP), better known as the Higgins boat, to the larger Landing Craft, Mechanized (LCM) and then to the still larger Landing Craft Tank, Mark 5 (LCT-5), which was the smallest boat that could carry up to five tanks. Much of the instruction was done in classrooms. Oscar and fellow amphibs found that Norfolk was not too friendly to the navy at the time. They saw signs posted in some yards and places of business that said "No sailors or dogs."

Oscar was assigned to an eleven-man crew that was sent to the U.S. Naval Amphibious Training Base at Camp Bradford, Virginia, not far from Norfolk. There they received intensive training on an LCT-5 boat. When they finished amphibious training they were sent to Lido Beach, Long Island, where they received a series of inoculations to prevent diseases wherever they were going overseas. A short time later, GM2c Russell and his group received orders to proceed to England.

From all the shots we had taken we thought we might be going to the jungles of the Pacific. We were relieved to instead be going to England. We laughed about all the shots. What the devil did the navy think we could catch in England? I was excited about going. I had hardly been out of Mississippi before volunteering for the navy.

Oscar joined a long line of soldiers and sailors walking up the gangplank onto the largest ship he had ever seen. Docked at pier 90 on the Hudson River between West 46th and West 54th Street was RMS *Mauritania*. She was built in 1939, the second liner of that name. Painted grey for wartime duty, she had been armed with two six-inch and three three-inch guns plus a mix of 20- and 40-millimeter antiaircraft cannon. She had been designed as a luxury liner to accommodate 1,360 passengers with a crew of 800, but now her duty was troop transport. All her luxury staterooms, beautiful lounges, and grand salons had been stripped out and the spaces filled with banks of bunks three high to accommodate seven thousand troops outbound for war. *Mauritania* cruised at twenty-three knots, and because of her speed she sailed alone without convoy protection.

Oscar described the conditions encountered aboard.

Not only was the sea rough, but the ship maneuvered in an irregular zigzag course as a precaution against submarines. She could really roll, especially when making those zigs and zags. Men were crowded together everywhere on the ship. Many who had never been on boats began to get seasick before we were out of sight of land. Some lay in their bunks nearly the whole time heaving into buckets or their helmets or onto the deck. The whole ship smelled of vomit. You could get fresh air topside but it was really cold up there, and, even in the cold wind, men lined the rails throwing up. Like most of the sailors who had received training on boats, I never got sick, but trying to eat in the crowded chow hall was an experience. We were fed only twice a day in shifts. The huge main dinning salon had been converted to long rows of tables with benches. There was hardly room to walk down the aisles in between. You picked up a tray and went down a serving line and then sat where you could. The North Atlantic in winter can get pretty rough. When the ship rolled, if you were not careful, your tray could quickly slide several seats down one way or the other. Trays on the end slid off onto the deck. Then, when the ship rolled the other way the trays'd slide back. Sometimes when a tray slid back to its owner he might find that during the roll someone had thrown up in it. You quickly learned to eat with one hand and hold the tray steady with the other.

The general misery went on from seven to eleven days; Oscar is not certain. It was a longer crossing than the fast ship usually made because it was diverted far up toward Iceland due to a submarine threat. Finally, *Mauritania* steamed down the North Channel between Scotland and Ireland into the Irish Sea to dock at Liverpool, England. Disembarking took time. There was a lot of confusion. Men were running up and down trying to find their outfits. Army sergeants and navy chiefs were forming up their units shouting out roll calls. Officers searched for assigned transportation. The biggest mess was sorting out the white navy sea bags and green army duffel bags that had been unloaded in huge piles on the dock. Each man had his name stenciled on his bag, but finding it in big piles was a problem.

Our amphibious crew finally boarded a train that took us up the line to a small station where we got off and marched to barracks-like quarters. We were assigned to an LCT-5, but the boat wasn't ready. It had been built in America, but lend-leased to Britain, and had been in the North African and Sicily landings. It was old, rusty, and banged up when brought to England for refurbishment. We figured amphibious landing craft were in short supply because our boat and many others were to be lend-leased from Britain back to the U.S. Besides our boat undergoing refurbishment, we learned it was receiving special modifications—the installation of armor plate. Her classification was changed from LCT-5 to LCT-5 (A), the

"A" designating armor. That should have given us a clue as to what her job might be, but we had other things to worry about.

Our pay had never caught up with us. At our quarters we were charged for meals and everything else we might need. Some of us had a little pay left over or money loved ones had given us before we left the States. Others had almost nothing. What we did was share what money we had among our crew, including our newly assigned boat captain, a Lt. JG. I don't remember his name because the only way we addressed him was "Skipper" or "Sir." He was down to eight dollars when our pay finally caught up with us. Every man was paid back what he had shared with his mates. We had a good crew; had trained together and had confidence and trust in each other and we liked the skipper.

While we didn't have any money to spend on recreation, we devised a game that, I am ashamed to say, fraudulently and frequently got us away from the barracks for a while. I think it was Vallario who thought it up. He was quite a character. We would get on a bus which always ran a few blocks before the conductor got to us to collect our fare. When he asked for our fare we would tell him we were going to some place we knew was in the opposite direction. He would kick us off without collecting a fare, telling us we needed to be on such and such bus going the other way. We would poke around shops or pubs or sightsee wherever we got off and then do the same thing going the other way. Sometimes we had a long walk to get back to the barracks, but we had fun and saw a little of the city. But like I said, we were a little ashamed of ourselves. Still it was the only recreation we had because of a lack of funds.

Speaking of funds, there was resentment by the British Army and Navy men because in the first place there were so many Americans all over England, and in the second place the Americans were paid better and spent their money freely. This meant competition for the girls and that was the real problem. It kept the British military police, the American Army MPs, and Navy SPs pretty busy. Our crew stayed out of it primarily because we weren't being paid at all.

The LCT was the smallest vessel in the navy to be formed up in independent flotillas like destroyers and larger ships, a fact that was looked down upon with some disgust by those who considered themselves in the "real navy." The LCT was first born as an English design at the urging of Winston Churchill. He envisioned a boat that could carry at least three tanks and deliver them right to the shore, "or pick them up like we might have done if we had had them at Dunkirk." Churchill set the specifications. It was to be a boat that had acceptable sea-keeping ability and could sustain itself and its crew for at least a week. The Americans improved on the British LCT with the American Mark 5 design. Even so, the sea-keeping characteristics of the flat-bottomed, blunt-nosed, shallow draft craft were minimal in rough seas and not so easy to steer on calm ones. The LCT-5 was 114 feet 2 inches long, 32 feet 8 inches in beam, and had a forward draft of 3 feet. Crew quarters were aft, separated from the tank deck by a bulkhead. Over it located on the quarterdeck was the wheelhouse. For armament, the LCT had two 20-millimeter antiaircraft guns, or two 50-caliber machine guns mounted in steel gun tubs, one to each side of the wheelhouse.

The craft was equipped with a sturdy bow ramp that could be lowered to allow loading and unloading of tanks and other vehicles. It could carry 150 tons on its open deck. To carry such loads, the LCT-5 was powered by three 675-horsepower Gray Marine Diesel engines. It was slow with a cruise speed of seven knots with a range of seven hundred miles.

All LCT vessels scheduled for the landings in France were modified with longitudinal strengthening to allow the cutting out of a middle section of each side of the hull down to the tank deck to allow side loading of tanks and vehicles direct from docks or larger ships when ramp loading was not practical. The theory was that an LCT could be loaded faster that way as opposed to slowly backing vehicles up the ramp one at a time. To cover the cutaway openings, removable steel bulwarks were bolted to each side. The fault lay in that they leaked in any kind of sea.

The crew quarters, located at the stern on LCTs, were small, roughly twenty-six feet wide and thirteen feet front to back. To accommodate eleven crew members and their personal gear, and serve as the crew mess, the open space was crowded with two triple-decked and two double-decked bunks placed amid vertical stanchions supporting the quarterdeck and wheelhouse above. In addition there was a galley stove, a coffee maker, a large sink, a counter with six stools where meals were eaten in shifts, and crew lockers. With only ten bunks, one man had to take turns sharing a bunk with a man on alternate duty watch. In port, if no standing watch was assigned, a hammock had to suffice for the eleventh man. To the port (left) side of the crew quarters there was a thin bulkhead that separated a tiny officer's quarters. The bulkhead was so thin conversations could be heard from either side.

Just forward of the officer's quarters, there was a tiny head (toilet) with a small lavatory accessible from the crew quarters. There was no heat except for the stove. Ventilation of fresh air was minimal. There was no shower facility. The dishwashing sink and a small lavatory in the head had to serve for crew washup. Because of limited fresh water, clothes had to be washed in a bucket of saltwater or dragged on a rope behind the boat. They came out salty but smelling better. To add to cruising discomfort, the three diesel engines were located in the hull below and partly forward of the crew quarters. Whether welcomed during cold weather or cursed in hot weather, heat radiated up from the engines to the crew quarters above. When under way the rumbling and vibration of engines and propeller shafts was constant as was the roar from the exhaust. There was also a syncopated banging of the kedge anchor hanging off the stern in its steel cradle. Even when at anchor with the three main engines secured, the diesel generator, necessary to run lights, fans, stove, anchor winch, and charge batteries, and an aid in starting the main engines, throbbed its protest. The crew had no choice but to get used to the cacophony of sounds and odors. A man tired enough can sleep through anything.

Such close living conditions led to a more relaxed atmosphere aboard LCTs, which, as one amphib officer stated, "horrified the regular navy." Perhaps with some justification the amphibs were often called "a bunch of pirates" because of their reputation for "foraging" parts and supplies, a practice they had to do because normal maintenance supply channels tended to ignore or lose the smaller boats' requisitions, or lose track of their locations. Every boat had an unofficial "chief of scrounge" chosen for the ability to make "midnight requisitions" of everything from ice cream to water pumps and engine injectors. It was such practices that kept them serviceable.

One journalist wrote,

> To the layman, the LCT-landing craft tank looks like a tin shed with a false front, traveling upside down and backwards through the water. The major difficulty of the LCT as a water-going vehicle is that is has no sense. Instead of trying to ride the waves, it tries to club them to death. Another difficulty is the skippers of these crafts. They are all male Tugboat Annies, ninety-day wonders, graduated as Ensigns, truculent, fretful, quarrelsome, eager and more friendly than anything else on two legs that I have found. They bow before nothing. An LCT in the South Pacific that cut across the bow of one of our mightiest battleships did not give way. Instead, the skipper grabbed up a megaphone and shouted in the direction of the Admiral on the bridge, "Can't you see where the hell you're going with that damn thing?" In general, an LCT is something only a mother can love, and their skippers love 'em. . . . They have bestowed on them fond names, the regular Navy's names for them are not so tender. They call them water mules or spitkits, seagoing jalopies, sea jeeps, or just plain four-letter words.
>
> —Ira Wolfert, *Saturday Evening Post* (January 8, 1944)

As Churchill had specified, the vessel was designed for a cruise duration (fuel, food, and water) of no more than seven days. On longer legs the crew had to depend upon larger vessels for resupply. For cross-ocean transport, an LCT was small enough to be loaded by harbor crane aboard the deck of an LST (landing ship tank). Upon reaching its destination it was launched by ballasting the LST to list to one side and then cutting the LCT loose to slide over the side into the water. Crude, but it worked.

Some thirty LCT-5s were selected to be armored. Two inches of armor plate was affixed to the aft bulkhead separating the crew quarters from the tank deck. Two and a half inches of armor plate was affixed to the front and sides of the wheelhouse situated at the stern on the quarterdeck over the crew's quarters. One inch of armor was provided at the sides of the bow to protect the ramp-operating crew. Flat armor plates were added to each of the 20-millimeter guns. The armor added some seventy-five tons to the vessel. The armored LCT-5s carried the new designation LCT-5 (A).

With the refurbishment complete, the LCT-5s were lend-leased back to the United States and assigned American crews. GM2c Russell and crew discovered that they had been assigned to one of the LCT-5 (A)s but were only mildly curious as to the difference between their boat and regular LCT-5s. They were just glad to have their own boat.

Our quarters were pretty basic, but we had a home at last and were glad to get it. We were assigned to Flotilla 18. No sooner was our boat ready than our skipper received orders. We sailed northward from Liverpool, around the Isle of Man, and eventually entered the Firth of Clyde in Scotland. After poring over the complicated chart of the Clyde estuary, our skipper discerned the proper channel and navigated its buoys well inland to the newly leased U.S. Navy Base at Rosenath, Dumbartonshire.

On this, the first long passage for the crew, they learned why their boat was designed for short-duration amphibious landings and not long sea voyages. With one cabin that served as sleeping, cooking, and off-duty living space combined, the LCT was not a cruising yacht no matter how calm the sea and fresh the breeze. After a few days running, the poorly ventilated quarters stank of diesel fuel, cooking odors, and unwashed bodies in sweat-stained clothes. Fresh water was limited. There was no shower. One could "sponge bathe" oneself in a bucket; in the dishwashing sink, which was usually coated with grease from washing pots and pans and food trays; or in the tiny lavatory in the head if it was vacant, which was rare considering it had to serve twelve men. The crew had little choice but to get used to the stink of the boat, their quarters, and each other. Still, they wouldn't trade for a berth aboard a "big ship" for anything.

They all had jobs to do and did them. Just as in the regular "big ship" navy, the crew stood watches at duty stations. While under way, the men in the wheelhouse worked hard. The coxswain and other able-bodied seaman qualified to handle the helm had a full-time job holding the flat-bottomed, blunt-nosed, shallow draft boat on course. It tended to pound and yaw from side to side in any kind of sea. There was never a moment you could hold the wheel steady. There were lookouts posted at the small viewing ports cut in the wheelhouse armor. They served as extra eyes for the helmsman who could see little ahead from his station behind the wheel. When running a narrow channel or in formation with other vessels or docking, the skipper, often standing outside on the quarterdeck for a better view, would call for the helmsman to steer port or starboard or steady-on while shouting instructions to the motor machinists controlling the throttles and gears of the three engines. For example, to maneuver a tight turn to port in narrow waters he might, in addition to rudder commands, take such action as backing down the port engine full, stopping the center engine, calling ahead full on the starboard engine, and then bringing them all on line at normal settings once the turn was completed. Handling an LCT was neither easy nor a task for the faint hearted. When a certain boat was known to have a brand-new skipper, it was given wide berth by other craft, and for good reason.

The care and feeding of the engines was a hot job that required motor machinists to make frequent visits to the cramped engine room below the main deck. The feeding of the crew was a hot job also, especially if the crew didn't like the cook's chow. The gun crews had constant drills and maintenance chores on their equipment. The anchor crew had to maintain the anchor winch motor, drum, brake, and cable. The ramp crew had to keep the forward, small, gasoline ramp engine, cables, and sheaves in shape. Since radio silence was often the case, the signalman had better know-how to read and send flag hoists, semaphore, and blinker-light Morse code. Then there were the universal boat duties of keeping the entire vessel shipshape—inspecting and wiping down engines and accessories, cleaning quarters, washing down decks, chipping and painting, splicing ropes, lubricating everything that moved, and holding firefighting and man overboard drills. Only the cook was excused from such chores, but if the food was lousy, he risked being thrown overboard.

Holding all together was the skipper, who on such a small boat could win a crews' respect and confidence if he knew what he was doing, or gain neither if he was incompetent or acted the part of a martinet. In any case, the boat was too small for the officer in command to remain isolated or aloof. He could relax formalities, but he had to remain the officer in charge if the boat was to be safely operated and properly maintained.

Gunner's mate Russell and the whole crew admired their skipper for his ability to navigate the boat up the coast of England and Scotland into the Firth of Clyde, busy with large navy and cargo ships, and up to Rosenath. After all, he had no fancy navigation instruments, only a magnetic compass, a set of charts, a watch, and a pair of binoculars.

Upon arrival they found Rosenath an extremely crowded and busy place. Every type of amphibious craft was involved in training exercises. Russell, his skipper, and the crew spent the rest of the winter receiving intense amphibious training in docking, loading, beaching, retracting, developing individual crew duties and skills, and cross-training in each. The whole crew had to perform well during flotilla exercises in close company with other vessels. Collisions were a serious risk, and some did occur. In addition there was the task of keeping the crew fit through physical training. One good thing about the base at Rosenath was that the crew was quartered onshore in a Quonset hut. The first order of business was a hot shower for every man.

The Skipper worked the crew hard, especially those in the wheelhouse, the helmsmen, and the men who controlled the engines and those who assisted as lookouts in directing the helmsman. One of the men who stood directly at one of the observation ports was Lenny Weinberger. He was the helmsman's second set of eyes. Lenny was only five feet two inches tall. We all wondered how he got in the navy in the first place. In order to see out, Lenny had to stand on a large block of wood. Whenever we came alongside another boat or ship, Lenny would swagger out on the quarterdeck and challenge the vessel to show a sailor shorter than himself. I think we always won in that category.

While all that was going on, I drilled my gunners on fire direction, which was my job, and in keeping the guns clean and oiled. In an environment of salt spray a neglected gun could rust up in a matter of hours. We conducted loading and aiming drills. A 20-millimeter antiaircraft gun is heavy to swing around, and we had to get accustomed to doing so with the added weight of the armor shields.

It was cold and we appreciated living in Quonset huts in Scotland as opposed to being confined to our boat, but we had to endure weekly inspections of the hut and our gear. Although amphibs were not known for "spit and polish," we did well, got good grades for the skipper. In return, he took us on long hikes into the hills instead of workouts and calisthenics at the base. The hikes served as physical fitness and recreation. Once in the hills away from the base we were free to do as we pleased. Being from the Deep South I had only seen a light snow once when a small boy. From the hills we had a vista of snow-covered Scottish mountains. I have never forgotten the beauty of that scene.

During the last weeks of March, Russell's LCT sailed around Scotland, meeting rough weather along the way, and down the coast of England hugging the shoreline and ever watching for German aircraft and fast E-boats. They refueled and restocked food along the way to reach Plymouth, England, on the south coast. There were more boats and ships in the area than Russell had ever seen. Many were anchored, but Russell's boat was directed to join LCT vessels docked side by side, bow-in along the harbor shore at Queen Ann's Battery. They spent the months of April and May taking part in flotilla exercises, landing in all weather and tides at such beaches within reach such as Slapton Sands, Devon, that were said to be similar to the landing beaches in France. It was at Slapton Sands where during a night amphibious exercise of LSTs on the 28th of April, several German torpedo E-boats sneaked in among the group, sank two, and damaged one of the amphibious ships, all loaded with troops to take part in a practice landing. The cost was high—the death of nearly eight hundred American soldiers and sailors. That incident was kept secret. Russell and his mates only heard rumors of the tragedy.

It was now no secret to the LCT crew as to where they were going. With the huge buildup of troops, vehicles, artillery, gasoline, and stores of every description, everyone in England as well as German headquarters in Berlin knew the invasion of France was coming and soon. They just didn't know when or where.

Then one morning toward the end of May, barbed-wire barricades suddenly appeared with MPs blocking off access to the port and armed sentries patrolling the entire area. All leaves were canceled. Troops marched or rode in but no one went out—neither did any mail or phone calls.

Seabees (members of Naval Construction Battalions) came aboard Russell's boat and built a heavy platform out of twelve-by-four-inch timbers on the deck some distance behind the ramp. The skipper did not speak about it. The boat took on fuel, and extra food was stored in a side storage locker.

Early on June 4 they motored their LCT to a vehicle loading dock. They lowered the ramp and two Sherman tanks, one with a bulldozer blade attached, carefully backed onto the boat and maneuvered up on the wooden platform side by side. It was easy to see that the purpose of the raised platform was to allow the tanks to fire forward over the bow ramp. The crew, adding up the fact that their boat was armored and that it had been further modified to allow tanks to fire over the ramp, began to get a little nervous.

As night fell, a Navy Combat Demolition Unit combined with an Army Engineer Demolition Team came on board and settled onto the open deck space behind the tanks. The combined group numbered forty-one souls including one officer. Their job, which they did not discuss with the boat crew, was to open fifty-yard gaps in the obstacles the Germans had planted to wreck landing craft. The purpose of the dozer tank was to help them.

As with all the troops scheduled for the invasion, they wore wool OD (olive drab) uniforms that had been impregnated with some sort of smelly waxlike substance. (Oscar Russell did not know it at the time, but he had played a part in the development of the protective clothing.)

During the night of June 4, the order was given to start engines. All three rumbled to life and sat idling as the skipper repeatedly checked his watch. The hands seemed to move agonizingly slow. The crew was uncharacteristically quiet. The demolition troops had settled down. Most were sitting; some were checking their gear one more time. The tank crews sat on the wooden platforms beside their tanks taking a last smoke. Then it was time. Lines were cast off. The LCT moved away from the dock out into the harbor where it took a waiting LCM (Landing Craft, Mechanized) under tow. They joined a long line of LCT-5 (A)s, each with a single blue light on its stern for the boat behind to follow. In the darkness and deteriorating weather they could sense more than see the enormous flotilla of ships and landing craft heading toward France.

Operation Overlord, the long-awaited invasion of Europe, was under way, transported and supported by Naval Operation Neptune involving some 2,493 vessels of all shapes and sizes. The first landings on French soil were scheduled for 06:30 on the morning of June 5.

Once at sea, Skipper stepped into his tiny compartment and, as instructed, removed sealed orders from the boat's safe and opened them. His boat, as with all LCT-5 (A)s, was assigned to O-1, the first wave to land. The orders designated his landing site as Fox Green, an area marked on the map at the east end of a five-mile section of the French coast code-named Omaha. When six thousand yards offshore, he was to transfer the combined demolition team from his LCT to the LCM they were towing. There were sixteen such teams scheduled to land in the first wave. Their job was to clear gaps fifty yards wide in the rows of obstacles the Germans had placed on the beaches. The LCM and the LCTs carrying tanks to support them would run in to the beach together.

The weather was ugly and getting worse. The wind had risen steadily and was now at force 6 on the Beaufort scale, building waves ten or more feet high. The LCT was having trouble keeping in formation. Intermittently they lost sight of the vessel they were following. Weighed down by the extra weight of added armor and the tanks they carried, they were shipping water and spray over the bow and sides—lots of it. The men they carried on the open deck had no shelter. They were miserable, wet, cold, scared, and seasick. The deck they tried to sit or sleep on was awash.

All ships and boats had to maintain strict radio silence lest the Germans detect the fleet and its intention. Some boats were already in trouble and would founder.

Sometime between the last hours of June 4 or the first hour of June 5, a PT (Patrol Torpedo) boat, riding the sea wildly as a bucking horse, managed to come alongside Russell's boat. Yelling through a hailer, they conveyed new orders. The landing was canceled. All boats were to return to their starting point.

To try to continue crossing the English Channel in such weather, much less attempting beach landings, would have ended in disaster. Yet, how most of the 2,493 ships and boats managed to reverse course in the dark and storm-tossed English Channel is beyond contemplation by the most experienced mariner. Even more remarkable is that the amphibious boats found their way back to sheltered harbors, inlets, and bays. June 5 was less than an auspicious beginning for the breaching of Hitler's Atlantic Wall.

Sadly there were boats that foundered. It is interesting to note that President Roosevelt, upon asking questions following a review of Overlord by General George Marshall's and Admiral Ernest King's staffs, discovered there were no dedicated sea rescue vessels included in the planning. He insisted that the oversight be corrected. At that late hour it was too near the proposed invasion date to design and build such specialized vessels in time to participate. The only solution, quickly decided upon, was to transport sixty eighty-three-foot, wooden, gasoline-powered U.S. Coast Guard (USCG) Cutters from the U.S. East Coast to England. Their orders were to perform rescue duty during Operation Neptune.

Because they were wood and used gasoline to power their engines, the navy used the pejorative term "The Matchbox Fleet" to describe them. It was the Coast Guard in those wooden patrol boats that courageously performed rescues during rough-weather channel crossings as well as close inshore under fire during the Normandy landings. They were the boats that rescued many men from the channel on the night of the aborted invasion of the fifth of June. On D-Day, sixth of June, they would pull more than four hundred men from the water.

With mention of the Coast Guard, it would be remiss not to note that during the Normandy landings as well as landings in North Africa, the Mediterranean, and the Pacific, USCG personnel manned U.S. and British supply ships, LSTs, Higgins boats, and rescue vessels. Their courageous contribution to victory has never received the recognition they deserve.

On the night of June 5, the fleet was ordered to sail once more for the invasion of France. The weather was not good, but it was somewhat abated from that of the day before. The LCT was designed for short-run transport of men, vehicles, and supplies onto shore. There were no provisions or facilities to sustain the forty-one demolition troops and ten tankers they had taken aboard. The troops had been confined to the vessel since early morning on June 4. They were wet, cold, and wretched, having had no food but the field rations they carried when they boarded and having tried to sleep on open decks awash and soiled with vomit and worse. Without respite they found themselves once more tossed by rough channel seas bound for landing on the coast of Nazi-held Normandy. About the best the boat crew could offer them was hot coffee for those who could keep it down.

The plan was to land at low water on a rising tide. The theory was that at low water the beach obstacles would be exposed, making it easy for the demolition teams to plant charges and destroy gaps in them, never mind that the Germans might not approve. The plans assumed the boats landing in following waves would have fifty-yard clear paths through the mined steel and log obstacles designed to rip open the bottoms of landing craft.

What the miserable soldiers and their amphibious boat crews, as well as those in command of Operation Overlord did not know, and what would later be called one of the great intelligence failures of the Allied planners in World War II, was what awaited the assault force on a five-mile stretch of beach on the northern coast of France code-named Omaha.

With great effort the Allies had successfully convinced the German high command that the invasion forces would cross the narrow Straits of Dover and land in the area of Calais. As a result, Allied intelligence confirmed that the best German troops available were all concentrated there. Intelligence determined that the German troops manning the Normandy defenses some 140 miles down the coast to the southwest were coastal defense regiments made up of mixed units of a type rated only fair in combat ability. What they did not know was that the 352nd Field Division of the German Army had been relocated as a precaution to strengthen the defense of Normandy. At least a third of the division and all the officers and cadre were combat-experienced troops from the Eastern Front. During the preceding months, the 352nd had been brought up to full strength and was a first-rate fighting force.

Omaha Beach stretched along a gentle crescent between rocky cliffs at each end and backed by bluffs rising 100 to 170 feet high. The bluffs were broken in five places by natural draws leading down to the beach, one of them with a paved road. The draws afforded the only way to get tanks and vehicles off the beach, up the bluffs, and onto the flat land beyond.

The 352nd Division at Omaha prepared the defense of those draws by creating fifteen strongpoints called Widerstandsnesters ("resistance nests"). The Allies knew the draws would be heavily defended. They knew about the big guns located in eight gun casemates and four open positions. They knew mines had been attached to beach obstacles and planted in beach sands and on bluffs. They knew the beach would be covered by machine guns from the bluffs, and mortars behind them, but there was much they did not know.

The invasion commanders had no idea that the 352nd Division had moved in to defend Omaha. The invasion planners did not know that the combat-hardened troops had brought with them sixty light artillery pieces (many of them captured Russian guns) and thirty-seven deadly 88-millimeter guns. Neither did they know there were pillboxes cleverly laid, not to provide light artillery and machine-gun fields of fire toward the sea, but rather to provide enfilading fire down the length of the beaches. These pillboxes were completely concealed from direct view from seaward by concrete walls that extended well beyond the barrels of the guns and were covered with earth. These acted as screens to hide muzzle flashes. These emplacements did not show up in aerial photographs. The use of flashless, smokeless powder ammunition and the fact that they used no tracer bullets made them extremely hard to locate. Along the bluffs, in between the draws and Widerstandsnesters, were trenches, rifle pits, and an additional eighty-five machine-gun emplacements, many connected by tunnels. There was no area of the beach that could not be covered by enfilading machine-gun and light artillery fire from pillboxes, frontal suppressive fire from the bluffs above, and indirect fire from mortar emplacements inland.

All of that is what awaited the already tired, ill-fed, spray-drenched, cold, and seasick men tossing through the night in rough seas headed for a five-mile stretch of French beach. Nearly one thousand of those men would die for every mile of sand on Omaha.

In the twilight before dawn, June 6, Oscar Russell and his crew got their first distant look at Normandy as the heavy guns of the naval task force, twelve thousand yards off the French coast, shelled the shore line. The troops had been told that a large flight of Allied bombers would drop bombs on the enemy positions and especially on the beaches to destroy mines and barbed wire and create craters to provide cover for men working their way across the sands to the bluffs. The bombers had come, but low cloud cover precluded bombardiers' visual sightings and forced them to use a radar technique to determine when to release their bombs. As a result, the closest bomb to the beach fell a quarter of a mile inland. None of the landing troops approaching the beach knew of this failure.

Plans called for special DD tanks (Duplex Drive tanks that had floatation skirts and propellers) to be launched and "swim in" to their designated zones on the beaches followed by demolition teams in their LCMs. The DD tanks were to provide cover for the demolition teams while they cleared fifty-yard gaps in the beach obstacles. The teams were to accomplish this in twenty to thirty minutes by setting and exploding charges on individual obstacles before the rapidly rising tide could cover them. The beach would then be open to wave after wave of infantry, vehicles, and supplies landing at preset intervals. Only minutes behind the teams, the LCT (A)s would land their tanks to begin destroying enemy emplacements. The first wave of infantry would follow. At least that was the plan.

The weather, though much improved from the day before, was still ugly with winds registering four on the Beaufort scale (eighteen knots) with waves six feet or greater at sea and surf breaking on the beach. Six thousand yards offshore the transfer of the demolition team from Russell's LCT (A) to their LCM, dangerously pitching and banging alongside, took longer than planned and delayed the start of both boats toward the beach. An LCT, five hundred yards to port, dropped its ramp to launch the three DD tanks it was carrying. Gunner's mate Russell, gunner's mate Dilbert Lyles, and their crews manning the 20-millimeter guns; the skipper and those in the wheelhouse; and the demolition teams in their LCM beside them watched in shock as one DD tank after another dropped off the ramp and, within twenty or thirty yards, were swamped in the six-foot seas and sank. Their flotation skirts had been designed for a maximum of 2.7 foot waves, not the six-foot waves into which they had launched. The tank crews were seen popping up to the surface floundering in their life belts.

> The 741st Tank Battalion launched twenty-nine of its thirty-two duplex-drive tanks offshore and immediately lost twenty-seven when they foundered and plunged to the bottom of the Channel. Only two swam ashore. The skipper of the LCT transporting the remaining three DD tanks refused to launch them. He ran them into shore where at water's edge they immediately fell prey to German gunners. (War Department, Center for Military History)

Russell's skipper, witnessing the failure of the DD tanks that were supposed to defend the men he had just put into an LCM, determined that he would put the tanks he carried up on the shore, obstacles or no obstacles.

The tank crews on board the LCT started their engines. At two thousand yards the tanks opened fire on the bluffs ahead, lowering the elevation of their gun barrels at intervals to maintain hits on the bluffs and any structures they could see as the distance to the targets closed. With the LCT rising, plunging, and yawing in the rough sea, few tank rounds landed where intended. At 1,500 yards GM2c Russell and his teams opened fire on the bluffs with their 20-millimeter guns. They could see very little on shore. The naval gunfire had started brush fires, the drifting smoke from which obscured not only targets on shore but also the landmarks the landing-craft skippers had been given to guide them in to assigned landing zones. In addition, the incoming tide was sweeping all boats eastward at a speed of more than two knots. Many would land as much as eight hundred yards or more from their assigned landing zones. As a result most Group 0-1 landings were made behind schedule and at the wrong place.

Russell's skipper had an unmistakable landmark to serve as a general guide: the jutting cliff east of his assigned zone, Fox Green. The inbound boats began to receive artillery and mortar fire. Several rounds splashed near Russell's boat. At eight hundred yards they began to hear scattered hammering sounds against the armor plate that rapidly grew in intensity as they closed to the beach. They were taking heavy machine-gun fire and more. Lenny Weinberger, standing on his wooden block searching for a gap in the obstacles, was yelling directions to Coxswain McClure at the helm when there was an ear-splitting metallic sound like no one aboard had ever heard. Something, likely an 88 shell, pierced low through the two-and-a-

LCT-5 A with tanks up on the forward platform. Note the rough sea with LCT-5 A riding low under the heavy load.

NATIONAL ARCHIVES

half-inch armor plate, knocked the wooden block out from under Lenny, and passed out the back of the wheelhouse without exploding. Lenny, lying on the deck stunned speechless, kept pointing wide-eyed at a hole about three inches in diameter in the armored wheelhouse bulkhead. The skipper took Lenny's lookout port and directed the helmsman and motor machinists manning the throttles and gears.

As we closed on the beach I could see more than a hundred holes right through our still-raised landing ramp. The tanks were OK. They could take machine-gun fire, but stuff was bouncing off our armored gun shield. We could not pick out specific targets so we fired like crazy along the crest of the bluff wherever we saw muzzle flashes. I expected my loader or the other gun crews would be hit any second. The skipper must have thought so, too. He yelled for us to get in the wheelhouse and somehow we did without losing a man.

Things were getting pretty chaotic in there, too. I just tried to stay out of the way. I was looking out the side port when I saw the LCM with the team we had carried coming in just ahead of us and off to the side about fifty yards. They had been taking fire inbound, but when they dropped their ramp I witnessed the first of the many horrible sights that became common that day. When the LCM dropped its ramp the men in front were hit before they got off, more than I could count cut down like nothing you can imagine. How any of them got off I don't know. Some were going over the sides. I couldn't believe the courage of those men. They spread out in the water and set to work doing their job trying to clear the obstacles. The water was kicking up with bullets all around them. Some were trying to pick up the wounded, trying to get them back on the LCM. Several of them were shot down. Others struggled to drag off a rubber raft loaded with their explosives. They were shot down. I looked to see if I could spot from where the fire was coming thinking I could go back to my gun, but I couldn't locate a target. I looked back and saw the sailor in charge of the LCM go berserk trying to retract from the beach. He backed away with his boat deck covered with the blood of the dead and wounded lying where they had been hit.

Skipper picked a spot and called for all engines full ahead. I think in the excitement he forgot to order the kedge anchor dropped on the way in. We were pretty close when we bumped a sandbar. It looked like there was a deep runnel between the bar and the beach. We had seen that in practice landings where we stopped on a bar and the water between the bar and the beach was deep enough to drown a man or a vehicle. Skipper took the wheel and wagged the rudder to port and starboard with the engines at full trying to work us on across the bar and somehow did it. The ramp was dropped and the tanks got off in about three feet of water. Skipper called to Joe Carman on the gears to reverse, and ordered Vallario on the throttles to go to full throttles to back off. The engines screamed like we had never heard. The whole boat shook like the engines were trying to jump off their mounts. Then things got silent except for the machine gun bullets hitting the boat and mortar rounds coming in close.

Skipper yelled at the engine men asking what they were doing and called for engines to be restarted and back down full. Nothing! Not even the generator. Vallario said the temperature gauges were all pegged in the red and volunteered to check the engine room. He

LCT-5 high and dry. Note that the anchor cage on right side of stern is empty.

made it there and back with bad news. He said the engines were red hot and the raw cooling water filters were jammed up with sand. He reasoned that when working across the sandbar a ton of sand had been sucked in the raw, cooling water intakes, all of them, the generator too. "The engines have had had it, Skipper, burned up," he said. We were stuck on the beach, boat and crew alike.

"What we gonna' do, Skipper?" the men asked. He tried to answer, but a mortar round landing beside us drown him out. It seemed that when a round hit in the water or went into the sand a lot of the shrapnel was contained, but still we heard pieces from near misses tear into the hull. If one hit the deck it would be bad. Skipper said to sit tight onboard as long as we can. I asked, "If we spot a target, can we fire what's left of our ammunition?" He wisely reckoned that since we lay immobile and our deck was empty, the Germans didn't seem too interested in us. We realized that was true. After a few minutes, we were no longer taking fire of any kind. They were interested in moving targets like the poor teams trying to clear the obstacles and the incoming boats. Skipper said, "Russell, you go out there and fire off that 20 millimeter with those damn tracers and all hell will come down on us." As if to confirm his point, way down the beach an LCM took a direct hit just off the beach. The explosion was huge. We were reminded that the LCMs bringing in the demolition teams carried rubber rafts loaded with a couple of hundred pounds of explosives besides the forty pounds each team member carried in his pack.

> The Navy and Army demolition teams in the first wave suffered forty-one percent casualties. (War Department, Center for Military History)

Things were to get a lot worse, and Russell and his mates would be witness to much of it. They had landed just down the beach from a draw, code named F-1, that was heavily defended by two of the Widerstandsnester-fortified strong points.

> The troops that came ashore at Fox Green took some of the heaviest casualties. On one Higgins boat carrying thirty-one men, only

seven got off the boat alive. (War Department, Center for Military History)

The tide was coming in. So was the first wave of infantry. The demolition teams in the vicinity of Fox Green, under heavy fire, had managed to wire up their explosives and were ready to set them off when the first Higgins boats, many caught on sandbars, dropped their ramps and disgorged their platoons of infantrymen into chest-deep water. Before the demolition charges could be fired, what was left of the navy and army special teams found the desperate infantrymen, many if not most facing combat for the first time, taking cover at the base of the very obstacles set to blow. As a result few gaps were cleared. What the landing troops faced was two hundred yards of sand beach that they had to cross under fire or die where they were.

Russell and his crew could do nothing but watch men fall under machine-gun, mortar, and artillery fire. And there were landmines, lots of them. There was no way army engineers could sweep the sands with mine detectors, most of which had been lost in the landings. The engineers, using bayonets for probes, crawled across the sand on their bellies finding and marking mines.

The tide was rising at the alarming rate of one inch a minute, five feet an hour. Russell watched the second wave coming in behind the first. There were already dead and wounded in the water and all over the beach. The second wave added to the count. Most of the tanks that had made it to shore to defend the landings had been knocked out. Many were burning, adding to the smoke obscuring the landing zones. One tank, immobilized with a track blown away, defiantly continued to fire until it was hit and set afire.

The dozer tank we brought in was trying to push away obstacles before the tide covered them but had to stop, not because of the tide or enemy fire, but because of troops seeking shelter around it. It could not maneuver for fear of backing over them. While a few men crossed the beach to the bluffs, many were crouching down in the water. What looked like a lot of floating helmets were troops crawling forward as the tide rose. From the wheelhouse we could see the wounded that had fallen on dry sand now being covered by the inrushing tide. It was terrible. The men too badly wounded to crawl ahead of the rising water were drowning. Some of us asked Skipper if we could try to help, but [he] said no, that we wouldn't stand a chance. He was right. We watched troops turn around to try to drag the wounded forward, but most of them were hit. I couldn't stand watching anymore and had to turn away. It was like looking into hell.

Radio silence had long been lifted, but communicating between units ashore and with headquarters at sea was difficult. Most of the radios brought in were dropped, shot, or disabled by salt water. Anyone on the beach that raised an antenna brought immediate mortar fire down on themselves. In addition, the Germans were jamming all frequencies.

Things were so bad and chaotic on the beach—wrecked boats, drowned-out vehicles in the surf, high casualties, and leaderless units due to dead or wounded commanders—that General Omar Bradley, Omaha commander onboard USS *Augusta* anchored twelve thousand yards offshore, stopped inbound landings at 08:30 and considered canceling further operations on Omaha. Then Bradley received word that small groups of men from mixed units were reaching the base of the bluffs.

Russell remembers what changed and what he believes saved the Omaha invasion that day. Navy destroyers had been ordered to screen the fleet twelve thousand yards out, but no German heavy artillery rounds reached farther than three thousand yards from shore and no aircraft or submarines threatened. With men ashore on the beach, the big gunned ships were afraid to fire on the bluffs lest heavy shells fell short and kill their own troops. The destroyer captains had been begging to be turned loose. They said they could get in close enough to see targets and deliver accurate fire. Finally permission was granted. Several destroyers went in to support the troops at Omaha. They risked running aground and shell fire by getting in as close as eight hundred yards.

I believe those destroyers saved the Omaha landing. There was the wreckage of some sort of stone structure on the bluff west of us. One of the remaining tanks was firing on it. I know now that it was the site of dug-in German guns that weren't being hurt by fire from down on the beach. I believe that destroyer must have seen where the tank rounds were exploding on the bluff and used that as a marker. In any case it fired a salvo of all its five-inch guns at that spot. Its 40-millimeter guns were working it, too. That German position went silent. That destroyer and several others began running close in parallel to the shore and pounding the defenses including the draws. I don't think they knocked them completely out, but they gave the men on the beach a chance to reach the bluffs. We could see small groups of them begin to climb between the strong points. Once on top they attacked the Germans from the flank and maybe from behind. I wonder how different it might have been, how many men could have been saved, if those destroyers had gotten in earlier.

About 1100 or 1130 hours the tide was at its high mark some twenty feet above where it was when we landed. With no engines and no kedge anchor to hold us, we floated further up on shore. It seemed to us that though we had been hit by lots of machine-gun fire and close mortar rounds, maybe once we were in close, the larger guns up on the bluff like the 88s couldn't depress their barrels low enough to hit us. I think that is what saved us that day. Anyway, as the tide receded we were left high and dry.

There was still some fire on the beach, but not much, mostly snipers I think. Troops were not having as much trouble making it across the beach. More tanks were fighting onshore and more men had made it up the bluffs. The tide was receding, and you could see the mass of wrecked boats, tanks, and vehicles that had been submerged by the high tide. They added to landing obstacles.

Skipper had been walking back and forth like a caged animal, stopping now and then to look out the ports. About noon he looked at us and announced he had had enough of doing nothing. He said we couldn't charge up the bluff and fight with only our 45 pistols but asked for volunteers to do what we could for the wounded. Every man volunteered. Army medics and navy corpsmen had come in with every unit including the team we had brought in, but many of them were killed trying to help the wounded. A medic leaning over a supine wounded man stood out as a target. More medical teams were arriving, but there weren't enough of them. Whether navy or army, they were dressed in the same OD uniforms impregnated with some sort of stuff. Some had blue bands around their helmets with a sort of rainbow crescent on the front and a red cross on their arm. Some had white circles with red crosses in the center painted on their helmets, but many took those off thinking they made them stand out as targets.

We were scared at first, at least I was, but we soon got too busy to be scared, didn't think about it. What we saw and what we had to do still haunts me at times. None of us were trained in anything but simple first aid. We spread out and started looking among the dead for the wounded. With some it was hard to tell the difference. You could hear those that were conscious cry out, but the unconscious were just laying there bleeding. There wasn't too much sniper fire, not the sweeping machine-gun fire that had killed so many. Maybe because we didn't look or act too much like combat soldiers they didn't waste ammo on us.

What we found on that beach was beyond awful. We didn't have but a couple of stretchers on our boat. When we found a live man, we carried him back to our boat, laid him as gently as possible on the deck, and took the stretcher out for more. Some of our guys and the skipper stayed to do what they could for the wounded. All they had was the boat first-aid box and the little first-aid kits on the soldiers themselves. All those kits had was a bandage and an envelope of sulfanilamide disinfectant to shake onto the wound. The guys receiving the wounded on our deck worked to stop bleeding, apply tourniquets to shattered limbs, and use water and rags to try and clean wounds and bandaged what they could. At the time, we didn't have any supplies of IVs or morphine or some new drug called penicillin. It was awful; the hurting and crying and moaning and dying. Sometimes we would bring in a man with an arm or leg bone exposed; the flesh just peeled wide open. There were a couple holding their insides in with their hands. We kept telling them they would be OK.

I don't like to talk about all this. You wouldn't either. There were body parts scattered around the beach, sometimes near the body they came from and sometimes not. I think some bodies were just blown to bits. One I can't forget was lying in two halves, insides stretched over the sand in between. We worked as fast as we could. The wounded had been out there since early morning, since the first, second, and third waves had landed. We found a medic and told him what we were doing and asked if he would come to the boat and help the wounded we had collected. He saw what we were doing and went out and got another medic. Before we knew it, we had an aid station on our deck. Our boat gave the wounded a little protection and the medics didn't have to waste time looking for the wounded. We did that, bringing them in one by one. The medics had lost most of their equipment and supplies landing in deep water. They had to do things like close open wounds with safety pins, but they did have some morphine.

It wasn't long before our deck was filled up. Then I guess word got around, and more stretchers and supplies showed up including morphine, IV bags, and needles. Every time the tide came we hailed Higgins boats and loaded the wounded on them to take out to LSTs that had been set up as hospital ships. They were anchored about two miles offshore.

There were still people crossing the beach that got hit by snipers, and more wounded were being brought down from the bluffs. Mortars were not shooting as often, but they were accurate and would hit a boat as it landed or a tank now and then. They had spotters up there somewhere. More gaps in the obstacles were being cleared, and the big LSTs began to arrive with vehicles, more tanks, and supplies. That added to the traffic jams. I think the draws must have still been closed because the tanks and trucks weren't getting off the beach.

When we caught up with the wounded in our area, we tried for a while to get the dead up on the beach out of the surf. It was so horrible and sad. Dead boys were rolling in the lapping waves. The wet sand at the water's edge was pink with blood. The bodies formed a line in the wash down the beach as far as you could see, all pushed to the shore by the rising tide. We didn't look at their faces. When I thought I just couldn't do it anymore, some outfit came in and started taking care of them, putting them up on the shore and covering them with blankets. They brought in a lot of blankets. We took a couple of big bundles of them for the wounded on our boat who up until then had none. Everything was in short supply.

> The plans for D-Day called for 2,400 tons of materiel to be landed on shore. At the end of the eighteen hour day only 100 tons had reached the beach. (War Department, Center for Military History)

The nights were the worst. We could only load the wounded on Higgins boats during the day. They couldn't see to come in at night. We couldn't show any lights, so the medics had to work by feel unless the moon was out. I really can't talk anymore about all that, the wounded and the dying and the dead. It never leaves you, you know, the sounds and scenes that pile up in memories you try to put away, far away.

I don't know how many days we were there, long enough to see medical teams organized with doctors and hospital tents, long enough to see burial teams pile the dead on trucks and drive them up the draws to bury on high ground. I think by June 12 the beach was pretty clear of enemy fire. Skipper gathered us together one day and said, "Boys, I thought we would get some kind of orders, but I think we've been forgotten. You men have done what you could, but looking at you I believe you have about had it. I know I have. Orders or no orders, I'm going to get us a ride out on the next boatload of wounded."

That's what he did. We rode a Higgins boat out to one of the LST hospital ships. The huge interior was loaded with about 140 wounded on stretchers hung on racks along each side and nearly a hundred walking wounded. They had doctors and medics on board and an operating room. Right after we got aboard, the ship took on a last load of wounded from a Higgins boat, closed the huge bow doors, weighed anchor, and made for England to unload, resupply and return.

Onshore we got a ride in a truck to our flotilla headquarters. Skipper asked them why we never received any orders or any messages at all. They told him they had written us off, that twenty-six LCT boats had been lost. Skipper asked when we would get a new boat. They told us there weren't any spare boats, that only nine out of the thirty-six LCT boats of Flotilla 18 were operational on D-Day + 1. Everything they had afloat was in use. They took our names and rates and told each of us to check with them in a few days for new orders.

It was more than a few days, but I got new orders. On the first page there was my name with some others that ordered us back to the States and said we would have ten days' leave. What a relief! I thought I was going home and my war would be over. That was before I read the second page. It said I was further ordered to proceed to Portland, Oregon. It didn't say why, but I had a feeling my war was not over.

I went by train to Liverpool where I had passage on a small ocean liner headed for its home port of Boston. They said it used to be named *Washington* but the name had been changed to *AP-22 Mount Vernon* when the military took it over. That ship had good food, better than I had had in a long time. The crew knew we were all going home and treated us really well. At Boston, I reported to the Argo building on D Street near the harbor. It was an old building about nine stories high serving as a navy receiving station. I lived there a few days until my travel orders were cut.

From Boston it was home to Mississippi. I was so happy to see my folks and all the people that stopped by to welcome me back, but they wanted to hear all about the war. I couldn't talk about it, not even a little. They quit asking. Mom fixed real good food like I hadn't eaten since I left home. At five feet eight inches, I left weighing 180 pounds but was down to 150.

One day Mom came from the grocery. She said because I was home, the butcher had cut some nice fresh pork chops for her even though she didn't have ration stamps for them. Fresh meat was rationed and hard to get at the time. She laid the package in the sink and asked me to unwrap them for her while she put away the other groceries. When I opened the butcher paper a lot of blood poured out. For a second there, I didn't see the sink; I saw the sand on Omaha Beach. I had to leave the kitchen for a minute or two.

While on leave I did things that folks at home took for granted, simple things for them I guess, but not for me. I would go down to the drugstore and get a milkshake, or sit at the kitchen table and eat a piece of pie and drink a cold glass of real milk—ordinary things to people in Natchez, I suppose, but at that moment in my life they were priceless. I was tired and the folks seemed to understand. They let me get a lot of rest, not just sleeping late, I had trouble sleeping, but sitting quietly on the porch or going down to the levee to sit and look out over the river.

Then it was time to leave home again. I packed, had all new uniforms, hugged my folks, told them not to worry, and boarded the first of many trains that took me across the whole country to Portland. I remember one station in a small town in the middle of the Great Plains where the ladies of the town passed out coffee, sandwiches, and cookies. The train was full of soldiers and marines and sailors. Those nice ladies made all of us feel good.

I reported in at Portland as a Gunner's Mate 3c. I had been promoted one rank. I was assigned to a boat called an LCS (L) (3), which I had never heard of. I learned it was Landing Craft Support, Large, Mark 3. I didn't know what it was. Turned out the LCS (L) was a mini-ship, 158 feet long, 23 feet wide, but with a flat bottom that drew only a little over six feet of water. It could make sixteen knots at full speed. The ship took a crew of up to six officers and sixty-five enlisted men. I figured that little ship was built for fighting. It was armed with a three-inch/fifty-bow gun; two twin 40-millimeter guns, one forward, one aft; four 20-millimeter guns; four 50-caliber machine guns; and ten Mark 7 rocket launchers. Somebody in the Pacific Theater knew what they were doing. With its shallow draft it could get close inshore to support landing troops. They sure could have used them at Omaha. I was informed that these little boats provided more firepower per ton than any ship built for the navy. I knew why I was there. It took a lot of gunner's mates and gunners to man them.

The one I reported to was LCS (L) (3) number 86. It was brand new, having just been completed and fitted out in Portsmouth at Commercial Iron Works. I found that most of the crew had been together since amphibious training in Maryland. That made me a new boy aboard, but when they learned I had been at Omaha Beach I had no trouble fitting in.

We left Portland about the 28th of December 1945, passed Astoria just downriver, and met the mouth of the Columbia River. Let me tell you, crossing the bar at the mouth of the Columbia River, we went through the roughest and wildest seas I have ever seen, and I had been in the English Channel in a gale. They call that bar the graveyard of ships and I know why. Those bar pilots earn their money.

LCS 86 was bound for San Diego. The trip down the Pacific Coast was without incident and served as a shakedown cruise for the crew. Once they reached San Diego they commenced crew training and gunnery exercises out around San Clemente Island. Given liberty, the crewmen of 86 found San Diego too full of sailors. Tijuana, Mexico, just across the border, was more to their liking. All returned with a picture to send home: a picture of themselves with a beer-bottle-drinking donkey. Russell reckoned the donkey's owner would retire a millionaire after the war.

Just before departing California for Pearl Harbor, LCS 86 received a new skipper, Lt.(jg) Houston. He was a no-nonsense boat commander. On the passage to Hawaii he worked the crew hard with all sorts of drills and frequent calls to general quarters until the crew could respond rapidly to his satisfaction. The sailors complained, but once on assignment they appreciated what he had taught them.

Number 86 arrived at Pearl Harbor around the 19th of February. The crew enjoyed a nine-day layover, taking in Waikiki Beach and such other cultural pastimes as studying the intricacies of the hula dance. At Pearl, Ensign William Wilhoit came aboard as gunnery officer. The crew discovered he had earned the Navy Cross and Purple Heart as skipper of an LCT at Normandy. From reading the personnel jackets of his gun crews, Wilhoit found out Russell had served on an LCT(A) at Omaha. The two got along well.

Resupplied, Number 86 received orders to lead a convoy of twelve LCTs to Eniwetok in the Marshall Islands. They departed Pearl Harbor on the first of March and began a long voyage toward an as yet unknown final destination. They passed Johnson Island,

Majuro, and were glad to drop off the slow-moving flotilla of LCTs at Eniwetok. From there they were ordered to Guam and from Guam to Saipan. All the Pacific islands they passed had been secured through hard and costly fighting by marine, army, and naval forces. The crew learned it was now to be their turn. As they departed Saipan, Captain Houston opened new orders. They were bound for the Japanese island of Okinawa. They did not know it, but they were headed for an invasion that would prove the most costly to both sides of any in the Pacific.

The little fighting boat, arriving just after the initial invasion, was assigned three duties: giving close inshore support to the troops fighting on the island, protecting the fleet on antiaircraft radar picket duty, and performing "skunk patrol," which entailed screening the fleet from small, fast Japanese suicide boats. Of the three, antiaircraft picket duty turned out to be the most hazardous.

On the 18th of April 1945, we ran across a Japanese supply barge trying to sneak in and sank it. A couple of days later, we supported an onshore marine/army action. We learned our rockets did more good marking targets for the big guns on ships offshore than the actual damage they caused to the enemy. Next, we were assigned our first night "skunk patrol" where we learned about suicide boats. They attacked only after dark. Any night there was bright moonlight meant extra danger. Enemy planes and suicide boats could easily see our ships in the moonlight. You hear a lot about the kamikazes, but not the suicide boats. There weren't a lot of them, but they had explosives packed in the bow. They could come out of nowhere and had the potential to do real damage. We were told that until they were sent on suicide missions at night they stayed camouflaged on small islands scattered around Okinawa like Tokashiki Shima, Ie Shima, and Izena Shima and the Kerma Retto Group. We later learned that most of them were small, carried about five hundred pounds of explosives, and had, of all things, Chevrolet automobile engines. They would sneak out at night running very slow and quiet to get on station, then make a short, fast run to their target. I don't think they were very effective. It was on the night of April 28 that we first met one coming out of Mae Shima. Out of nowhere we heard an engine roar at high speed, but at first could not see the craft. Then some of our sharp-eyed gunners picked it up and let loose. That thing blew up in a terrific fireball.

A few days later, we were on our first picket duty. Radar-equipped destroyers patrolled outside the fleet and coordinated target sightings with the Combat Air Patrol center. They would pick up incoming kamikaze flights and steer our fighters to intercept them. The Japs picked up on the radar destroyers pretty quickly and determined that if they could knock out the picket ships they would have a much better chance of getting through under the combat air patrols to attack our capital ships, especially carriers. As a result, two or three LCS boats would be assigned to provide extra antiaircraft support to protect the radar destroyers.

We were new at the game. LCS 63 was on station with us when we saw a single plane coming our way. The officers spent time trying to identify it as a friend or foe. The last thing we wanted to do was shoot down a friendly plane. Well that thing suddenly dove on LCS 63, missed them, and crashed just off our bow. Not a shot had been fired. The only thing that saved us was bad piloting on the Jap's part. It was a real wakeup call. We all, officers and men, got out the books and flash cards to study aircraft identification.

Not all the Jap planes were kamikazes. On bright moonlit nights it was easy for the enemy pilots to see our ships. At night they would send bombers as well as kamikazes. I was told we did not have many night fighters to cover the fleet. About the middle of May, after running on skunk patrol a few days, we were back on picket duty, station #5. One night we were on station with the destroyer *Braine* when five Jap planes attacked us. Together we shot down four of the five. The fifth one came over our fantail and dropped a bomb that exploded close off our stern. We felt it all right, but it did no damage.

A few days later, we were still with the destroyer *Braine* when three Jap planes in formation attacked our picket group. We shot down one and set another one on fire, but trailing flames it came right over us and hit DD *Braine*, setting her on fire. Then the second undamaged plane hit *Braine* and started a second fire. Sailors with nowhere to go jumped overboard to avoid the flames. We picked up about forty survivors and then pulled alongside *Braine* to fight her fires. LCSs were pretty good fire fighters. We had a water manifold forward of the bow gun and two monitors just in front of the aft gun. It took a while, but all of Skipper Huston's fire drills paid off. We put the fires out and took off some badly injured crewmen. We found out later that the fire had gutted not only the superstructure but much of the ship down below. If *Braine's* magazines had cooked off they would have taken us along with her.

A few days later, we joined a destroyer and two other LCS boats on picket station #15. Greater numbers of enemy planes were coming over, sometimes more than a hundred in one flight. It seemed we were at GQ (general battle stations) almost all the time. Nobody got much sleep. About the fifth day on station a lone plane came right through a hail of rounds and struck the stern of destroyer *Porter*. Again we were the first to get along side. We vainly fought the fires for three hours. Her skipper finally ordered the crew to transfer to our boat. The captain was the last to board us. *Porter* sank stern first as we pulled away. Her bow pointed straight sky-ward before she slipped beneath the waves. We had over 150 sur-vivors aboard which we later transferred to a DM (a mine warfare ship) and returned to patrol.

The next day on patrol with LCS 122, and 19, four Jap planes came at us. We shot the first one down. The second one, carrying a bomb, was hit and set on fire, but kept coming. It looked like it would hit us, came so close we could see the pilot, but flew past to hit 122 at the base of her structure and start a fire. Fortunately the bomb it was carrying went all the way through the ship and out the other side before exploding. The third kamikaze came low and straight at our fantail. The crew on gun #7 knocked it down with 40-milimeter rounds. It splashed just off our stern. Boy, did we cheer the gunners on #7, the only ones that could sight on the low-flying plane coming straight in on our stern at about three hundred miles an hour. Some math wiz on board figured it was just one second away from hitting us. The fourth plane turned away and climbed into the clouds. We and LCS 19 came along on each side of 122 and put out her fires. We and 19 took off the wounded, dead, and remaining crew except for volunteers who stayed aboard, got her engines started, and operated her from the aft steering station until a tug took her under tow.

The last half of July we patrolled station #16. Jap planes came in great numbers. A Combat Air Patrol engaged a huge flock of them right over us. We did not fire for fear we would hit our own planes. As I watched from my gun station I saw our pilots shoot down sixteen or seventeen of them, but two of our planes went down too. Our aviators did a good job, but they couldn't get them all. There were just too many. No vessel on our picket station was attacked.

Besides all their guns, the LCS boats were equipped with smoke generators used to cover the fleet on bright, moonlit nights. One evening we were making smoke upwind from the fleet. We covered them, but to do so we had to steam out in the moonlight. With no warning at all, a Jap plane came diving out of the darkness and missed us by maybe fifty feet. It hit the water and exploded right beside us. Nobody onboard will forget that near miss.

After eighty-one days, Okinawa was secured. LCS 86 with its flotilla was ordered to Leyte in the Philippines. The voyage was uneventful. Shortly after they dropped anchor the crew got a sure sign that the waters there were secure: a small boatload of nurses passed close by. From all the whistles, waves, and howls it would seem as if the men of 86 hadn't seen a woman in ages, which was true. At Leyte, the men got liberty, beer, ball games, and fun, but also plenty of work putting LCS 86 back in shipshape in preparation for what, after seeing the cost of taking Okinawa, every service member in the Pacific faced with bottomless dread: the invasion of Japan.

The eighty-one days of fighting on Okinawa had cost the United States, including a British carrier flotilla, fourteen thousand dead including five thousand American sailors. For the first time in the war, more sailors were killed than either marines or army men. The total estimate was 65,000 casualties wounded, dead, or missing; 26 ships sunk and 368 damaged; and 768 aircraft lost, including those lost on raids on Kyushu, Japan, 340 miles away. This was the cost of taking a Japanese homeland island only sixty miles long and four to six miles wide. No one wanted to think of what the cost of an invasion of Japan proper would be.

Two months later on August 6, while preparation for the invasion of Japan was well under way, an atomic bomb was dropped on Hiroshima, Japan. The world was stunned, but Japan refused to surrender. A second bomb was dropped on Nagasaki. Not until August 15, 1945, did Japan surrender. About 2100 hours, news of the surrender flashed around the harbor at Leyte. For several minutes many stood in dazed silence. Some men fell to their knees and thanked God. Then, as if a switch had been thrown, everyone went wild. Ships' whistles blew, ship's bells clanged, and flares of all colors sailed into the night sky along with sweeping beams of searchlights.

Oscar Russell's duty was not quite over. The flotilla of LCS (L) (3)s sailed on to Japan to aid in ensuring that Tokyo Bay was and remained secure. On September 2, 1945, GM3c Oscar L. Russell and crew aboard their LCS 86 were just across the harbor from the moored U.S. ship BB-63. From their small fighting vessel they were privileged to witness the formal surrender of Japan as it took place on the deck of battleship USS *Missouri*, BB-63.

A navy admiral dubbed the little LCS ships the "Mighty Midgets," a sobriquet they had justly earned in combat. LCS (L) (3) 86 received the Naval Unit Citation for "meritorious service and heroism in action against enemy Japanese aircraft and suicide boats during the Okinawa Operation from April 18 to June 21, 1945." GM3c Russell and all his fellow crew members were authorized to wear the Navy Unit Commendation Ribbon Bar. Years later, Russell would be awarded the French Legion of Honor for his service at Omaha.

Oscar went home, married a lovely lady named Helen, and got a good job. Still, after all he had been through, all he had seen, a deep calling came to him he could not ignore. After talking his feelings over with Helen, the couple sold their home so that Oscar could enroll as a student at a Baptist seminary. Oscar Russell spent the rest of his working life as a Baptist minister.

Near his retirement, rather strange ailments began to appear. One was an uncomfortable skin rash that with treatment would abate for a while only to reappear. Another more serious problem manifested itself. He began to lose his sight due to chronic conjunctivitis, keratitis, and corneal opacities. The Veterans Administration, after many consultations, could not determine that the cause was service related. You see, even though Oscar suspected the cause, he still honored the oath he had signed to never talk of the secret tests involving his and others' exposure to mustard agents including sulfur mustard, nitrogen mustard, and lewisite.

Those volunteers were never told that the purpose of the tests was to develop antigas protective clothing. They never knew the tests resulted in the formulation and manufacture of CC-2 antigas paste, a greasy, foul-smelling coating used to impregnate the uniforms that all combat troops wore during the invasion of Normandy. There had been reports that Hitler had used mustard gas during the invasion of Poland in 1939, after Mussolini had used it in Ethiopia in 1936. That intelligence generated great fear that Hitler would resort to poison gas to stop the Allied invasion of Normandy.

By 1991 Oscar, in his late sixties, and other ex-servicemen were losing their sight and being diagnosed with skin cancer. As they sought treatment at veterans' hospitals around the country, the Veterans Administration could find no information of human mustard gas testing, no medical records, and no follow-up records. The veterans could present no proof that the ailments were service connected. Finally, in 1993, after many complaints were filed, a study was conducted of the claims. The results released in 1999 stated that an estimated four thousand servicemen may have participated in secret chemical tests. Still, it was not until 2005 that the top secret testing program was declassified. At the time Oscar was eighty-two years old. By this time many of his fellow volunteers who had suffered similar ailments were deceased and never received any compensation (VA Fact Sheet, April 1999; VA news release, March 2005; letter to Oscar Russell from the undersecretary of Veterans Affairs, November 28, 2005).

Oscar is still trying to subdue memories of war that disturb his sleep, and after suffering from skin cancer and blindness, you might be surprised at what retired reverend Oscar L. Russell had to say about it all.

I'm just glad that when the call came to help keep our nation free, I was able to serve my country and my God. I am proud to be called Christian and an American and to salute Old Glory flapping free in the wind.

Oscar L. Russell is in his early nineties at this writing.

CHAPTER 8

MIKE KELLY

JUST ANOTHER MILK RUN?

Y OU WALK AROUND THE C-47 one last time after performing the pre-flight check. Personally you supervise the tail hookup, checking the release mechanism. Satisfied, you climb aboard, walk up the cargo deck to the cockpit, strap into your seat, and complete the cockpit check before starting engines.

In the darkness outside, the field is alive with activity. Men loading aboard aircraft, the sound of hundreds of engines roaring to life, vehicles scurrying back and forth as they haul crews and troops to their assigned planes. The night air fills with the mixed smell of hot oil and engine exhaust.

You and your copilot run up the engines, test the flight controls, and complete the pretakeoff checklist. Your mouth is dry, there are butterflies in your stomach, but you know they will go away as soon as you clear the ground. You've been through it all before. You'll be too busy concentrating on flying your bird to think about what lies ahead.

"Cadet Kelly!" the instructor barks. "Are you going up today?"

"Hell no! And I'm not gettin' in one of those damn things tomorrow, either."

147

Mike Kelly volunteered for flight training in late 1942. After ground school, he found himself in Arcadia, Florida, strapped into the back seat of a PT-17 open-cockpit biplane for his first lesson at primary flight school. He was excited, enthusiastic, and totally ignorant of the sensations of flying.

In 1942 the army air corps was in desperate need of pilot instructors. To fill that need they hired older civilian pilots, held young pilot officers over a few months for a tour of instructing, and assigned instructor duty to veteran air corps pilots considered too old to fly combat. Many of the latter were generally bored with instructing, harbored a biting desire to "get into action," and envied the young pilot trainees who, with far less experience and skill, would soon be flying combat in the European or Pacific theaters and earning quick promotions.

Such instructors could be short on patience with the junior birdmen placed under their tutelage. Some developed the philosophy that they should not waste time on any but the most able and most determined to learn to fly. What better way to find out which students qualified than to wring 'em out on their first flight? Never mind that these instructors gleefully scared the hell out of most of the trainees in the process. Those who showed up for the second lesson likely wouldn't waste an instructor's time or turn out to be an embarrassment. Those who didn't—well, flying was a volunteer pursuit. No one had to go up.

Kelly fell into the clutches of one of these air corps types who considered aviation cadets as useless as tits on a boar hog. Mike was all smiles when he got into the PT-17 trainer for his first flight. By the time he got out of it he was as disoriented as a drunken monkey. He had been flipped, yelled at, rolled, yelled at, spun, yelled at, looped, yelled at, acrobatted a hundred ways, and yelled at for more than an hour.

By the time the plane landed, Kelly had lost his breakfast, his enthusiasm, his desire, and his pride. "To hell with it," he said and refused to go up the next day and for four days thereafter. Then he heard the "rumor."

The air corps needed pilots fast, and someone noticed they were losing a lot of cadets from the training program. Some had to be washed out, those cadets who for various reasons were determined to be unsuited—"Son, that's it. I'm gonna do you a favor and wash you

Generally known as the C-47, this versatile transport aircraft came to be known by many nicknames, not all of which were complimentary. Dizzy Three, Dakota, Skytrain, Gooney Bird, and Spooky are but a small sampling.

out of the program before you kill us both." The critical problem with the training program was that it was losing too many qualified candidates who, of their own volition, quit the program.

One deterrent to that was the policy that anyone leaving the program was subject to the draft, but that in itself didn't seem to prevent the high rate of dropouts until the rumor began to circulate. Word got around that any cadets who voluntarily dropped out of pilot training would be rewarded with the permanent rank of private and given such choice assignments as tending pack mules in Burma, guard duty in the Arctic, or testing parachutes for the duration. Maybe the rumor was true, maybe not, but no one wanted to find out. Kelly reported to the flight line.

Mike threw up a few more times, but he got the hang of flying. In fact, he turned out to be very good at it and quickly grew to love it. He went on to advanced training, was commissioned a lieutenant, and was awarded his pilot's wings in early March 1943.

At the time, too many graduating pilots wanted to be fighter jocks. The invasion of Europe was being planned, and there was a growing need for bomber and transport pilots to support it. The army brought in a brand-new B-17 bomber and C-47 transport to show off to Mike's graduating class. Most of the new pilots had never seen a large plane up close.

"What do you think, Kelly?" a pal asked.

"Hell, I like 'em big."

Kelly claims he was looking at the well-endowed girlfriend of a fellow lieutenant at the time. Whatever the truth, Lt. Mike Kelly received orders to report to Columbus Army Airfield, Mississippi, for training in multi-engine AT-9s and 10s.

When the orders came in, the pilots assigned to the fighters and the bombers razzed those who had been assigned to the transports, calling them Gooney Bird pilots and saying that all they would do was haul toilet paper, beans, and VIPs on "milk runs" while the fighters and bombers would see all the action. It didn't turn out quite that way.

Later, in England, sometime after midnight on June 5, 1944, you watch a green flare arc lazily across the overcast night sky. It is the signal for your group, seventy-two planes in all, to begin taking off in sequence. You hold the brakes, pull the yoke all the way back, and ease the throttles of the big radial engines forward to full takeoff power. The C-47 stands quivering from wingtips to tail in anticipation of being set free.

You check the engine gauges once more. They're all in the green. You release the brakes. The C-47 tugs at its load, begins to move forward. You gain speed slower than normal. Trailing behind at the end of a 250-foot nylon line is a Waco glider packed with airborne troops and their combat gear.

Your tail comes up, and the glider gets airborne while you continue to lumber across the ground, struggling for flying speed. Finally you have enough. You ease back on the control yoke, and the C-47 lifts off.

The weather is not as rotten as yesterday, but still it's not good. You climb to five hundred feet, proceed to the assembly point, and circle while the rest of your group joins up. Occasionally the glider pulls your aircraft's tail to the right or left or up or down as the glider pilot struggles to maintain his tow position at the end of the nylon tether, struggles to stay out of your prop wash and vortex. You have to constantly work the controls to maintain course and altitude. It's a little like dragging a live fish on a line.

Everyone is up, no aborts. Each C-47 has struggled to take up its prearranged position in the formation. There is no room for mistakes.

The group turns out on course, on time, flying four abreast to the row, eighteen rows deep, all towing gliders. Timing is all important. There's a group ahead of yours and others behind.

Formation flying in the dark is not fun for most pilots. It is even less fun tonight, considering that more than 800 heavily loaded gliders are being towed through a black sky crowded with 1,086 other C-47s carrying paratroopers. You're all part of the largest air invasion in history—D-Day, Normandy.

You concentrate on maintaining course and altitude at five hundred feet. As low as you are, you still cannot see the angry, wave-tossed Channel below, but you know it's there. You are lead: front row, left. All the other pilots have to continuously make slight adjustments to their power settings to maintain their position in relation to you. You can barely make out the transport off your right wing. The copilot keeps a close watch on it. The last thing any of you want to do is to slide into another transport or glider or towline in the dark.

Your copilot calls out, "French coastline coming up, Skipper."

You start a prearranged climb to cross the coastal defenses at fifteen hundred feet. You are now flying low, slow, and noisy over enemy-occupied territory. Somebody's waking up down there. You see muzzle flashes winking below, and tracers begin to stitch up the black sky. You know it will get worse.

Ease the yoke forward now in a descent. The formation descends to level off again at five hundred feet for the run inland to the assigned drop zone (DZ).

"Where the hell are the Pathfinders? Dammit! We are supposed to have navigation guides down there somewhere."

Your copilot has been trying to pick up their signal. "They're not coming up, Skipper, I can't get a damn one of them."

Eighteen planes loaded with Pathfinder parachute teams had taken off ahead of the formations at 11 P.M. The teams were to jump with special devices to light up the DZs and use homing signals to guide the transports to their designated DZs. One of the Pathfinder planes disappeared over the Channel. Others encountered low cloud banks, which obscured their assigned zones. Several others were shot down. The few Pathfinders who did land near their assigned DZs couldn't light them up because of the close proximity of enemy troops.

You ask your copilot again if he marked the time you crossed the coastline. You are navigating by dead reckoning—time, speed, and compass—correcting for forecast winds. It's all you have. You concentrate on holding course, altitude, and airspeed steady. If you can't visually recognize the DZ, you'll have to depend on the clock. When the watch says you're there, you'll release the glider and hope you're over the DZ. The low overcast doesn't help matters; you can't see a damn thing on the ground below.

You think about the airborne troops packed into the glider behind you. In your mind's eye you can see them sitting back there, scared, silent, waiting—the sweat on their blackened young faces reflecting the glow of antiaircraft (AA) tracers lighting up the sky around them.

It's getting worse. Somewhere off to you left you see a C-47 with an engine on fire. You are determined to hold your course steady at release altitude in spite of the AA fire and poor weather.

Damn! Was that a hit you just felt? Are you taking hits? The formation is getting loose. Some of the planes begin to turn and twist, trying to avoid the increasing AA fire, trying to survive.

Your copilot screams, "Jesus! Look there!" A trail of fire marks the path of a dying transport trailing the group ahead of you. It slides down the night sky to end its flight as a morbid beacon marking the way in for those yet to run the gauntlet. You fly on . . .

If it was bad for the transport pilots, it was worse for the glider pilots and the men riding with them. Unseen below, the open fields are planted with thousands of posts (known as "Rommel's Asparagus") designed to thwart glider landings. After being released from the tow plane, the glider pilots have only seconds to quickly pick their spot, dive steeply to shorten their exposure to enemy fire, level off, and set her down. It worked well enough in practice . . . in daylight, but now they have to do it in the dark gray overcast before dawn. What light there is comes from AA fire and flares, all of which serve only to blind them. To land, all they had to do was pick a clear bit of earth, set up their approach, avoid the trees, hedgerows, farm buildings, ditches, and all the "asparagus" the Germans have planted.

To make matters worse, before this all began, there was a shortage of trained glider pilots. The deficit was filled expediently by assigning airborne troops as copilots, thereby freeing trained copilots for reassignment as glider command pilots. The training for the new copilots took place about thirty minutes before takeoff and consisted of a few minutes' ground instruction by their respective command pilots. "If I get wounded or killed going over, here's what you do to land . . ." Some glider pilots were hit, and their instant copilots had to take over and land. Airborne Gen. James M. Gavin later said of them, "Having to land a glider for the first time in combat is a chastening experience; it gives a man religion."

It's time now. You signal for the release and feel your C-47 surge forward, free of its load. The truth is you don't know if you're over the DZ or not. The clock says you are there. You have done the best you could. You cross over a crashed transport as you climb for altitude. Like a huge torch from hell, the burning plane on the ground illuminates the running figures of the soldiers in the field below. You don't know if they are friend or foe.

The scene slides quickly behind as you climb into the darkness and clouds above and head back to England on the assigned route. There you will land, hook up another glider, and do it all again. You don't think about that. It's your job, and you will do it. It's better to concentrate on your flying for now.

The invasion of Fortress Europe is under way. Few gliders or paratroopers land on their assigned DZs. Lack of Pathfinder beacons, intense German AA fire, and low ceilings result in a scattering of the airborne forces all over the Normandy countryside. Worse, three out of every four gliders are destroyed on landing. They fall victim to Rommel's posts, hedgerows, stone walls, trees, ditches, buildings, shearing wings, breaking fuselages, flipping upside down, or combinations of the above. The cost of the glider landings alone, in terms of dead and injured, is 11 percent of the airborne force. Many of those who aren't killed or badly injured during the landings find themselves lost and under fire from Germans. The enemy, however, is as confused as the American troops landing all around them.

The second wave fares little better. These glider pilots have the dim light of the dawn to help them survey their landing zones. What they see are fields strewn with obstacles, broken gliders, abandoned parachutes, littered with supply packs, corpses, and the flashes of enemy ground fire. Dawn's early light also helps the German gunners see the approaching air armada. Like the first waves before them, many glider troops and parachutists are dead before they hit the ground.

D-Day was the second time that Mike Kelly had carried airborne troops into combat, but it would not be the last. Kelly would fly in three of the four largest airborne assaults in the European theater. He doesn't talk much about the rough parts, preferring instead to recall the humorous happenstances of his service, like the time he was flying copilot on the airborne invasion of Sicily. It was the first large-scale airborne assault in history, the first for any American division, the first to invade Europe, the first to be attempted at night. The operation was the proving ground for later airborne assaults at Salerno, Normandy, Holland, southern France, and across the Rhine.

In the middle of the night on July 9, 1943, four months after receiving my wings, I loaded eighteen parachutists (two "sticks" of nine) from the Eighty-second Airborne aboard our transport at a windy,

The men of the 82d and 101st Airborne were the first Allied troops to invade Europe, and C-47s carried every one of them there. For D-Day the C-47 pulled double duty as a transport for paratroops (below) or a tow plane for gliders.

U.S. AIR FORCE

desert field in Tunisia. We flew over Malta and headed directly for the Sicilian coast.

We had been briefed to be alert for enemy night fighters—told that they could come out of a black sky and flame your ass before you knew they were there. I was copilot, and a guy I'll call Sheffield was pilot. (He might not want me to use his real name.)

Usually, about fifteen or twenty minutes out from the drop zone, we turned on a signal light in the back to alert the paratroops to get ready. When we were about fifty or so miles from Sicily and still over the Mediterranean, I told Sheffield it was about that time. Some genius had installed the prepare-to-jump and jump light switches on the pilot's side of the instrument panel next to the landing light switch. When Sheffield reached for the standby switch, he acciden-tally flipped both it *and* the landing lights on.

Suddenly the plane to our front was bathed in brilliant light. The startled pilot of the illuminated plane broke radio silence, screaming, "Night fighters! Night fighters!" and peeled off in an evasive dive that scared the hell out of everybody.

Sheffield, not realizing the light was from our plane, also took violent evasive action. So did several other planes in front that found themselves suddenly lit up. Those pilots behind us saw exactly what had transpired, but the formation had orders to maintain radio silence. All they could do was continue on course.

To his credit, Sheffield caught on pretty quick, snapped off the landing lights, and along with the other dodgers, sheepishly sneaked back into formation, hoping that in the darkness and the surprise of the event, no one could identify the planes involved. (No one ever did.)

As soon as Sheffield ceased gyrating the plane around the sky, I went back to check on the paratroopers. I stepped into chaos. There were piles of tangled, cursing troopers from one end of the plane to the other, all trying to get back on their feet, which wasn't easy since they each had about a hundred pounds of parachute, combat pack, weapons, and ammo strapped to their bodies. The jumpmaster was hanging halfway out the open doorway, and one fellow had somehow gotten hung upside down from the overhead ripcord static line.

When the standby signal had lit up back there, the troops had just enough time to stand up and start checking their gear before

Sheffield whipped the plane into a violent, diving, twisting maneuver. They had all floated up off the deck, banged into the overhead, and been slung all over the place. Of all the troops that jumped that night, none were more enthusiastic to leave their plane than our bunch.

What Kelly doesn't talk about is what happened when they reached the Sicilian coast, namely, the C-47s that were lost. Earlier that day, while the Allied invasion fleet was forming off the coast of Sicily, Italian and German planes repeatedly bombed them from 6:30 in the morning until 3:40 that afternoon. The ammunition ship USS *Robert Rowan* was blown to bits, and the British hospital ship HMS *Talambia* was sunk.

That night, following the prescribed inbound air route, the C-47s loaded with paratroops started descending for their drop zones. The route was supposed to take them down the shoreline with a turn inland for the DZ. The winds were strong, as much as thirty-five miles an hour. Many planes were blown offshore and unknowingly turned inland over the blacked-out invasion fleet. When they did, some scared kid on an antiaircraft gun thought the enemy bombers had returned and opened fire. After he opened fire, the whole fleet opened up on the friendly aircraft overhead.

The planes were so low over the water it was hard to take evasive action, but the pilots tried. Machine gun and 20- and 40-millimeter AA cannon fire tore through the crowded jump planes and wreaked havoc on the men inside. Six C-47s immediately broke up and crashed in flames with all their troops. Others, badly crippled, went down spilling parachutes on the way. Many of the paratroopers who jumped in time for their chutes to open, or who made it out of the aircraft after crashing into the water, were too loaded down to stay afloat and drowned. Those who managed to survive were later picked up in boats manned by deeply remorseful sailors. In all, 318 paratroopers and pilots were killed or wounded by friendly fire.

This tragedy was not over, however, since the fire from the fleet alerted the enemy on shore of the incoming aircraft. Those transports lucky enough to survive the friendly fire offshore were met by fierce enemy fire once they crossed the Sicilian coast. Out of a total of 144 planes, 23 were shot down. Of the remaining 121 planes, 87 limped back to their bases in Tunisia badly shot up, 37 of them so severely damaged that they were out of action for months or scrapped altogether. The remaining 50 shot-up planes, Kelly's among them, required a week or more for repairs. It was reported that one C-47 landed with more than two thousand holes in it. Of the 121 shot-up planes that returned, many landed with dead and wounded airborne troops aboard. Of the 144 planes launched on the mission, only 34 landed in flight-worthy condition. When later asked about the flight by a few fighter jocks, Kelly said, "It was just another milk run, fellas."

Two days later the tragedy was repeated when 124 C-47s were flying British airborne troops to Sicily to reinforce the invasion. Just offshore, 11 of the planes were shot down and 27 were so shot up they had to turn back. All were the victims of friendly naval fire. Of the remaining 86 transports that made it to the DZ, 50 suffered severe damage from enemy fire. To make matters worse, as the devil's chance would have it, the Germans had designated the very same DZ to drop their airborne reinforcements. British and German paratroops landed on the same DZ only minutes apart. The result was one of the most confused, hard-fought close engagements of the war.

Kelly's last airborne missions were flown into Holland as part of British F.M. Bernard Montgomery's ill-fated plan, Market Garden. Kelly favors another comical tale rather than discuss the difficulties faced by everyone involved in the campaign.

On the fourth day of the operation, I took off from England, this time towing a glider full of troops from the First Free Polish Parachute Brigade. The weather was not good. When we reached the Dutch coast, the cloud cover was very low and building. Our group leader decided to take the formation over the clouds, betting the drop zone would be clear by the time we reached it. The cloud tops were still climbing in front of us when we reached twelve thousand feet. We couldn't go any higher because the glider troops had no oxygen. We didn't dare descend for fear there were formations somewhere in the soup below. There was nothing to do but abort the mission and return to base.

When our formation broke out of the low overcast over England, we cut the gliders loose over various auxiliary airfields. There was just one problem. We had no way to communicate with the gliders.

The Polish paratroopers had been dragged all over the sky for hours without seeing the ground. Upon landing they charged out of their gliders with guns loaded at the ready just as they had been trained. They thought they were in Holland. We later learned that one of our Polish glider troop captured a British airfield before the very surprised Brits could sort out the situation. I think even a few rounds were fired. Anyway, it was all hushed up. As soon as the weather permitted, we loaded the Poles up and towed them across again.

That day only 53 of the 110 transports that took off got through. All the rest, including my group, had to temporarily return to England.

What Kelly doesn't mention are the conditions under which he flew across Holland during Market Garden. The planes had to fly eighty miles across German-occupied Holland in daylight to reach the drop zones. The first flight consisted of 1,545 C-47s, 478 of them towing gliders, with 1,100 fighter escorts. They crossed the coast at an altitude of only four hundred feet.

The formations were so large it took nearly an hour for the strings of planes to pass over any given point on the ground. This gave the German gunners ample time to find their targets.

Maybe it was the surprise or the fighter escorts or poor German marksmanship or luck or God, but aircraft losses were less than expected. That doesn't mean there weren't any. The first wave of Brits got in okay, but by the time the planes of the Eighty-second Airborne (including Kelly's) came in, the Germans pretty well understood the game and were moving more AA guns into position.

Because of the criticism the C-47 pilots had taken from missing their DZs and scattering troops during the Normandy drops, they doggedly stuck to their course in spite of ground fire all along their route. Many planes were seriously damaged. Sixty-eight were lost. Still, it was considered the best airborne delivery of the war. On Market Garden D-Day Plus One, American C-47s again ran the gauntlet, this time towing 428 gliders filled with troops from the 101st Airborne and 450 gliders jammed with troops from the 82d Airborne. Drops continued for four days. Kelly flew them all.

It wasn't enough. If the airborne delivery was successful, the same cannot be said for Market Garden. Montgomery's plan called for Amer-

C-47s not only carried the paratroopers into action but also served to tow the glider-borne troops as well.

ican and British airborne divisions to surprise the enemy, secure the bridges across the Rhine and its Dutch tributaries, and hold them for three days while British and American armored columns raced across Holland to link up, cross the Rhine, and make a sweeping end-run attack into Germany. The airborne troops took the bridges in spite of unexpected heavy resistance from crack German units the Allies didn't know were in the area. The bridges were held for the planned three days, but Montgomery's column didn't show. The bridges were held for a week. Still Montgomery's column didn't show. Desperately short of supplies and without reinforcements, the airborne troops held for two whole weeks. Finally they ran out of ammunition, medicine, food, and blood. Montgomery's relief column couldn't fight its way through. It never reached the bridges. The cost, measured in dead, wounded, and captured, was very high.

Mike Kelly won't talk about the planes and crews and friends who never returned, but he will talk about a wild, clandestine operation he flew out of Italy. By 1944 the partisan bands fighting the Nazis in the mountains of Yugoslavia were desperately short of supplies. A small unit of volunteer American pilots, Kelly among them, took on the task of supplying them.

Our base of operations was at an airfield in Brindishi, Italy. The operation was kept pretty secret. We flew only at night. In the late afternoons our plane were loaded with all kinds of stuff: guns, ammo, food, medical supplies, explosives, blankets, tents, goats, chickens, rubber ducks, a kitchen sink, you name it. After dark we took off alone, crossed the Adriatic Sea, and flew into Yugoslavia.

For each mission we were given a set of coordinates and a pre-arranged recognition light signal. When we reached the designated area, we circled and waited for a signal from the ground. We often saw signals coming from two different places at the same time. The Germans tried to lure us down with false signals.

Some nights we never saw a proper signal and returned home. Only the partisans had the prearranged signal for a given mission . . . we hoped, but we knew the Germans might get lucky. They recorded previous signals and would flash them at us. It got so bad that the partisans were issued colored lights to mix into the coded signals. A week later, the Germans were down there trying out colored lights. There was always the chance they might capture a partisan having a given night's code signal and beat it out of him. That thought was so unpleasant, it never crossed our minds—except when we were on a short final approach just about to touch down.

If we saw the proper signal, we started a descent among the hills and mountains. Somewhere below, two rows of small fires would appear; smudge pots of burning, oil-soaked rags. There would be a signal at one end indicating in which direction we were to land. If we were lucky, the partisan leader would have picked a spot long enough to allow us to land and take off in one piece.

The partisans, men and women, would snuff out the smudge pots as soon as our wheels touched. While some maintained a defensive perimeter around the field, others raced out of the darkness and unloaded the supplies fast so we could all get out of there before German troops arrived. The mountains had German eyes and ears.

These landings were always interesting. We didn't dare use landing lights, and we never knew the exact elevation of the fields. We just lined up on the rows of little fires, judged their elevation as best we could, and put down between them as close to the near-end markers as we could. We approached with flaps and gear down, low and slow so we wouldn't overshoot the short little strips. There were a lot of reasons why you didn't want to have to make a go-around. One, you might not make it. Sometimes we landed one way and had to take off the opposite direction because a chosen strip might have something just beyond the far end—like a hill or a ridge or a mountain. Two, we might be landing on a meadow four or five thousand feet high. Heavy as we were going in, our acceleration and climb rate for a go-around wouldn't be too spectacular at that altitude. Three, if we made the go-around okay, by the time we made a second approach and landed, the Germans might have time to get there before we could be unloaded and take off again.

What would really get your attention on final approach would be to have the torch-lit runway suddenly disappear. If that happened, you had just seconds to jam the throttles forward and persuade the ole girl to climb while you got the gear and flaps up. Landing field lights only disappear that fast if you have descended below the level of something blocking your line of sight—like trees or a hill lying in the darkness between you and the strip.

Takeoffs were equally entertaining. Before takeoff, the partisans would tell us the lay of the land, if any of them spoke English . . . things like only fly that way, big mountain over there. Moonlight could help. On nights when there was a low overcast, or patches of ground fog, things got a little crazy. Rolling along bumpy terrain in the dark at full throttle you couldn't help but think up all sorts of fun things that might be lying in front of you . . . a stump hole, a tree, boulders, hills, a German machine gun.

I'd keep my eyes on the gyro-compass to keep the takeoff roll straight, while my copilot stared at the airspeed indicator, humming that old hymn "I'll Go Anywhere If Jesus Goes with Me," and biting buttons off the seat cushion with his rear end. Actually, we both did a lot of button biting. The second we reached flying speed, we pulled her off, got the gear up, and established our maximum climb rate. If we knew we were in a long valley, we might fly down it while climbing. If we were in a little pocket, or just didn't know, we followed the partisans' advice, or lacking that, climbed in a tight circle until we reckoned we had enough altitude to clear the immediate terrain. Looking back, I think it's probably good that we made all the flights at night. We might not have even attempted to land in some of those places if we could have seen what they looked like in broad daylight.

Kelly doesn't mention that the mountains in Yugoslavia reach elevations of nine thousand feet. Of course, flying at night they wouldn't have to hit a mountain to make their mark in life. Hitting trees or stumps or boulders or a little rise in the terrain on landing or takeoff could have produced much the same results.

Meeting the partisans was always interesting. "When we first started," he recalled, "we would be met by joint representatives of two different partisan groups who were supposed to divide the supplies evenly between them. The two groups tended to argue about who got what, and the arguments were not always friendly. Their mutual dislike for one another was eclipsed only by their mutual dislike of the Germans. I think one group was Serbian and the other something else. We finally had to start making separate deliveries to each group. That was bad enough, but there were other Yugoslavs who hated both of those groups so much they supported the Germans."

MIKE KELLY'S flying didn't end with the surrender of the Axis powers. He retired as a lieutenant colonel after a long and distinguished career in the air force, including a tour flying helicopters with a rescue squadron. Not a bad record for a cadet who had vowed never again to get "in one of those damn things!"

CHAPTER 9

HARRY BELL

PRESENT AND ACCOUNTED FOR!

EIGHTEEN-YEAR-OLD HARRY BELL—a mortar gunner in Weapons Platoon, F Company, 422d Infantry Regiment, 106th Division—was among ten thousand men crowded aboard the aging British ocean queen *Aquitania,* which had been built prior to World War I. She zigzagged a lonely course across the Atlantic, depending upon her speed alone to protect her from German U-boats. On October 27, 1944, she arrived at Greenock, Scotland, and disgorged her cargo of troops weary of crowding, poor food, and the awful aroma below decks of unwashed bodies and the stench of vomit from the seasick. Harry and the 422d were trucked to an assembly camp at Adderbury, England. Their training was over. The 422d drew combat supplies, readied their weapons, and waited.

With little to do, Bell and his friends quickly discovered the Kingston Pub, where beer and ale were plentiful and young Americans were warmly received by the locals. Harry particularly remembers one evening when a dignified elderly couple walked outside with him and his buddies. A Rolls-Royce eased to the curb, but instead of getting in, the couple instructed the driver to follow them. They walked along and talked with the young soldiers, asking about their homes and families. When they reached the camp gate, the gentleman turned to the young Americans and said, "We think you Yanks are very valiant to take up the fight. We English appreciate so great a sacrifice, and we want you men to know it." The Americans were a little embarrassed by the Englishman's sincere and gracious words. They shouldn't have been. Their sacrifice would be great.

We received our orders and crossed the English Channel aboard the *Monowai,* landing at Le Havre on December 6, 1944. The port was war scarred. We disembarked from the ship, walked through mud and snow directly to a line of trucks, and immediately began a long, dreary, cold, wet ride across France and into Belgium. Not too terribly long after we passed through the crossroads village of Saint-Vith, we reached our destination: a hogback ridge called the Schnee Eifel in the Ardennes region along a section of the Siegfried line. The Ninth Infantry had driven the Germans from that portion of the concrete fortified line. The Germans still held the Siegfried line to the north and south of this position.

The 422d arrived on 10 December and relieved the 9th Infantry man for man and gun for gun. The newly arrived troops, cold and wet to the bone, dug in, established forward outposts, and sent out patrols. To this point, we had never been under fire. My team set up the 60-millimeter mortar, unpacked and readied our ammunition, dug foxholes, and waited.

Everything was quiet until, somewhere directly to the front, we heard a distant strange noise. One of the men from the Ninth Infantry said that the Germans were launching a V-1 buzz bomb. Seconds later the thing flew right over us. We couldn't see it because of low clouds and fog, but we could hear the peculiar sound made by the pulse-jet engine. When another one was fired after dark, I saw a speeding orange glow through the low overcast as the missile flashed over us.

The sunless, fog-shrouded terrain was part of the heavily forested Ardennes along the border between Belgium and Germany. To the frontline troops of the 422d, it was a strange, almost surreal setting.

Above is an aerial view of a portion of the Siegfried line revealing rows of antitank obstacles zigzagging across the countryside. A short distance to the rear of the line, a series of pillboxes, bunkers, and command blockhouses were concealed.

The days seemed ghostly as the dark forest appeared and disappeared in the swirling fog. At night the stillness was broken by occasional gunfire, the strange pulsating roar of the V-1s, and the eerie light from parachute flares dropped through the overcast.

On December 12, my weapons platoon received a sudden desperate fire mission from an outpost a few hundred yards to our front. They said they were being overrun and called for fire on top of their position. My squad answered quickly with the mortar. A relief patrol sent out immediately found only stillness and American and German dead lying together in the snow.

The 422d had suffered its first combat casualties after two days in an area considered to be a "quiet zone" by Supreme Headquarters of the Allied Expeditionary Force (SHAEF) under the command of Gen. Dwight D. Eisenhower.

The next morning, the overcast lifted to maybe fifteen hundred feet. The sky had lightened just a little, but the overcast was still pretty low when I heard a roar behind me. I looked up just in time to see a P-47 Thunderbolt shoot down a homeward-bound Nazi plane. We watched the German pilot bail out. His parachute carried him behind his own lines out in front of us.

"What's a lone German plane doing over the Ardennes?"

"Taking our picture. Next time let's give 'em the bird."

"You think the Krauts are planning something?"

"Why don't you guys ring up Ike and ask him?"

That night and the next day, 14 December, we began to hear the sounds of heavy engines drifting through the forest from the German lines, sounds like those made by tanks.

The 422d Regiment reported what they heard to the 106th Division headquarters, which was getting the same reports from other units up and down the line. The reports were relayed to SHAEF, and patrols were sent out to determine what the enemy was up to.

The Germans, in fact, were preparing to launch the greatest surprise attack of the war since Pearl Harbor and the largest offensive of the war on the western front. What's more, they were being diabolically clever about it. Notably, they relied on seasonal weather—low cloud cover and heavy fog—to prevent aerial observation of their activities in the Ardennes. Cloud and fog might prevent aerial observation of the massing of mechanized troops and armored panzer forces, but how does an army hide the sound of heavy mechanized equipment moving into attack positions? The answer is that it can't. Instead, an army feeds the enemy an acceptable explanation.

What the patrols from the 106th Division saw and reported were German trucks running up and down the line, broadcasting the sounds of tank engines through huge loudspeakers. Eisenhower's staff examined the reports and concluded, logically, that the Germans wanted the Allies to believe that large armor forces and mechanized infantry were being moved into the Ardennes in preparation for an attack. SHAEF was so smugly confident of this interpretation of events, no other possibilities were explored seriously. It was one of the greatest blunders of the war.

SHAEF believed the goal of the German deception was to trick the Allies into pulling troops out of France to beef up Belgium, thereby relieving pressure on the main German forces. Such insight seemed very clever to Eisenhower's staff. In conclusion, SHAEF interpreted this subterfuge as a sure sign that the Germans, steadily being driven out of France, were incapable of mounting a serious offensive, and certainly not through the Ardennes with its narrow roads and valleys squeezed between thickly forested hills. This conclusion was made despite the fact that in World War I, and again in 1940, the Ardennes had been a German invasion route into Belgium, France, and Holland. SHAEF informed the 106th Division headquarters of its conclusions along with orders to pass the word to the 422d, 423d, and 424th Regiments. No troops would be pulled out of France to reinforce the Ardennes. Even worse, no special warning was given to the troops on the line.

At 5:30 on the morning of December 16, 1944, only six days after Harry Bell's division had taken up position on the frontline, twenty-two German divisions attacked across a seventy-five-mile front in the Ardennes. Opposing them were six American infantry divisions, two armored divisions, and one cavalry group, all thinly stretched along the same seventy-five-mile front. The odds were twenty-two to eight, worse when you consider that ten of the German divisions were armored panzer units.

The German plan was to split the Allied forces in two and capture Antwerp, which was, at the time, the only fully operational Allied winter supply port. Antwerp was vital to the continuation of the drive across France and into Germany. Other French ports had been either damaged by Allied bombing or sabotaged by retreating Germans, and thus were far from being fully operational.

The German 66th Corps broke through the Losheim Gap to the north of the 422d Regiment, annihilating the 14th Cavalry Group in the process. To the south of Harry's regiment, they drove a huge wedge between the 423d and 424th Regiments, chopping them to pieces. Confusion reigned as the Germans poured through the American lines, penetrating deeply into Allied territory with astonishing speed.

Harry Bell's platoon was in the center of the first line of defense in the greatest and most confused battle of the western front during World War II—the Battle of the Bulge. They had been green troops on the morning of the attack; they were veterans by nightfall. Sustaining heavy casualties, the 422th managed to hold its section of the line.

From Saint-Vith to SHAEF, the commanding generals and most of their staffs had been sound asleep when the phones started ringing. A short time later telephone lines were cut in the forward areas. All that was left were short-range radios, and in the hills of the Schnee Eifel in the Ardennes, these were unreliable. Rear command centers were unable to find out what was happening. Frontline units were on their own. Stunned, SHAEF fought confusion and panic while the Americans on the frontline fought to survive.

What made the situation even more critical, most of the American reserve units were widely scattered far to the rear, many in rest areas with much of their equipment—trucks, tanks, artillery—down for maintenance. They had been busy preparing to celebrate Christmas, not halt a blitzkrieg.

The 422d Infantry was ordered to hold at all costs. By the second day they reported by radio that they were holding but were running out of ammunition. They received a radio message from divisional headquarters at Saint-Vith that they were to continue to hold, that they

German panzer regiments and mechanized infantry attacked unexpectedly and broke through the American lines in mid-December 1944. The ensuing Battle of the Bulge was the largest engagement in the European theater of operations.

U.S. ARMY

would be resupplied by air. It didn't happen. For three long days the novice troops of the 422d Regiment held out against enormous odds. All the while the pincer movement of the German 66th Corps was closing behind them, racing for the all-important road-and-rail junctions at Saint-Vith and Bastogne.

At 8 P.M. on 18 December, their third night under attack, F Company received its last radio message: The 422d was to pull back to Schonberg immediately. An armored column was being dispatched there to provide a protected escape corridor to Saint-Vith.

Well-planned night withdrawals are difficult at best. With the main lines of communication severed, an unprepared night withdrawal while under attack, with no idea of the developing military situation, is no fun at all. Bell's squad got the word to take what they could carry and fall back fast. Fast!

Bell's platoon moved quickly into the forest with their weapons, what little ammunition they had left, and almost no rations. While moving on foot in the bitter cold through the dark of night over unfamiliar, heavily wooded, hilly terrain, many units were separated, companies from battalions, platoons from companies.

What was left of the entire regiment was crossing unreconnoitered ground while fighting rear-guard skirmishes and being harassed by sporadic incoming artillery. Communication was lost all over the sector. No one knew where the enemy forces were or where friendly forces could be found.

Bell's platoon became separated but kept moving toward Schonberg as ordered. Along the way they picked up stragglers and learned that Schonberg had been captured. That meant there would be no armored relief column and, worse, the Germans were in front of them.

On December 19, Bell's platoon, moving west-northwest up a narrow valley, had no choice but to move out of the cover of the forest and into open ground. They waited, watched, saw no indication of the enemy. Then the order came to spread out and move out fast.

The platoon was about halfway across the open ground when German 88-millimeter guns opened up on them from the far end of the valley. Almost before the Americans could react, the fire lifted.

"We had all thrown ourselves to the ground at the first shot," Harry recalled. "When the firing stopped, I raised my head and saw a lone

German with a white flag several hundred yards away tramping through the snow toward us. He was an officer and spoke perfect English: 'You have ten minutes to decide to surrender or be annihilated.' To emphasize the latter option, he calmly pointed to our front and waved his flag. German troops moved out of the forest to reveal their positions. The lieutenant looked at us then at the German and nodded."

Bell's platoon leader had little choice. They were nearly out of ammunition (Harry's squad, what was left of it, had one mortar round), out of food, hadn't been able to communicate with anyone since the day before, had no idea where they were. When Harry's platoon surrendered, it was one of the last units left out of the 422d. By that time almost the entire regiment had been wiped out or captured.

The German declared, "You and your men are my prisoners. Wait here. If a single one of you moves from this spot, we will open fire." He then turned and marched back toward his lines.

I felt awful, but there was little any of us could do. I figured at least I wouldn't give them my gun. I field-stripped my .45 pistol and scattered the parts in the snow. Before I knew it, all the other guys around me did the same. It wasn't much of a defiant gesture, but it made us feel better.

A German platoon emerged from the forest and moved toward us, guns at the ready. When they reached us, their officer assigned a man to search each prisoner.

The young German who searched me had a bloody bandage around his head and acted more nervous than I was. He kept a pistol aimed right at my face the whole time. I think he was in pain from his wound and still shaken from combat. He looked at me with wild, excited eyes. I have absolutely no doubt that he would have shot me at the slightest provocation.

We were formed into two columns and moved out in the direction from which we had just come, back toward Germany. They marched us for miles, not stopping until, just before sundown, we reached a small rural crossroads. There we were herded into an open animal stockade to spend a cold rainy night sitting in frozen mud.

The next morning we were marched down a road for some distance and joined a huge column of prisoners that stretched as far as

U.S. ARMY

More than 300,000 German troops were involved in the Battle of the Bulge, and their spirits were high, almost foolhardy. Many compared their ardor to the old enthusiasm that had emboldened the blitzkrieg successes of 1940.

we could see. I think there must have been several thousand in all. The first few miles we marched past the fresh evidence of battle scattered along the roadside—bodies and burned-out vehicles, Allied and German alike. We had had no food or water since the morning we were captured. Rest stops were rare and short. We drank water from ditches when we could. I recall only two occasions when we were allowed to go into the fields by the roadside and pull up sugar beets to eat raw. I remember marching in the dark, but I can't remember if we ever stopped to sleep.

Mile after mile, no matter how tired, cold, and hungry, everyone tried their damnedest to keep marching. Some just couldn't. Those who collapsed, the wounded among them, were shot and left on the side of the road. Even today I can close my eyes and hear those shots, some from behind and some from up ahead.

The column was comprised of remnants from the 422d, 423d, and 424th, practically the entire 106th Division. After sixty long, freezing miles, we reached a German rail junction and were loaded

Isolated groups of American G.I.'s tried to hold out in the Ardennes forests. Some joined up with other units, some, like Harry Bell's, were captured when they exhausted their ammunition.

into railcars. (This march was equal in length and cruelty to the infamous Bataan Death March in the Philippines, but it is unknown to most Americans today.)

I was racked from fatigue, hunger, and freezing cold then shoved into a boxcar packed with as many standing men as the car would hold. The train rolled out with no water, no food, and no sanitary facilities for the prisoners crowded inside.

We were packed so tightly, no one could sit. If you fell asleep, you might slump a little, but that's all. The train rolled into a rail yard at dusk and stopped. We saw a sign that said Cologne. The Germans left us locked in the cars.

During the night we heard the drone of approaching planes. Then bombs began to pound across the rail yard. The explosions were terrible. They walked toward us and beyond. We could feel the concussion from the explosions. Some men screamed and pounded on the doors. Our car was hit with shrapnel, but no one inside was seriously hurt.

The next morning our section of the train was backed up and switched to another track. Those of us along the sides of the car could see out of the cracks in the wood siding. As we pulled out of the yard we surveyed the damage the raid had caused and recognized what had been the forward part of our train. Eight of the railcars in front had been destroyed in the bombing. It was a horrible sight. The seven or eight hundred prisoners locked in those boxcars had been blown to bits. Their bodies and parts were hanging out of the wreckage and scattered all over the yard. Someone remembered that it was Christmas Day.

At Frankfurt am Main we were given water for the first time since the march had begun—one bucket to each car. Somewhere up the line the train stopped, and we were transferred to trucks and driven into the mountains.

Shortly after passing through the former vacation village of Bad Orb, we came to what had been a summer youth camp before the war. High barbed-wire fences with guard towers surrounded row upon row of wooden barracks. The cold, filthy, starving, new arrivals climbed down from the trucks only to be made to stand for hours in the snow as we awaited interrogation.

Once we had been interrogated, each man was issued a blanket, a tin cup, and a prison dog tag. (I still have mine: Stalag 1XB, Number 24661.) We were divided into groups of two hundred, and each group was marched to a barracks. I found my building to be as cold inside as it was outside. There was one toilet, one water tap, and a small fireplace. Crude wooden bunks were built like shelves, three high, against the walls.

It wasn't until the next morning that we had our first meal since being captured. The meals were exactly the same every single day. Breakfast was a cup of barely warm, sugary dark tea. For lunch we were given beet tops in a watery soup. One loaf of black bread was issued for every eight men. The bread was part flour and part sawdust; it had the scent of pine. There was no supper. We were issued no utensils. One guy in my squad had somehow managed to hang on to his pocket knife. He lent it to some of us to carve wooden spoons from a plank taken from a bed. That spoon was a luxury, and I still have mine.

The prisoners in each barracks were divided into twenty-five squads of eight men each. I was elected leader of my group. We bunked near the windows at the front of the barracks. One of the few rules I instituted was that the men in my squad would rotate the duty of meticulously dividing our daily loaf of bread into eight equal pieces. That way each man would share the extra privilege of gathering and eating the resulting crumbs. We were all starving.

One morning the Germans set up machine guns in front of each row of barracks and turned out all of us to stand at attention in groups of two hundred. Guards went through each group then randomly pulled ten prisoners out of ranks and marched them in front of the nearest machine gun. An English-speaking officer announced that a prisoner had broken into the Germans' kitchen and killed a guard. Then he screamed at us, "If the guilty criminal is not turned over to us these men will be shot. You have four hours."

We stood at attention for almost four hours, then the officer gave an order to the machine gunners. We heard the bolts clang and knew the guns were ready to fire. Our group was in the front row, and I could see the prisoners standing in front of the guns. Some of them had their eyes closed. I stood there waiting, knowing they would shoot those men.

A sudden movement down the line to my far right caught my attention. A kid stepped out of ranks and walked to the officer in charge. He confessed that he had tried to steal a little food for himself and his squad.

We watched the guards take him away; we never saw him again. We later heard that while he was stealing the food, a guard surprised him and somehow, in the struggle that followed, the guy grabbed the guard's bayonet and killed him with it.

As far as being a prisoner, there was little difference from one day to the next. Twice we received small Red Cross boxes, four men to a box—crackers, candy, cigarettes, soap, and toothbrushes. That was like Christmas. I carefully divided everything evenly among my squad, right down to cutting the pieces of chewing gum into even shares. It was a little bit of badly needed cheer.

Another thing that lifted our spirits was the increasing frequency of Allied bomber formations high overhead. We could see the vapor trails of the big planes and of the fighters crossing back and forth over them. But there was one day that brought no cheer at all. A lot of us were in the yard when two P-47 fighters came out of nowhere and strafed the camp. Eight prisoners were killed. I believe the pilots realized their tragic mistake and broke off the attack. We all fell on the ground when they circled and came in low over the camp again, but they didn't fire that time and just flew away.

The German guards offered us no help. The frozen ground was too hard for us to dig graves. All we could do was wrap the dead in their blankets and shove them under the barracks to freeze. Whenever we walked past, none of us could look at them.

There were other deaths—men who became seriously ill, and there were many who were taken to the camp infirmary. Most never returned. When any of my squad got sick, we hid the fact from the guards and nursed them ourselves as best we could. We were all getting weaker from lack of food.

Finally the season started to change to early spring, and we begin to hear a new sound—distant gunfire! Then the younger German guards began to drift away, leaving only the old men to guard us. By then it didn't matter. We were too weak to escape. We lay in our bunks and listened to the sounds of fighting grow ever closer. We

Liberation required a little paperwork for the former prisoners at the Bad Orb camp near Frankfurt am Main. One of Harry Bell's fellow captives, Pvt. Douglas Profitt, gladly complies with the certification procedure.

U.S. ARMY

encouraged the sickest among us, told them to hang on a little longer. We now had hope of rescue, but damn little else to keep us alive.

There came an evening when no German could be seen in camp. The following morning we heard the rumble of tanks. At first no one could see them, didn't know if they were friend or foe. No words can describe the emotion that ran through us when we saw two tanks approach. Each bore a big white star on its frontal armor. We watched the machines knock down the prison gate then roll into the yard.

FIVE-FOOT-ELEVEN-INCH Pfc. Harry Bell, weighing barely ninety pounds, led his prison squad out to meet the tanks. Too weak to walk, they crawled on their hands and knees. The stunned crew of the lead tank climbed down to help nineteen-year-old Bell to his feet. He saluted then proudly announced, "All present and accounted for." And he collapsed into the arms of the tank commander.

American losses during the Battle of the Bulge totaled 76,890 men—8,607 killed, 47,139 wounded, and 21,144 missing. The 106th Division (of which Harry Bell's unit was a part) was virtually destroyed, losing three entire regiments. By delaying the advance of a large number of the enemy during the first crucial days of the attack, they bought time for reinforcements to be organized. As a result, F.M. Karl Rudolf Gerd von Rundstedt's timetable was irretrievably lost, and with it, the victory he so desperately sought.

Mortar gunner Harry Bell was officially listed as missing in action until May 1945. Just weeks after the survivors of Stalag 1XB were liberated, Germany surrendered. After a lengthy stay in an army hospital, Harry was sent home.

CHAPTER 10

KNOX WHITE

THE LAST BLITZKRIEG

S OMETIME AROUND MIDNIGHT ON December 16, 1944, the peace and quiet around a rest area in Holland was shattered with shouts of "Everybody up! We're moving out! Now! Draw all the ammunition you can carry—you're gonna need it."

Pfc. Knox White crossed the Atlantic aboard the good ship *New Amsterdam* with eight thousand other young, green troops headed for Europe. In late November 1944, nearly six months after the landings at Normandy, White disembarked on Omaha Beach and joined a contingent of replacements loading onto a train of "forty and eights"* bound for Holland.

It was stuffy in the boxcars, and you couldn't see the countryside, so a lot of us climbed up on top. Rocking along perched on the roofs of the cars was fun, in spite of the cold, until we passed into a landscape

---

*French railcars designed during World War I to carry either forty soldiers or eight horses (not forty soldiers *and* eight horses per some sources).

littered with the debris from recent heavy fighting. The reality that we were on our way to take the place of the dead and wounded began to register in the pits of our stomachs.

My orders were to report to the Seventh Armored Division. I found them in a rear area near Heerlen, Holland. I was assigned to D Troop, Eighty-seventh Cavalry Recon Squadron-Mechanized. Before I could unpack my duffel bag, I was summoned by the outfit's executive officer. I wondered what kind of trouble I could possibly be in so soon after just getting there, but when I reported, the officer looked up from his desk and said, "Private White, according to your records here, you have a college ROTC background. Is that correct?" I told him it was, and he said, "Good! I'm promoting you to corporal and assigning you to lead a squad in third platoon."

I felt pretty good about the promotion until I learned that the Seventh was short of a lot of squad leaders, noncoms, and officers and that, along with troop replacements, they were receiving new tanks and vehicles. I heard that the Seventh had recently suffered heavy losses during a disastrous attempt to break through to the Rhine and its Dutch tributaries and turn Germany's flank.* It dawned on me that I was taking the place of some poor devil who hadn't made it back.

I put on the best "military command presence" I could muster and reported to third platoon. The sergeant looked me up and down, nodded for me to follow him, then introduced me to my squad. I found myself suddenly responsible for ten men, two Jeeps with light machine guns, and an armored car with a turret-mounted 37-mm cannon and heavy machine gun.

Next I met the platoon leader, a lieutenant about my age. He looked up from his desk. "I see you've had some college and ROTC. Glad to have you, Corporal." And that was that.

I thought I had better get to know my squad, so the next day I got the men together to clean up our vehicles and equipment. As it turned out, I never got a chance to know them well.

Conditions were pretty relaxed. The general attitude of the troops and the officers alike was that Germany was about whipped. The Sev-

---

*The Seventh had been part of the failed Operation Market Garden.

enth Division commander, Gen. Robert W. Hasbrouck, put out the word that we would spend Christmas in the rest area and celebrate as best we could, "maybe even get some turkey."

My platoon was scattered around the town, quartered in nice, warm Dutch homes and buildings. Like everyone else, I settled in and expected light duty over the holidays. It would be my first Christmas away from home.

In the middle of the night of December 16, I was roused from a deep, warm sleep by my platoon sergeant. Shaking my shoulder and shining a flashlight in my face, he bellowed, "Corporal White! Get your squad together! Full fuel and ammo! We're moving out!"

That jarred me awake fast. I hadn't been out of the States a month and was about as green as a replacement could be; I had no real field experience at all. I got dressed and rushed around waking up all the members of my squad. They had a few things to say about being rousted out of their warm beds: "What's going on? For crying out loud, it's the middle of the night," and a great many other more colorful comments and complaints. We got our vehicles started, waited our turn to fuel up, drew ammunition and rations, and moved to our platoon's assembly point.

There was confusion everywhere. It was pitch dark and freezing cold. Drivers and mechanics were working to get cold, balky vehicles started. Officers and sergeants were yelling to be heard over the noise of the engines. Some of the vehicles and tanks were down for long-overdue maintenance and couldn't be put back into action on short notice. Unit commanders were running up and down in Jeeps, trying to organize the whole division into a road convoy while the MPs worked to unsnarl traffic jams.

No one seemed to know what was happening or where we were going. One thing everyone knew was that this was no training drill. I was trying to put up a good front for my new squad, but I was really scared. D Troop was a recon outfit. Our job was to scout ahead and make contact with the enemy. Like I said, I was plenty scared when we pulled out well ahead of Seventh Division.

By 3:30 A.M. on December 17 my squad was rolling through the darkness in a freezing rain toward the village of Saint-Vith. I drove the lead Jeep and was followed by the armored car with the second Jeep

behind. According to my map we were heading toward a quiet back-
water of the front—the Ardennes.

At the time, Knox had no way of knowing that the Seventh Armored
Division was heading directly into what would be the greatest and
most confused battle of the western front in World War II. To the Germans it was Operation *Wacht am Rhein;* the Allies would know it as
the Battle of the Bulge.

By December 1944, Supreme Allied Headquarters was convinced
that Germany, after six years of war, was incapable of mounting a large
offensive. They were wrong. Taking advantage of seasonal bad weather
(low overcast and fog), the German army managed to assemble an
enormous force in the forest of the Ardennes on Germany's border
with Belgium. German intelligence knew that the Allies considered
the Ardennes a relatively quiet area and that it was lightly defended.
Their plan was to launch a surprise attack, quickly break out of the
Ardennes, and drive across the open lowlands to capture the port of
Antwerp—at the time the only fully functional port in Europe capable
of sustaining the Allied campaign against Germany.

At 5:30 A.M. on December 16, twenty-two German divisions, ten
of which were panzer, struck across a seventy-five-mile front thinly
defended by only eight Allied divisions and one small cavalry unit.
The attack came as a total surprise and represented the greatest failure of Allied intelligence since Pearl Harbor. German mechanized
infantry and armor poured through the lines, immediately annihilating the Fourteenth Cavalry, punching through and encircling the
frontline Allied divisions, and cutting lines of communication everywhere across the front.

At their headquarters far to the rear, American division commanders had no idea of what they were up against, nor could they contact
their forward units to determine the situation. Based on the only news
he had, that frontline units had reported they were under attack, just
before communication with them was broken, Gen. Dwight D. Eisenhower, the supreme Allied commander, ordered up what slim
reserves were immediately available.

The 7th Armored Division was ordered to the vital crossroads
hub of Saint-Vith, the 101st Airborne Division to the crossroads town

KNOX WHITE

An M8 Greyhound, mounting a 37-mm gun in addition to two machine guns, was the most formidable element in Knox White's three-vehicle squad. It was no match for the German panzers that swarmed the Ardennes during the Battle of the Bulge.

of Bastogne. All that was left in reserve was the 1st Army, and its units were widely scattered in rest areas all over Holland. Further complicating the response to the attack, much of the Allied equipment was undergoing maintenance and repairs and could not be rushed immediately into the fight.

Geographically, the terrain of the Ardennes was mostly thickly forested hills, which were largely impassible by motorized vehicles. What limited roads and railroads existed to allow for the advance or withdrawal of troops were confined to narrow valleys. The key to the Germans' success was Saint-Vith, a crossroads of three railroads and six roads. Once they had secured it, the vital hub would allow the simultaneous rapid advance of mechanized columns out of the confined Ardennes by these roads and railroads leading to the open lowlands, which were much more favorable to the Germans' panzer divisions. Only by quickly taking Saint-Vith could they sustain the drive to Antwerp. Any delay would allow the Allies enough time to mount a defense.

By dawn on December 17 the narrow torturous roads leading from Saint-Vith to the lowlands were impossibly jammed with American noncombat units trying to move to the rear at the same time that U.S. reserve combat units were trying desperately to move to the front. At times traffic snarled to a halt.

The Seventh Armored split into two columns to try to get through to Saint-Vith by alternate routes. Knox White's D Troop, hours ahead of the Seventh Armored, was assigned to scout the route that led east to the village of Malmedy then south to Saint-Vith. They had no way of knowing that the entire German Sixth Panzer Army was racing west on the same road. The sky was heavily overcast with ceilings too low to allow aircraft reconnaissance.

When D troop reached the junction at Malmedy and turned south, the lead units of the Sixth Panzer were only minutes away. D Troop cleared the junction not knowing how lucky they were.*

D Troop had left Heerlen at three in the morning on December 17. It arrived at Saint-Vith a little after noon. Slowed by traffic evacuating to the rear, it had taken the normally fast-moving, fully mechanized recon squadron nine hours to move seventy miles, an average speed of less than eight miles per hour. Even at that, they were far ahead of the main body of the Seventh Armored Division.

When we arrived at Saint-Vith, I didn't have time to get out of the Jeep. D Troop was ordered to establish an outpost at the nearby town of Wallerode. Third platoon was given the point.

Before heading out, my platoon leader asked a sergeant who was directing traffic at Saint-Vith where the frontline was.

The soldier answered, "Hell, Lieutenant, there ain't one. Germans are all over the damn place. We don't even know where half our own units are."

After hearing that, the lieutenant told my platoon sergeant to take someone ahead to reconnoiter. To my surprise, he turned to me,

---

*Trailing D Troop by a few minutes was Battery B of the 285th Field Artillery, which ran head-on into the Sixth Panzer and was annihilated. Eighty-six prisoners were subsequently taken to an open field and murdered by an SS panzer platoon. This atrocity is remembered as the infamous Malmedy Massacre.

ordered my men out of my Jeep, jumped in beside me, and told me to drive. I left my assistant squad leader in charge, and we took off.

Not more than three or four miles out of Saint-Vith we were sniped at—dust kicked up to the side and in front of us. It was a first for me, and I was scared stiff, the sergeant too, I think, but we kept going, both of us bent down as low as we could get and still see the road.

When we pulled into Wallerode we found the village deserted except for two G.I.'s burning papers in an empty oil drum. They told us their battalion had been ordered out that morning; they threw the last of their documents into the fire and took off. Sarge told me to get out and look for a building suitable to serve as a command post while he took the Jeep to scout positions for D Troop's armored cars.

I was in a building on the edge of the village when a plane roared low directly overhead. I jumped to the window in time to see a P-47 flash over me and fire at something out in front of my position. My sergeant and I probably owe our lives to that foolhardy pilot who was out alone that afternoon and braving a thick overcast so low it almost touched the hilltops. I couldn't see what he was shooting at because of forest, but I knew it had to be the enemy.

A few minutes later a whole line of Germans emerged out of the tree line less than three hundred yards away. They were the first German soldiers I ever saw. All I had was a pistol, and I can tell you I was one lonely, scared soldier.

The sergeant could have left me, but he didn't. I heard him roar up and yell my name. I could have kissed him. I ran out of the building, jumped in the Jeep, and we got out of there as fast as that thing would go. Shots rang out behind us, but we made it.

We reported that we had found the Germans, lots of them. Instead of going on to Wallerode, D Troop turned around and was ordered to dig in about a mile east of Saint-Vith. By that time Saint-Vith was a mass confusion of evacuating quartermasters, maintenance personnel, transport units, and kitchens. Someone had ordered a whole battery of big 8-inch artillery pieces to be spiked and their carriages burned. I guess they figured the roads were too clogged with traffic to get them out and didn't want them falling into the hands of the Germans.

That night the town was shelled. Nobody slept. The next morning, December 18, German tanks appeared in the tree line to our front and began firing at us. The 37-millimeter guns on our armored scout cars were useless against the armor of their tanks. We might have scared them a little, but that's all. What we did have, however, was enough machine guns to discourage the tanks' accompanying infantry, and their tanks wouldn't advance without infantry to cover their flanks.

For the moment, Saint-Vith's defenders consisted of our small outfit, a combat engineer outfit, a headquarters company, and bits and pieces of outfits that had managed to straggle into town ahead of the Germans. We held, barely, until the main body of Seventh Armored finally arrived with their tanks to beef up the town's defenses.*

About eleven in the morning of December 20, D Troop was ordered a few miles west to the village of Samree to beef up the left flank. At a crossroads named Baraque de Fraiture, the main body of D Troop proceeded on down the direct road to Samree while my squad was assigned to scout a secondary road.

I led in my Jeep with the armored car and the second Jeep in trail. We made good time for a while and didn't see a soul. There was no other traffic on the road, which should have told me something. Rounding a sharp curve, we drew a hail of small-arms and machine-gun fire. Tree branches just over my head splintered and dropped in my lap. Maybe from their dug-in positions on the hill above, the Germans couldn't depress their machine guns enough to hit us. Whatever the reason, they kept firing high.

We couldn't see them in the woods above us, but our two Jeeps and the scout car opened up with everything we had. Still their fire continued to hit the trees just over our heads.

We backed out of there around the curve, got on the radio, and warned D Troop that the Germans were on the secondary road and could get behind them at Samree.

My squad managed to get to the main road and find D Troop pulling back. They had arrived at Samree to find a battalion of infantry and a company of tanks already there—all of which were German. We pulled back to the intersection of the two main roads at

---

*At the time the Americans did not know that as many as six German divisions were converging on the front and flanks of Saint-Vith while, in spite of the low overcast, German paratroopers were dropping to the rear.

Fraiture and dug in at the junction to prevent the Germans at Samree from hitting the division's flank.*

We put the scout cars in defensive positions, dug foxholes, and waited. About 2 A.M. the platoon sergeant told me to take a Jeep and try to make it to division headquarters at Vielsalm to get some new radio codebooks. D Troop had received word that the current code and all three alternates had been captured. Without new codes, no one would believe our radio transmissions since the Germans already had English-speaking operators using captured radios and codes to try to confuse us.

I took off for Vielsalm alone and scared. I got sniped at in the dark, but I don't know if it was Germans or nervous Americans. The village wasn't that far away, but I couldn't use headlights and could barely make out the roads. I drove as fast as I dared in the dark, nearly running off the road a couple of times.

Things seemed pretty confused at headquarters, but I got the new codes and made it back to Fraiture about dawn.

During the night, crews with two 105-millimeter howitzers had stumbled into our group. As far as they knew, they were all the artillery left from their battalion. They said that the 106th Division had lost two whole regiments—nine thousand men.

As bad as that news was, we didn't have much time to dwell on it. Not twenty minutes after I returned from Vielsalm, the Germans attacked our position from behind us—down the same road I had just driven! They must have seen me but let me pass rather than give away their position.

Just as they attacked, a heavy fog settled in. It was a crazy battle. We couldn't see a thing. We fired blindly down the road, and they fired blindly up the road. After an hour or so the Germans ceased firing. I don't think they realized we were a mechanized cavalry recon unit and didn't expect to meet so many machine guns and cannon at point-blank range. The two howitzers we had picked up added greatly to our firepower.

---

*This was the correct tactical decision based on available information, but unknown to the small recon troop, Fraiture was on the main route of advance for the Fifth Panzer Army.

A little while later two antiaircraft sections straggled into the road junction along with what was left of a company of parachute infantry separated from the Eighty-second Airborne, which was somewhere to the northwest. They were just in time to help us throw back two more attacks.

It was pretty obvious, with retreating stragglers coming in from one direction and the Germans firing at us from another, that we were pretty well surrounded. Nobody knew what the hell was really going on, what the situation was, except that Germans were all over the place, lots of them, and that we couldn't be in much more trouble.

Later, on December 21, my platoon sergeant told me that he and I had volunteered to try to get through to Vielsalm to report D Troop's critical situation and request reinforcements and ammo. He said he had volunteered me because I was good at map reading and knew the way. We started out on the main route but ran into a German road-block. We finally worked our way around by using side roads. Looking back now at what eventually happened to my outfit, it may have been that the Germans again let two men in a Jeep through rather than give away their positions.

On the outskirts of Vielsalm we saw a German run into a house just off the road ahead of us. We figured he was a forward artillery observer or a sniper. Either way he could do a lot of harm. We pulled up, got out, and busted into the house shooting. I don't know if he took a bullet from me or the sergeant, but one of us hit him and he surrendered. We got him in the Jeep and went on into the village.

Things were pretty tight in Vielsalm. We found a colonel and his staff officers on the line, defending their own command post. We turned the German prisoner over to the colonel and informed him of D Troop's desperate situation, told him we were holding Fraiture but running out of ammunition. He told us that he understood but couldn't help us. In fact, he was surprised we got through; Vielsalm was surrounded. He said he didn't have a man to spare, that his clerks, drivers, and cooks were in the line, but he would see what he could do about ammo and got on the radio.

I don't know who he talked to, the division commander I think, but the news wasn't good. Division had no ammunition to spare; every unit was already into their reserves and running low. That wasn't the worst of it: Division considered it critical that D Troop hold the crossroads at all cost. Fraiture was on the only possible escape route open to the division at the time.

We climbed back into the Jeep and set out with the bad news the way we had come. Almost immediately we ran into trouble. We tried one road then another. Each time we saw either German vehicles or troops ahead and had to turn around and run.

We kept trying and finally worked our way down a narrow side road I was sure would take us close to Fraiture. Then, around a blind curve, we ran smack into a roadblock. I think the Germans were as surprised as we were. I threw the Jeep in reverse and backed around the curve out of range while the sarge covered us by firing all the machine gun ammunition we had left.

While sitting around the curve, trying to decide what to do next, three Americans came running out of the trees, yelling at us. They startled the hell out of us. The sergeant nearly opened up on them with his carbine. They were from D Troop. The three had been cut off while manning an outpost and had gotten past the Germans through the forest on foot. They told us D Troop was surrounded, that we couldn't get through with a whole tank company.

We loaded them on the Jeep and backtracked to Vielsalm to beg once again for help to rescue our unit. Once again we were told there was no help available. All five of us were ordered to join the remnants of several other recon troops consolidated into one ragged unit.

I felt angry and damned guilty for not being back there with D Troop. I still feel guilty for not being with them. They held the Fraiture crossroads at all cost, and the cost was high.*

---

*Days later Knox White learned the fate of D Troop. The news hit him hard. Surrounded and vastly outnumbered, D Troop held the Germans at Fraiture for three long days. Finally, at 6 P.M. on December 23, they were overrun. It took two German infantry battalions and a company of tanks supported by artillery to do it. Every man of D Troop at the crossroads was either killed, wounded, or captured. Every tank, armored car, and vehicle was lost. White and his platoon sergeant, by a quirk of chance (and a hazardous assignment), had missed death or capture by a hair.

Shortly after we joined up with the rest of the division at Vielsalm, we were ordered to disengage and withdraw to save ourselves—if we could. Disengagement was difficult; some units were fighting hand to hand with the Germans inside their lines. The entire division was in danger of being surrounded and cut off.

Our little ragtag, composite recon unit pulled back with the division. We were all that was left of the Eighty-seventh Recon Squadron, Mechanized. We had lost most of our troops and almost all of our vehicles. When we reached the lines of the First Army, the Seventh Division, including our small unit, we drew new vehicles, resupplied, rearmed, and turned around. Along with the First Army, we went on the offensive and fought our way back to Saint-Vith.

On Christmas Day the skies cleared, and we finally got some air support. We were close enough to Saint-Vith to see the airdrops to the 101st surrounded at Bastogne. While Patton's Third Army broke through to relieve Bastogne, Seventh Division retook Saint-Vith.*

A LITTLE over two weeks after arriving in Europe, nineteen-year-old Knox White was thrown into the center of the largest single battle on the western front of World War II. Between the two sides, more than a quarter of a million men were wounded, captured, or killed.

For White, this battle was not the end but the beginning of his war. The Eighty-seventh Recon Squadron, reformed and reequipped, went on to fight its way across the Rhine, through the deadly Ruhr pocket, across the Elbe, and to the Baltic Sea. White was there all the way but mentioned only two incidents that occurred during the last hundred days of the war.

---

*Although Bastogne received (and continues to receive) the most attention in regard to the Battle of the Bulge, the delay in taking Saint-Vith was more crucial to the failure of the German offensive. Had Saint-Vith fallen to the Germans during the first two or three days of the offensive, F.M. Karl Rudolf Gerd von Rundstedt would likely have bypassed Bastogne and moved his vast reinforcements, many of whom were waiting in the rear on railcars and truck convoys, through Saint-Vith and into the open lowlands beyond with little to stop him.

The first occurred just before his unit crossed the Rhine. They liberated a famous hotel in Bad Godesberg, about five miles above Remagen. While White crouched on the hotel balcony overlooking the Rhine, directing artillery fire, the irony of the moment wasn't lost on his very fine sense of history.

"It had been at this hotel," he recalled, "that British prime minister Neville Chamberlain met with the French to plan the infamous meeting with Hitler at Munich. In 1938 Czechoslovakia was both willing and able to fight. Few would argue—and in fact, we now know that Hitler's own generals believed—that England and France could have joined the Czechs and stopped Hitler cold. Instead, without even discussing the matter with the Czech leadership, England and France appeased Hitler by handing him Czechoslovakia in return for a piece of paper promising an end to German aggression. It's been said that as many as a third of the tanks Hitler used to invade Poland a few months later were Czechoslovakian, handed to him by those cowards."

German troops began to withdraw on January 8, and American units linked up eight days later. Many of the withdrawing Germans were shuttled to the eastern front in response to a new Soviet offensive. In the end, the price of the Battle of the Bulge amounted to 100,000 German and 77,000 American casualties.

U.S. ARMY

Knox bitterly recalled a second incident of appeasement, one that occurred after the fighting had ended. "We were ordered to pull back from the Baltic to appease the Russians, to give up that territory we had fought hard to win, but that wasn't the worst of it. I can still see the civilians, running beside our tanks and vehicles, holding up their children, crying, begging to be allowed to go, begging us to at least take their children before the Russians came. Can you imagine begging soldiers to take your child? Leaving those people behind was as hard on us as the fighting we had done."

Knox White never told his wife or children the details that are related here of his experiences during the Battle of the Bulge. Even as he recalled them a half-century later, he would not refer to the men he saw dying all around him, of killing the enemy, of the sounds and smells of battle. There is no doubt, however, that those experiences still linger vividly deep in his memory.

CHAPTER 11

AMOS S. POLLARD

CALHOUN 88, WHERE ARE YOU?

YOU'RE ONLY TWENTY-FIVE, but you're the old man to the crew. You hope they're sleeping better tonight than you are. Their average age is twenty-two; the youngest is nineteen. They have been with you since July 1944. You haven't lost one of them . . . yet. You're taking them to Munich tomorrow. You wish sleep would come.

"Captain Pollard! Wake up! It's time, sir."

There's a flashlight in your face. It's 4:30 A.M. in January 1945, a cold morning in Torretta, Italy. You feel like you haven't slept in a week.

"Okay, Sergeant. Make sure Lieutenant Smith is up."

Lt. James S. Smith III is your copilot and best friend. You're both members of the 827th Squadron, 484th Bomb Group, 15th Air Force.

You clean up, get dressed, and by 5 A.M. you're sitting in the mess hall forcing down a blob of powdered eggs, stale toast, and crankcase coffee. There's not much talk, not any joking around. It will be different when the mission is over, when the crews come back from seven and a half hours of flying, those who do come back. They'll blow off the tension with loud talk and jokes and hot coffee and maybe donuts after debriefing. There won't be much talk about those who don't return, or those who have to be lifted out of the planes and carried to

191

the hospital . . . or the morgue. That will come later. Right now it's 6 A.M. and time for briefing.

The briefing officer follows the same old routine. "Gentlemen, your target today is Munich. Start engines at 0740. Taxi out at 0750. Take off at 0800."

That means you'll have to cross the Alps to get to the target and cross them again to get home.

"Weather shouldn't be a factor—except for wind at altitude. It will be strong out of the north. No rendezvous with other groups today. All groups will leave departure point Bovino. Route out will be base to TP [Turning Point] number one to TP number 2 to TP number three to IP [Initial Point] to target. From TP number one follow the Italian shore up the Adriatic Sea and off the coast to avoid flak from enemy AA guns along the Italian boot.

"At TP number two bear northwest and parallel the Swiss border to try to avoid the enemy fighters out of Udine. Be careful not to violate Swiss airspace. Swiss fighters are usually patrolling the border to enforce their neutrality. You've seen them. We don't know if they have actually shot up any Allied planes, but they have forced bombers crossing their border to land and have interned both plane and crew for the duration.

"At TP number three friendly fighters are to pick you up. You'll turn northeast for the IP and target. Estimated target time 1145. Bombing altitude will be twenty-three thousand feet."

That means you'll have to climb the entire route to reach altitude before crossing the IP for the bomb run.

"After the drop, rally right. The route back will be TP number four, TP number five to base. Bomb load will consist of 250-pound general-purpose bombs [four tons of them]. This is a planned visual mission. Bombing will be by individual boxes. Bombardiers should expect excessive drift over the target. Your radio range will be Lake Lesina, call sign LA, frequency 263 kcs. Tower frequency: channel B. Interplane: channel B. VHF channel A for fighters. Designated emergency landing fields are Falconara, Iesi, and Biferno. Check the sheet for your call signs and those of your fighter escort. Any questions? . . . Good luck!"

You stand up to leave and note a couple of fresh replacement crews that will experience their first taste of combat today. You know how they feel. You remember your own introduction on that first mission to Vienna. You were plenty scared. Flak was heavy and accurate, and fighters jumped your group coming and going. It was a hell of a day. You brought home a plane full of holes with the hydraulics shot out. Your copilot had to hand-crank the gear down. You landed with no brakes and no flaps and ran off the far end of the runway through a field of wheat and into a ditch. Scratch one B-24, but you and the crew walked away okay. The C.O. thought you did a good job. You thought you were just damn lucky.

You're an old hand now, experienced enough to know how your day will go. You woke up groggy, but you'll fly wide awake, routinely, carefully, the best you can do. At first you'll be busy with checkout, start-up, taxi, and takeoff, but after you get on course and settle down, you'll have time to think . . . about what can go wrong with the plane, about enemy fighters that may be waiting as you approach the target and again as you leave the target, about the flak over the target.

And you know that you will transition from being scared to being terrified and finally to an overwhelming feeling of relief when you get back home—if you get back home. Once back at base you'll experience the incompatible postmission twins—one, an emotional high from the excitement and having survived, the other, the physical low of bone-numbing fatigue. The first will cry for celebration, the second for sleep. There won't be much of either.

You won't show any of your feelings to your crew if you can help it . . . for as long as you can help it. But right now it's time to go.

Today you're flight leader for the fourth squadron group, call sign Calhoun 88. You'll be flying a Mickey, one of two radar-equipped B-24s in the outfit. The radar ships are supposed to allow you to identify the target through cloud cover. They're called Mickies because the target radars they carry are about as reliable as a kid's Mickey Mouse watch— more than half the time they don't work. You'll have two extra crew members, a radar operator and a mission photographer. That will make twelve souls aboard for this flight, twelve souls you'll try your best to bring home in one piece.

You leave the briefing hut, step into snow-melt muddy slush, and walk to a vehicle piled hood to spare tire with your crew and their parachutes and gear. Stuffed into their flying suits they all look like teddy bears.

You reach the big, gangly, four-engine B-24 and pile out. While the crew climbs aboard, you and Jim Smith walk around the plane for a preflight checkout with your crew chief. His boys have been working all night in the freezing cold to get your plane ready to fly. Checking engines and electrical, mechanical, and hydraulic systems. Loading bombs, fuel, ammunition, oxygen, and signal flares. The ground crew is as important to the mission as your flight crew, and they know it. You let them know that you know it, too. It's their plane. They just let you borrow it to fly missions.

What they try not to show is how much they care about you and the crew. Dog-tired from working all night, they'll stay to watch you take off then get some chow and go to their tents to sleep awhile. Late in the afternoon they'll get up and stand around in the cold, watching, waiting, looking at their watches, hoping their plane will get back okay. All the ground crews will be there. They'll tense up when they hear the planes returning. They'll count them as they come in, note the ones having trouble, note the ones firing flares in the landing pattern, alerting emergency personnel that they have wounded aboard.

If a crew's plane is missing, they will keep a lonely vigil long after the field grows silent, watching the empty sky, hoping their bomber will limp into view. They'll wait until there's no hope, until they know the plane would be out of fuel, until they know it's not coming home. Then they will walk away silently, feeling lost themselves, wondering if they are somehow partly to blame. Did anything go wrong with the plane? Did they miss something in maintenance? They won't talk about it. In a few days they'll be assigned a new bomber and crew—strangers. They'll go back to working long, cold nights, and from somewhere they'll gather the strength to watch the new crew take off and wait for their return.

You finish the preflight, pick up your flight gear and parachute, throw it through the hatch, climb aboard, and make your way to the cockpit. Your crew reports in on the intercom while you and Jim go through your cockpit checklist.

You'll be short two guns on this mission. The twin fifties have been removed from the ball turret in the belly. Radar antennas now stick out in their place. That means if a German fighter attacks from beneath, he gets a free shot.

The ground crew has already warmed up the engines. They start easily except for number four, which is a little balky at first.

As flight leader you taxi first, and the rest of the group falls in behind. You sit on the runway waiting for the signal from the tower to start your takeoff.

The runway is dirt—no matting, just hard-packed dirt. You had never seen B-24s operate off unpaved dirt until you got to Torretta. There are no runway lights either. On missions when you return after dark, they light off three railroad flares at each end. You line them up and set down in the blackness between them. The runway is just over two thousand yards long. When it is dry it is dusty, but you get off with a little runway to spare. When it's muddy, like today, the plane is slow to accelerate. You'll use every bit of the runway. When you reach the end, you'll pull back on the yoke and hope the bird will fly. If it doesn't, with full fuel and bombs aboard . . . well, you don't want to think about it.

There's the signal from the tower. You move all four throttles forward and monitor all four sets of engine instruments to make sure each is developing takeoff power. Your bomber is heavy, grossed out at a little over thirty tons. The big four-blade propellers chew into the air, and the plane lurches forward. You feel the wheels drag through patches of mud and standing water, and you have to play the big twin rudders to keep the nose pointed straight. Your copilot calls out the air speed. The needle on the gauge creeps up slowly. "Come on, baby." You're barely off the ground when the end of the runway flashes beneath you.

Smith clears the gear and flaps. You pull the throttles back to ease the strain on the engines and start a shallow climbing turn around the field so your flight can form up on you. There are no aborts today. Your squadron of seven lumbering B-24s forms into a self-defense box. Three other boxes from the three remaining 484th Group squadrons form up on your unit, and you begin the long, slow climb to twenty-three thousand feet.

The book says the B-24 has a maximum speed of 300 miles per hour. That's a joke. Maybe with everything buttoned up tight, no

A flight of B-24 Liberator bombers releases its load over the target.

guns, ammo, or bombs, light on fuel, no nose turret, and the belly turret retracted, one of these old girls may have danced to that tune. But fully loaded, with all guns hanging out in firing positions, you've never gotten more than 240 out of her in level flight. German fighters, however, can do 400.

Right now, climbing for altitude, you are indicating about 180. Out over the Adriatic you call for the gunners to test-fire their weapons. As you reach ten thousand feet you have each crewman check his oxygen mask and report that it's working. You're going to twenty-three thousand feet. At that level, without oxygen, a man can easily die from hypoxia. No problems are reported.

Each plane is carrying 8,000 pounds of bombs; each flight of seven carries 56,000 pounds, and the four flights together total a bomb load of 224,000 thousand pounds. Somewhere around 11:45 this morning, all 112 tons of high explosives will fall on Munich. The Germans know it. They'll do what they can to stop you. You try not to think about what the bombs will do. Your job is to drop them.

Your fighter escort is supposed to meet you at TP number three. There's been a foul-up. They fail to show. It's happened before.

Just short of the IP you finally reach twenty-three thousand feet and level off. Winds are sixty miles an hour out of the north. The sixty-mile-an-hour headwind slows your speed over the ground by an equal amount. The heavy bombers are slow enough as it is. If you approach the target upwind, you'll remain over the target much longer than you care to and be a sitting duck for the heavy antiaircraft guns below.

You lead the flight in a wide arc around Munich to the north so you can turn downwind for the bomb run and pick up a tailwind that will effectively increase your ground speed across the target by sixty miles an hour.

The temperature is thirty degrees below zero (F). The fuselage is not pressurized or heated. The waist gunners are standing at open ports. The crewmen wear electrically heated, leather fur-lined suits, but they are still cold. Remove your gloves, and you risk frostbitten hands. Touch guns or exposed parts of the aircraft with bare fingers, and your skin will freeze to the metal. It is not a nice place to be even when no one is shooting at you.

Every man scans the sky for enemy fighters. They are absent today, but the flak comes up to welcome you. Black puffs of smoke begin to appear slightly below and ahead of the flight. They look innocent, but you know each one marks the explosion of a shell into sharp shards of metal capable of tearing ragged holes through anything they hit: engines, wing spars, fuel tanks, men. The German gunners soon get the altitude right. Ugly black splotches appear around you as if the sky has contracted some hideous plague.

Just as you begin the turn downwind onto the bomb run, your number-two (left inside) engine loses power. Jim grabs the engine controls. He quickly adjusts the throttle and mixture and is able to keep it running, but only at partial power. You suspect the supercharger has failed. Whatever the problem, you won't feather it unless it catches fire; partial engine power is better than none. You assign Cpl. Marvin Goldstein, the assistant flight engineer manning the top gun turret, to keep an eye on the crippled engine.

You hand off the lead to the plane on your left because you are losing speed with one engine sick and falling back through the formation. You lower the nose a little to try to make up some of the loss in speed. It costs you altitude, but you want to clear the target area as quickly as you can. Your bombardier, Lt. Dan Paul, is no longer lead bombardier. He releases the bombs when he sees the closest plane ahead drop its bombs.

By now the entire group has passed you. They have cleared the target; you haven't. Suddenly your number-three (right inside) engine shuts down. Mechanical failure? More likely a piece of shrapnel. Fly the plane. Maintain control. Let your copilot deal with the engine. The flight engineer, Sgt. August Kovacic, leaves his gun momentarily to help Jim try a restart. It's no good. Some kind of liquid is streaming off the wing behind the dead engine.

"Feather number three."

You have only two and a half engines, but at least you don't have a fire. Your speed drops way back. By now you've fallen so far behind you can't see any of your group up ahead. You are slow and alone and losing altitude—and the Alps are in front of you.

The intercom comes alive. Sgt. Tom Fitzmaurice is the first to suggest jettisoning all the guns and ammo to lighten the plane. The tail gunner thinks maybe the crew should bail out. You tell them no one is to jump unless you say so, and no one is to throw out any guns or ammo—not yet anyway. You tell them that you're still flying, you've got the aircraft under control. You remind them that they are still deep in enemy territory, that they may need their guns.

You are no longer cold. You are sweating from an adrenaline furnace deep inside your gut. You are running the two good outboard engines hard and praying they will hold together. You ask your navigator, Lt. Robert Babcock, for a direct course south over the mountains for home. It will carry you closer to the enemy fighter base at Udine, but you don't have much choice. You can't hold altitude. You have to cross the Alps now by the most direct route or you won't cross them at all.

You're below eighteen thousand and descending as you enter the mountains. You abandon your navigator's course because you can't hold a straight line of flight. You must fly around individual mountain peaks because you can't fly over them. You find a cut toward the south between two peaks and take it. Then you have to fly east or west until you find another one and another. The peaks and ridges seem to be growing around you as your plane continues to lose altitude. If you make a wrong turn, you could become trapped in a blind bowl. You thank the good Lord there are only a few clouds and light snow flurries. If cloud cover were thick, and you had to fly instruments, you would never get through the mountains.

You are down to twelve thousand feet, and you just barely clear a ridge. Then you look up and can see the Adriatic far ahead. You're on the downside of the Alps. If you can hold your present rate of descent you will make it. If you have to put the bomber down or bail out, at least there's flat land ahead even though it belongs to the enemy.

It is at that moment the intercom comes alive with a voice crowding panic. "Bogies! Two Bandits at three o'clock!"

You don't have to ask if the spotter is sure. If he might have mistaken friendlies for enemy fighters. The voice is that of waist gunner Loran Conner. He's officially credited with shooting down at least one enemy fighter. He knows the difference. Besides, sitting beside you, Jim says he sees them, too.

"They're hanging out there, looking us over. I don't know why they don't come on in. We're a sitting duck."

A smoking engine jeopardized a plane's crew in that the potential loss of power forced the aircraft to drop out of the attack group. The plane below was likely hit by flak over the target (antiaircraft fire, which formed the black splotches in the photo). Trailing smoke also attracted enemy fighters.

U.S. AIR FORCE

You get on the radio, the fighter frequency. You don't believe it will do any good; you haven't seen a friendly all day, but maybe . . .

"This is Calhoun 88. Calhoun 88 calling anyone that can hear me. Over . . . This is Calhoun 88 calling. We're in real trouble. Over."

You wait a few long seconds for someone to answer. Nothing but silence. You try again. And again.

"This is Calhoun 88 to anyone who can hear me. Over."

Cpl. Clarence Causey Jr. calls. "They're swinging around, Skipper, still looking us over."

Cpl. Carlon Pinnegar adds, "Maybe they're new and don't know what they're doing."

You think to yourself, *Maybe they're pros and are taking their time trying to determine if any of our gunners are knocked out. They'd rather come in on a dead gunner.*

Jim Smith adds to what you're thinking, "I hope to hell they think the radar antennas sticking out of the ball turret are guns. We're naked below."

You try the fighter frequency again.

"This is Calhoun 88 in big trouble. Anybody out there?"

You think it's hopeless, but you keep calling to give you crew hope.

Suddenly your radio comes alive. A deep, resonant voice booms out, "Calhoun 88, where are you?"

You know your own slow drawl marks you as a white southerner. And you know unmistakably that the voice you hear is that of another southerner, one of a different color.

"This is Calhoun 88. We're clearing the mountains, southbound about fifty miles north of the coast. Altitude eleven thousand, descending. We're crippled and have two Me-109s closing in on us. Can you help?"

"Looks like you got yo'self in a pack a'trouble, Calhoun, but I do believe I see you. Just where did you boys come up with a call sign like Calhoun anyway?"

Something catches the corner of your left eye—two tiny specks rapidly growing in size. A moment or two later you look out your side window and watch a P-51 Mustang slide up on your left wing. The pilot takes off his oxygen mask and grins at you with the whitest teeth you ever saw. A moment later a second Mustang, his wingman, joins him. The lead black pilot gives you a salute and is gone as fast as he arrived.

"You boys head on home, now. We gonna take care of Fritz."

The tails of the two Mustangs are painted bright red. You've heard of them, the Tuskegee Airmen. They're based at Manfredonia on the spur of Italy. You don't know where they came from so quickly. Maybe they were on a fighter sweep over Udine, or maybe they just finished an escort mission. You don't care. You're so damned glad to see them that you could kiss 'em.

The German hunters quickly become the hunted. Your tail gunner sees one go down and the other run for home.

The Red Tails stay with Calhoun 88 until it is picked up over the Adriatic by a couple of B-24s sent out to watch over them just in case they have to ditch.

Back at Torretta, the ground crew stands waiting alone out on the field. They see the two search planes returning—and something more. Between them is a third bomber. Calhoun 88! Bomber crews pour out of tents and shacks to welcome home one of their own returning from the lost. They watch Capt. Amos S. Pollard bring in his crippled plane.

Amos and his crew have made it home once again. Within a couple of days the damaged engines will be repaired or replaced, and Pollard and his crew will go out to do it all over again. Before it's over, they will have flown thirty-four such combat missions.

THE 484TH BOMB GROUP began operations in Italy in April 1944 with four squadrons and a total strength of 61 aircraft. The war ended a year later. During that time, it took a total of 118 replacement aircraft to keep them at full strength. Capt. Amos S. Pollard survived the war. So did every member of his crew. He's proud of that fact. Others were not so fortunate. In its year of operations out of Torretta, 484th losses to enemy action (killed, wounded, or missing in action) totaled sixty-six crews—660 men. More than 100 percent of its original strength.

Of all the missions Amos Pollard flew, the one described here stands out most in his memory. He came from a rural community in Choctaw County, Mississippi, near the small town of Mathiston. He grew up in a segregated South and served in a segregated army air force and never thought much about it. Then, high in a lonely, hostile sky, two black men saved his life and the lives of his crew at great risk to themselves. For Amos, it changed a whole way of thinking.

"I'll forever be grateful to those Red Tail pilots. I deeply regret that I never was able to find out who they were to thank them personally. As their reputation grew, bomber pilots began asking specifically for the Red Tails to escort them. I was one of them."

Records indicate that not a single bomber under escort by the Red Tails was lost to enemy fighters during the war.

After the war Pollard and his copilot, Jim Smith, stayed in touch, corresponded, and occasionally got together. More than fifty years later, while Pollard was visiting Smith on the coast of Maine, the two took a rowing dory across a small inlet.

While they were rowing, Smith paused and said, "Amos, there's something I always wanted to say to you and just never got around to it. I figure we won't live forever so I might as well tell you now."

Amos kept rowing. Smith said, "I just want to tell you that I thought you exhibited one hell of a lot of personal courage back when we flew those missions together."

Amos stopped rowing and replied, "Hell, Jim, don't you know I was scared to death!"

"I didn't back then," Smith said. "You carried fear better than anyone I knew. You set an example for me and the crew. I just wanted you to know. Now get back to your oars before we drift out to sea."

Although Pollard never mentioned it, records show that he received numerous honors, among them the Distinguished Flying Cross and the Air Medal with oak leaf clusters.

OWEN T. PALMER JR.

GROWS THE SEA INTO SLIDING MOUNTAINS

A ROUND NOON, I WAS sitting in the student union grill at Ole Miss, eating a hamburger steak and listening to a Tommy Dorsey record on the jukebox. Someone ran in and yelled, "The Japs just bombed Pearl Harbor!" Everybody in the place was stunned.

Immediately after graduation, I volunteered for a crash program set up by the Department of the Navy designed to turn college graduates into naval officers in the shortest possible time. I was introduced to marching, saluting, and military conduct and learned pretty quickly a whole new language—the front of a ship was the bow, the back was the stern, ropes were lines, floors were decks, walls were bulkheads, ceilings were overheads, and bathrooms were heads.

Owen Palmer and thousands like him were given courses in leadership, tactics, damage control, Morse code, ship propulsion, gunnery, and first aid. They were taught, in theory at least, how to maneuver, navigate, and fight a ship. The program was designed to give them a rudimentary base of knowledge from which, it was fervently hoped, they could learn "on the job" all that was necessary to successfully fulfill the missions to which they would be assigned. In just ninety days they found themselves officers and gentlemen in the U.S. Navy.

Old hands—those who had come up the hard, slow way, languishing without promotion in the years before the war—resented and derided the Ninety-day Wonders. But even the old salts couldn't deny that the navy needed all the officers it could get. New ships and planes were being built faster than crews could be trained to man them. Within a very short time, the old hands noticed that the college boys learned fast, and most of them made damn fine officers. The Ninety-day Wonders manned the ships and planes and lived, fought, and died alongside the best the regular navy could muster. This is the story of one of them.

After receiving their commissions, Owen's class was given fifteen days' leave before going on to receive training in assigned special fields. It would be a long time before Ensign Palmer saw home again. This was in December 1942.

Owen was sent to radar and sonar ASW (Antisubmarine Warfare) school. He was destined to serve aboard a destroyer, one of the small vessels that made up the protective screens around the mighty task forces sent in harm's way.

On June 1, 1943, the new Fletcher-class destroyer, USS *Clarence King Bronson* (DD-668) was commissioned at Kearny, New Jersey. Aboard her as she sailed to join Task Force (TF) 58 in the Pacific was Ens. Owen T. Palmer Jr.

There are many stories that could be told about his time aboard *Bronson*. All one has to do is review the ship's combat log. She helped screen TF 58 during strikes on Kwajalein in support of the landings there and raids on Truk, Saipan, and Guam. She screened carriers covering the landings in the Bismarck Archipelago and on New Guinea. She returned to raid Truk again and shelled Saipan as the assault began on that island. She screened the carriers as they launched their planes during the decisive battle of the Philippine Sea.

DD-668 was there with TF 58 to cover the invasion of Guam and the capture of Palaus in September 1944. She took part in the battle of Leyte Gulf, the battle of Cape Ergano, and strikes in support of the Mindoro landings. *Bronson* steamed off Japan itself to shell inshore as part of the strategic plan to assault the island of Iwo Jima. On February 18 she left the main body of her task force to escort two cruisers to Iwo Jima for the pre-invasion bombardment and provided fire support to the forces ashore after the assault of February 19.

After the initial landings at Iwo Jima, Lieutenant Palmer was sent ashore to assess the effectiveness of the naval bombardment. "The bodies of our assault forces," he recalled, "covered the beach. I mean the whole beach as far as I could see. The stench of death lay like an invisible fog, a sickening smell that was even stronger than that of the sulfurous, volcanic gases that seeped from the earth."

There were better moments he remembers, such as the victories at sea and the rescue of downed pilots. There were so many of those that Palmer hardly recalled the day (June 19, 1944) when the combat log of the *Bronson* recorded the following:

> 1201: Observed three enemy torpedo planes attack from astern formation. All were shot down by AA fire from screen [destroyers]. 1214: Enemy aircraft reported bearing 263 degrees, twenty miles. Friendly fighters intercepting. 1215 to 1237: numerous small groups of enemy planes closing from westward—all intercepted by friendly fighters. 1309: Friendly TBM [torpedo bomber] from USS San Jacinto crashed in water. 1310: Stationed rescue party. Picked up crew: Ens. Bush, G, USNR, Pilot; Nadeau, L.W.; AOM 2/c and Delaney, J.L.; ARM 3/c.

The same pilot was, three months later, shot down off Saipan and again rescued, this time by the submarine USS *Finback*. (In 1992, President George H. W. Bush was reminded of the incident when he met Owen.)

Low points include the day *Bronson* and her sister destroyers fired every AA gun they had at attacking Japanese dive bombers only to see the carrier *Princeton* take a mortal hit. As the carrier burned out of control, the cruiser *Birmingham* came alongside her to rescue the crew. During the operation, fire reached *Princeton*'s bomb magazine. The resulting explosion killed many of the crewmen of both ships. At the time, *Bronson* had her own problems. She barely escaped damage when her gunners splashed an attacking twin-engine "Betty" bomber just yards off her port bow.

Bronson was assigned to Third Fleet, TF 38, which was primarily a carrier task force, in support of the invasion of the Philippines. While

Seventh Fleet had a defensive mission to escort Douglas MacArthur's invasion forces to the Philippines, Third Fleet had an offensive mission to strike where it thought most effective: ahead of and in support of MacArthur's forces. Beginning on December 13, 1944, carrier-based planes from TF 38 smothered the Japanese air bases on Luzon and Mindanao and wreaked havoc with Japanese shipping trying to reinforce the defending troops.

Combat, though never routine, had become a common experience aboard *Bronson,* but there was one battle of a different sort that stands out in Owen Palmer's mind above all other experiences during the war. The ordeal began in the Philippine Sea during the week of Christmas 1944.

Of all the ships in the task force, the destroyers were the most fuel critical. The small, fast vessels spent their time protecting the task force, providing an antiaircraft and antisubmarine screen around the fleet. *Bronson* had twin screws and sixty thousand horsepower. She had a top speed of thirty-nine knots. At the rate destroyers burned fuel darting in, out, and around the fleet, they required fueling every few days, sometimes more often. Unable to wait for the fleet tankers that plied between the task force and oil supply points, destroyers were frequently fueled from the battleships and carriers they escorted.

When the Philippines operation began, the fleet had already been engaged in operations for several weeks. It was low on fuel. On Sunday morning, December 17, in the face of worsening weather, TF 38 was ordered to commence fueling operations.

First to raise the scent of serious trouble that morning was the USS *Hull.* In the early hour darkness the destroyer joined the task force; it carried the mail for more than thirty of the ships.

Just after dawn *Hull* begins the task of delivering the mail. Before the sun has cleared the eastern horizon, *Hull* reports that she has managed "with great difficulty" to transfer forty sacks of mail to the battleship *South Dakota.* "Great difficulty" is an understatement. The wind is rising, and the sea with it.

To remain properly ballasted as they burn fuel, destroyers pump seawater into their empty tanks. As soon as the order is issued to initiate refueling, in spite of the rising wind and seas, the ballast is

COURTESY OF MRS. OWEN PALMER JR.

The Fletcher-class destroyer *Bronson*, on which Owen Palmer served, was photographed while transferring rescued pilots back to their home carrier.

pumped out of those destroyers that are scheduled to be refueled first. The process takes time and leaves the vessels floating high in the water.

At 1107 that morning, the destroyer *Spence* comes alongside the battleship *New Jersey* to fuel. The wind is blowing twenty-six knots, and the sea is already at force five. Waves trapped between the parallel vessels pound from one hull to the other, flooding the deck of the smaller vessel and threatening to wash her fueling crew overboard. The destroyer fires hauling lines across to the battleship, and with superhuman effort the heavy fuel hoses are drawn across the wave-tossed gap. After only a few hundred gallons have been transferred, both the fore and aft hoses suddenly part as *Spence* is tossed off station like a piece of driftwood caught in an angry surf. Her deck is covered with spilled oil and foaming sea, increasing the danger of the already hazardous task of securing fueling operations.

The same mishaps are happening to other ships, large and small. The light carrier *San Jacinto* manages to take on 170,000 gallons from a fleet tanker before being forced to discontinue fueling. The destroyer

Buchanan comes close alongside the light carrier *Altamaha,* and through the courageous efforts of her deck crew, manages to rig a boatswain's chair to transfer several rescued pilots back to their carrier. They abandon the exercise as being too dangerous. By early afternoon the fleet commander orders the suspension of all fueling operations.

A course change to the northwest is given to TF 38 and quickly followed by another to the southwest as the task force tries to determine the position and direction of the approaching storm and move from its path. Darkness falls, and the wind begins to howl; the seas grow. Aboard the destroyers, those on watch grow more than uneasy while those off watch spend sleepless hours simply trying not to be thrown from their bunks.

The ships begin to moan and creak and echo with drumlike sounds as huge waves slam into them, stressing their hulls with twisting and bowing moments. The barometer drops precipitously. The voice of the wind changes from low howls to high-pitched shrieks, driving the rain horizontally and shearing the tops of waves into spume so thick as to blur the dawn and reduce visibility to the point that station keeping becomes almost impossible. Fleet command faces the realization that the task force ships are in the grip of a full-blown typhoon under the worst of conditions—the ships are fuel critical.

On the morning of December 18 fuel reports from the destroyers are alarming. All but *Hull* were at minimums when the fueling was canceled the day before. Most have only 10 percent fuel remaining. Worse, those that have deballasted for refueling are tossed about the sea like corks. Water seeping through leaking plates and hatches begins to short out electrical systems, including ballast pumps, precluding their ability to reballast the empty fuel tanks.

The December 18 log of the *Bronson* reads: "0730: Dortch and Porterfield attempted unsuccessfully to fuel from Essex and Ticonderoga. Heavy seas and high winds caused the larger ships to drift down on destroyers attempting to fuel." With no hope of refueling, *Bronson* wisely remains ballasted with seawater.

The weather continues to worsen. *Bronson*'s log reports: "1200-1700: Heavy typhoon weather with winds over 100 knots and huge seas." To the northeast, a part of the Third Fleet reports: "The eye of the storm." It is the first positive report of the typhoon's position.

TF 38 is ordered to change course again, this time to due south in an attempt to break out of the storm. It is a futile effort. The full force of the great typhoon is upon them with all the fury nature can unleash. The fleet is locked in a battle with an enemy impervious to all the guns and planes and might of man.

The destroyers have difficulty coming to the new course. They try going full flank speed on both propellers with full rudders and fail. They try reversing one propeller and going full on the other with rudders full over and fail. They try every combination of rudder and power. The fury of the huge waves and high winds slam them back into the trough, pushing them over to dangerous degrees of roll unheard-of by even the oldest of hands.

The destroyers try again and again, only to be picked up and thrown over on their sides. The course change becomes irrelevant. The fight becomes one of survival.

The small ships are not the only ones in trouble. On the battleships, the huge forward gun turrets submerge as the heavy bows plunge into the enormous waves. Cruisers began to report structural damage. The heavily laden fleet tankers steam almost submerged under the enormous waves. All that can be seen of them is their superstructure. Their lifeboats are swept away.

Aboard the *Bronson* and other destroyers, men on duty or off hold a death grip on anything handy. Those who don't are tossed about like rag dolls. Men throw up. They fight a clawing terror deep inside them, but they somehow do their duty whether down below in the engine rooms, up in the pilothouse, performing damage control, or waiting their turn to relieve those on duty. Sick bays began to fill with the injured—men with broken arms, shoulders, legs, concussions—all from being tossed into bulkheads and equipment by the violent movement of their vessels. Reports begin to come in of ships losing men overboard. Not even the most experienced sailor in TF 38 has seen anything like this storm.

It is worse aboard the light aircraft carriers. Because of their high freeboard they experience the same problems of steering as the smaller destroyers. At full power they bring their bows into the wind and seas only to find themselves sliding sideways off immense waves and rolling violently down into deep troughs only to be slammed by the next huge wave. Frightening reports begin to come in. The aircraft carrier *San Jacinto* is the first to report fires due to planes breaking lose from their moorings. Then the carriers *Cowpens, Monterey, Altamaha,* and *Cape Esperance* all report planes breaking lose, tearing away from double and triple lashings and slamming wildly about. Their fuel tanks rupture, spilling high-octane aviation gasoline that ignites into raging fires. Fuel and ammunition stores are threatened. If they go, the ships go. There is no choice but to send men where even the devil would fear to go. The light carriers are rolling as much as forty-five degrees. Crates of spare parts and engines, bomb carts, and aircraft tear loose and slam back and forth across the hangar decks, striking bulkheads with plate-buckling force, creating giant meat grinders in the very spaces men must fight the fires to save their ships. Nonetheless, firefighting crews respond. They are no longer mere sailors. They are, to the man, extraordinary heroes. No log entry can express the bravery of the damage-control crews nor the pain of the badly burned and crushed nor the agony of those who die in the flames.

Now the wind grows the sea into sliding mountains. Ships large and small lose communications. Radar masts are carried away. Several 40-mm AA gun tubs and sponsons are torn loose and dangle

One of the few images of the typhoon-stricken task force captures the rolling of the light aircraft carrier *Langley*. The storm took a toll in ships, men, and in such instances as this, aircraft. *Langley* lost none, but three other carriers lost fifty.

over the side. Depth charges are lost overboard from their launchers and racks. Lifeboats are smashed. Below deck, gear, supplies, ammunition stores all break loose and slam wildly about. On some vessels the loose debris threatens to punch through the ship's outer skin. Loose gear slides en masse to the low side during deep rolls, making it all the harder for ships to right themselves. Men are sent below to relash the lose gear. They are sent at great risk . . . because their ship is at great risk.

Aboard *Bronson*, Owen Palmer is officer of the deck when the destroyer *Spence* sends a chilling radio signal: "Dead in the water, driven hard over, taking on water." It is her last message.

Spence's crewmen are forced into a sea so violent that life vests are torn from their bodies. There is so much horizontally blown rain and spume in the air that a man with his head above water can drown just breathing.

The fact that *Bronson* is a Fletcher-class destroyer, the same as *Spence,* does not escape Palmer. At the time, *Bronson* is rolling more than forty-five degrees and recovering sluggishly only to be knocked down again. Wind gusts of 150 knots are reported. *Bronson* moans and bangs, sounding as if its steel-plate hull might tear open. Each time it is knocked down it shakes and shudders and staggers like a mortally wounded bull trying to remain on its feet. Owen knows the distance from his ship's water line to the top of her mast is eighty-four feet. When *Bronson* rolls upright at the bottom of a trough, he is awestruck to see that the tops of the monstrous waves on either side are higher than her mast. He shoves the image out of his mind. There are more important things to think about . . . survival of the ship.

The destroyer *Monaghan* radios, "Am unable to come to base course." She is a proud old warrior that has earned twelve battle stars fighting from Pearl Harbor to the Philippines. A few moments later *Bronson* picks up a weak signal from *Monaghan:* "Am dead in the water." It is her last transmission. Eighteen officers and 238 men go down with her.

A radio signal from the carrier *Wasp* reports, "Sighted raft with men aboard." A few minutes later the *Independence* radios, "Men overboard!" There is little they or anyone in the fleet can do for them but pray.

By early afternoon TF 38 is scattered far and wide. The highest seas any sailor in the fleet has ever seen become confused by backing winds as the storm begins to pass. Monstrous seas that have lost their rhythm and direction attack the ships from all sides, wildly rolling them beyond anything recorded.

Bronson is fighting for her life. Owen recalls, "One roll nearly dipped her stacks. I think we rolled as much as sixty degrees. You could look down through the side glass of the pilothouse directly into the sea only a few feet away. She hung there for what seemed an immeasurable amount of time before somehow staggering upright only to be knocked down again, albeit not as far."

Hull is a smaller, older destroyer. She has just joined the fleet to deliver mail and is well ballasted with 70 percent or better of her fuel on board. The old destroyer is fighting her way through the weather like the veteran of the sea she is, but she is paying a price. Her young captain, Lt. Comdr. James Alexander Marks, finds that he, like many other destroyer captains, can no longer coax his ship to respond to her rudders. Her hull plates are leaking at their seams. Saltwater is intruding into passageways, cable trays, and sensitive electronics, causing wiring and high-voltage switches to arc, shorting out the ship's electrical systems. With the wind and waves off her port bow, *Hull* is repeatedly forced over onto her starboard side. Suddenly a huge wave rolls her so far over she takes water into her pilothouse. Before she can recover, a second terrible wave throws her hard down, and she lays there, held on her side by the wind as the sea pours into her. Marks gives the order to abandon ship and steps from the pilot-house directly into the sea; he has lost his first command. Of the three lost destroyers, he is the only captain to survive and will pay a terrible price for having done so.

The destroyer *Dewey* almost follows *Hull.* Her number-one stack goes over the side, leaving a hole in her deck that is open to the sea. She loses vital steam pressure through a broken line that fed the whistle mounted on the lost stack. Ironically, losing the stack may have saved her. Her skipper has the presence of mind to pump all her remaining fuel to the port-side tanks in an attempt to counter her constant, wind-driven list to starboard. The loss of the tall stack reduces her wind resistance. The combination possibly prevents the lightly ballasted *Dewey* from being knocked all the way down on her side to suffer the same fate as *Hull.*

Finally, those who have been in the worst of it, Owen and *Bronson* among them, detect a slacking off of the storm's fury and dare hope they have survived.

On December 19 the wind begins to die, although the seas remain troubled. Those ships fit enough to do so turn about and begin a search for survivors. Cries are heard or imagined by lookouts desperate to find lost shipmates. Some are found and rescued, a precious few. The search continues for days.

Reports gradually reveal the terrible toll the typhoon has taken. Task Force 38 has lost 3 destroyers, 150 combat planes, 800 dead or missing men, and hundreds of injured. Of its 16 remaining ships (6 light carriers, 8 destroyers, and 2 cruisers), all are so badly damaged they must limp into the naval base at Ulithi Atoll for extensive repairs. With losses greater than any suffered during battle with the enemy, the task force is too crippled to carry out its mission. Its combat operations are canceled.

Little notice of the ordeal at sea ever appeared in the newspapers at home. At the time, the raging Battle of the Bulge in Europe occupied the headlines.

For the survivors, the seas rolled on and the war continued. Owen Palmer was executive officer aboard *Bronson* as she steamed proudly into Tokyo Bay to witness the unconditional surrender of Japan.

Ironically, her captain was Comdr. James Alexander Marks, the fateful skipper of the lost destroyer *Hull.* After medical rehabilitation and numerous boards of inquiry, Marks was given command of *Bronson.* Palmer well remembers what Marks said to him shortly after coming aboard: "On a destroyer, either the captain or the executive officer must be an SOB. You have been aboard the *Bronson* since she was christened. The crew already knows that I am an SOB. You carry on."

"Marks's private war was with the sea, and he knew his enemy," Owen commented. "He never went to his station on the bridge without his life jacket, even on the calmest of days, but no member of the crew could blame him in the least nor was one word spoken about it. Marks was a very meticulous, strict captain. The *Bronson* maintained its degree of readiness even after the war ended. Looking back, I think it is perhaps for this very reason that more crew members of the *Hull* survived than did from the other destroyers that were lost in that terrible typhoon. He somehow kept those around him in the sea together and alive."

On December 5, 1945, DD-668 finally received orders for home. Home! It is hard to imagine what those orders must have meant to the crew of *Bronson*. Theirs was a proud ship. On her bridge, homeward bound, she carried nine battle stars. (Later she would earn a tenth during the Korean War.)

When *Bronson* docked in New York, only 3 officers and 25 enlisted crew from the original commissioning detail of approximately 350 men were aboard. One was her executive officer, Owen T. Palmer Jr., who had done his duty with courage, determination, and professional skill. He was but one among the thousands of Ninety-day Wonders who proved themselves worthy and contributed mightily to the Allied victory at sea.

THERE WAS a late and sad casualty of the deadly typhoon of December 1944. Upon his return to the United States, Comdr. James A. Marks was hounded by endless navy boards of inquiry into the loss of the destroyer *Hull*. Never mind that he had done his best to save his ship and his men . . . as well as any mariner could have done. Never mind that the navy thought enough of his seamanship to give him a second destroyer command—*Bronson*. Never mind that many believed that the additional armaments the navy added to the destroyers of *Hull's* class made them top heavy. Of the three destroyers lost, he was the only captain to survive, and therefore the only one whom navy bureaucrats could blame.

Maybe it was the ordeal of those boards of inquiry, or the cries of his men in the water around him that echoed in his memory, or the common but intense guilt so often felt by those who survive when so many around them do not. For whatever reason, a year or so after he returned home, Commander Marks committed suicide.

E. D. "DEE" HAMILTON AND JOSEPH H. IRBY

ISLANDS

TAKEN SEPARATELY FROM TWO men, the story begins the same way. Evasively, shyly, each talks in general terms, avoiding any sense of personal investment. Slowly the scattered intimate sketches unfold as though the teller is outside, detached from the scenes of battle, glancing at the action and only occasionally commenting on what little part of it he sees. Gradually the storytellers return to 1944. As each describes his recollection, his eyes and hands follow the action. They see the past, hear it, smell it, feel it as they speak.

Seventeen-year-old Pfc. E. D. Hamilton is a rifleman in A Company, First Battalion, Twenty-fourth Combat Regimental Team. Seventeen-year-old Pfc. Joseph H. Irby is a machine gunner in I Company, Third Battalion, Twenty-fifth Combat Regimental Team. Neither man knew the other until after the war, but both ship out of San Diego with the Fourth Marine Division on January 13, 1944. Eighteen days later they are in combat. The experience will never leave them. Semper fi.

Dear Mom, how are you? I am fine. This is the last letter I'll write for a while that won't be censored, so I guess I can tell you we ship

215

out tomorrow, but don't tell anyone. I don't know where we're going, but don't worry about me. We are the best trained outfit there is and we are ready. I thought I might be nervous, but I'm not. None of us are. We're excited and raring to go! We don't have to be on the ship until tonight so we're going downtown to a movie. I'll write soon.

Love, Dee

Joe Irby wrote a similar letter home before shipping out. All the young guys did. It would be the last innocent and truthful letter the men of the Fourth Marine Division would write home. All the others would still begin, "Dear Mom, I'm fine," but they would not be written by innocent kids, and they would not contain the truth, for the truth might have destroyed their mothers.

KWAJALEIN ATOLL
January 31, 1944

Unlike prior units on their way to combat in the Pacific, the Fourth Marine Division made no stopover in Hawaii for a last month or two of training to boost morale before deployment. Except for a brief pause en route to take aboard fuel and food, the ships carrying the Fourth Division steamed 4,430 miles directly to Kwajalein Atoll, part of the Marshall Islands in the Central Pacific. For the first time, America was taking the war into Japanese territory.

The atoll doesn't look like much. It is just a number of tiny islands and islets strung sparingly around an oblong coral reef that forms a lagoon sixty-five miles long and eighteen miles across—a huge, deep, natural harbor. The main U.S. objectives are the twin islands of Roi and Namur, which are connected by a causeway. Together Roi and Namur total less than one square mile of land; Roi is 1,200 yards long and 1,200 yards across, Namur is smaller—900 by 800. The larger island was cleared to accommodate an airfield. The smaller is lush with vegetation and man-made structures and provides the occupying Japanese with both concealment and cover. The atoll is used as a naval repair and supply point, and it is well prepared for defense. All but a few hundred of the estimated defending force of three thousand Japanese soldiers are dug in and waiting for the marines on Namur. They averaged one defender for every 240 square yards.

For two days prior to the U.S. landings, naval guns and aircraft pounded the twin islands with 2,655 tons of shells and bombs (181 pounds of explosives for each Japanese soldier on the islands). It appeared to the marines watching from the troop ships that every square yard of the islands had been hit. They were confident that the imminent landings would be easy, that few of the enemy could survive such a heavy bombardment concentrated on so small an area.

DEE HAMILTON

They get us up in the middle of the night. No one was sleeping anyway. I pick up my combat pack—poncho, extra pair of socks, D rations, mess kit, a few personal items—and strap on my web belt festooned with two canteens, K-Bar knife, field dressing, ammo pouches, bayonet, entrenching tool, and an old World War I–vintage gas mask—marines mostly get hand-me-down equipment. I stuff grenades in my pockets and sling my carbine across my shoulder. That's it, I guess. We receive a final briefing from the company commander and line up on deck to await our turn to transfer into the small Higgins boats (known officially as Landing Craft, Vehicle and Personnel—LCVPs). The fleet is anchored inside the huge lagoon. We're going in the back door.

Climb down the cargo net to the boat. Try not to fall. Try not to step on the guy climbing below you. Try not to get crushed between the boat and the ship. Try not to look scared. Boats mill about in the predawn gray, going around in big circles on calm water made sloppy by their wakes, waiting for the signal to form into assault waves and head for the beach. Navy still shelling the islands. Flaming big guns splitting the darkness. Hate waiting. Dawn flooding the darkness. Hours more waiting. The whole platoon stuffed in the wallowing landing craft. Not until midmorning do we form up in a wave of boats abreast and go for the beach four thousand yards away. Sky is bright blue, water clear, islands beautiful, green, a tropical paradise marred by smoke from the shelling. Damn scared, maybe terrified.

For the men of the Fourth Marine Division, the Kwajalein landing was the beginning of a new style of combat against a relentless foe.

Joe Irby

It's dark when we get up. Line up for breakfast call. By the time it's my squad's turn, we're out of food. I eat the last of my candy bars. We strap on our gear and wait to climb down cargo nets into a landing craft. It's not easy with a carbine and a .30-caliber machine gun strapped to my back. The boats take us to a large landing ship, and we transfer to an LVT (Landing Vehicle, Tracked). We call them amphtracks, short for amphibious tracks. They're open, armor-plated amphibious tracked vehicles armed with a machine gun or two and designed to "swim" to shore, climb up on the beach, and move inland carrying a couple of squads of men each. Our job is to secure all the tiny islands around the reef while the main force takes Roi-Namur.

The amphtracks crawl off the ship's open ramp into the water and start for the islands. The things are so noisy you can't hear yourself think. They float, but not by much. The tracks are churning the water like crazy, but we aren't moving very fast. A couple of the guys stick their heads up to look out as we approach the first tiny island southeast of Namur. Sergeant tells them to damn well get their heads down. He doesn't have to tell me. I'm scared as hell and crouched down about as low as I can get.

Dee Hamilton

We're getting close. Enemy shells start falling in the water. Everyone jerks forward as the boat hits the beach. Ramp is down. Everybody out! Wade ashore. Mortars! Japs have the beach zeroed in! Rifle fire and machine guns, too. Some don't make it. I'm okay. So is my best friend, Anthony. For some crazy reason, we call him Sam. We shoot back. Sam, me, and every other mother's son on the beach. Some of our guys are falling, Chaos and noise everywhere. It's awful. Never seen dying before, not like this. People screaming. We can hear navy shells going over us. After watching the shelling from the ship, we thought nothing would have survived on this tiny island, but there's plenty of Japs left all over the place. We move off the beach fast.

The company is trying to get organized, forming a perimeter, lots of confusion. Trying to move inland. Can see dead Japs killed by the bombardment, but can't see the live ones shooting at us. We don't have much cover. Fire like hell, move up a little, then do it again. Navy corpsmen tend wounded, leave dead. I'm all right, so is Sam.

Navy planes coming in. Damn! Huge explosion. Big concrete building, only one left standing from earlier shelling, must have been full of ammunition.*

Joe Irby

Our amphtrack crawls up on the beach of a tiny islet a few hundred yards down the reef from Namur. We go over the sides of the thing, and I land right on top of a dead Jap. It's a startling introduction to war. He must have been killed in the bombardment. No one shoots at us. All the action is on Namur; sounds like heavy fighting. We fan out

---

*This large concrete blockhouse had walls three feet thick and was filled with naval shells and torpedo warheads. Flying debris, huge chunks of concrete, and exploding munitions killed many marines in the area.

and start our sweep. A huge explosion over on Namur! [Same munitions building Dee mentioned.] Damn thing nearly knocked us down way over here.

We think most of the Japanese abandoned this islet before the invasion began, but we're surprised by a handful of Japs holding out in a small building. It's the first time I ever shot at anyone. It's not a good feeling, but they're trying to kill us. We shoot the hell out of them. I hope the rest of the little islands are this easy. The guys over on Namur are catching hell.

Dee Hamilton

We've been at it all day and have gotten only a few hundred yards inland. Lots of guys have been hit already. It's hard seeing 'em, hearing 'em scream and cry out for help. I feel bad they've been hit, and I feel guilty for being glad it's not me. When there's shooting I'm too busy to think about anything but staying alive, but when there's a lull, like now, I think about those guys I've seen hit, and I'm scared as hell. That's not true. I'm scared all the time, just more scared when I'm not real busy.

Sun's going down and we're crawling across an open area, crawling on grass, green grass, short, like someone's lawn. No cover, but at least it's getting dark. Can't dig in because the coral beneath the grass is too hard. Can't see to go farther.

I'm with Capt. Buck Schechter, company commander. A good man. I hope he thinks I'm doing all right. We're not on the perimeter, so we lie in the grass facing each other, covering each other's back. We've been told the Japs like to fight at night. Don't know what to expect; maybe counterattack, maybe they'll try to sneak in one or two at a time with grenades. We have to cover our outfit and each other from all sides.

In the middle of the night, hear rifle fire somewhere to the far side of our position, then not much else, shooting now and then, flares going off above. Afraid to sleep. Long night. Glad to see the dawn.

A terrible thing! During the night a private somehow got outside our perimeter, maybe to get ammunition from the beach or something, I don't know. Nobody got the word he was out there. The next morning he was found alive but with part of his head shot away.

We were told that, coming back in, he was challenged and couldn't give the password. Maybe he didn't know it. Maybe he thought the guys were joking. They weren't. Maybe they were trigger happy. It was dark, and when he couldn't come up with the password, they shot him. They must have thought he was one of the Japs who speak English. We had been told Japs would trick their way into our lines by speaking English. He was carried back to the beach aid station. Horrible! Half his brain was shot away, but the body kept breathing. He was gone, but his body wasn't dead.

We heard the medics did what they could, covered him with a poncho, gave him morphine, but they had to go on to others, those who had a chance. We were told that he stayed like that on the beach, a brainless body, his breathing sounding ragged like snoring for nearly two days. I didn't know him, but later learned he was a Private Hopkins, the son of Harry Hopkins, special assistant to President Roosevelt. (Special Assistant Hopkins was told that his son had volunteered to go for ammunition and was killed by a Jap rifleman.)

At daylight we figure we're three or four hundred yards inland. You would think we could quickly cross the remaining four hundred yards of the island. You could run that distance in a minute or two, but nobody stands up and runs, not more than a yard or two at a time.

The enemy is dug-in: machine guns, blockhouses, concrete pillboxes, antitank trenches, barbed wire, rifle trenches. You stay low even when not engaged because snipers are everywhere. Some of them climb to the tops of palm trees and tie themselves up there with wire to keep from falling. We can't see them, so we just shoot up at the trees.

The pillboxes are the worst. They are so well camouflaged, we don't see them until they open up on us. They get some of us every time. We lay down covering fire until someone can get close enough to throw in a grenade or satchel charge or use a flamethrower to knock it out. Then we move forward a few yards and have to do it all over again.*

Toward noon of the second day we're almost across the island and hope that it's almost over. Then we encounter strong resistance behind an antitank trench. They pin us down pretty good. Nobody's moving.

---

*There were fifty-two concrete pillboxes on Namur, an island less than a quarter of a square mile. None of them surrendered.

Suddenly our battalion commander, Lt. Col. Aquilla J. "Big Red" Dyess, comes up and asks what the hell is holding us up. He yells, "Come on, marines!" and stands up and leads a charge right at the enemy, pointing out targets as he goes. I was close to him when he started, so I had little choice but to stick with him.

None of us has ever seen a colonel out in front of the troops. He has a Thompson submachine gun and is blasting away at the trees as we move forward. Several snipers fall but are caught by their wire bindings and dangle from the treetops. I look behind us. The colonel has gotten the whole unit up and charging. He's not even wearing a helmet.

We take the trench and move up on the other side. The colonel stands up on the parapet of the trench to direct a bunch of marines to flank the last enemy position. I'm next to him, but I'm not standing. He puts a fresh drum in the Thompson.

Then an enemy machine gun we've all missed opens up. The colonel's head jerks back. He drops the Thompson beside me and falls to the ground like a rock. He stares up at me. He's taken a bullet right between the eyes.*

I pick up the Thompson, and the whole outfit goes for the Jap machine gun.

Joe Irby

Our small assault force meets little resistance on the tiny islands we reconnoiter. On the second day we come ashore on one of the outer islands down the lagoon, which is untouched by the initial bombardment. The island is covered with palm trees and tall grass. Just into the brush, we hear strange noises and see movement in the grass in front of us. I'm quickly called up to set up the machine gun.

Everyone is tense, ready. I listen and listen some more.

"Hell! Just shoot in there, Irby!" someone whispers.

I motion him to be quiet. This sound is familiar. I'm a country boy. I unsling my carbine, crawl out in front of the machine gun, and disappear into the grass.

---

*Lt. Col. Aquilla J. Dyess was awarded the Medal of Honor posthumously for his actions on Roi-Namur.

About ten yards in, I confirm what I thought I had heard—a big fat sow suckling eight piglets. I crawl back to the squad and tell 'em it's pigs, not Japs.

A few minutes later we see a white flag wave from the bushes. An island native walks out holding the flag, and several others peep out as he introduces himself in perfect English. He says he was educated in California; he's the village leader. His people had left Namur to hide from the fighting. He says there are no Japanese on the little island and insists that the entire platoon go through a receiving line of villagers.

We have to shake hands with all three hundred of them. We are a little embarrassed at first because the women don't wear any tops, but when a young woman climbs up a tree to get us some coconuts, we discover that they wear bloomers under their skirts.

The villagers are gracious toward us. They say they are happy to be liberated from the Japanese. (And happy that we had not shot their pig.)

Dee Hamilton

By midafternoon of the second day, Namur is secure except for mopping up small isolated pockets of resistance. Several thousand Japanese and several hundred marines, scattered all over the island, lay dead in the hot sun. The sickening, putrid smell of decomposition fills the air.

Sam and I find ourselves sitting around with nothing to do. It makes us nervous. We came ashore as green kids who had never hurt anyone. Then for two days we killed a lot of Japanese and watched fellow marines scream and die all around us. It all came so fast, the noise and fury and killing and dying. We didn't know what to do next.

We sit there hot, sweaty, gritty, dirty, tired, relieved it was over. I had put a big bar of yellow saltwater soap in my pack and pull it out to show Sam.

He laughs, "Hell, where did you get that? Let's go clean up a little!"

We drop our packs and the Thompson, sling our weapons, and walk to the shore. We step over and around dead bodies and pieces of dead bodies. We don't look at them. Across the way we see graves registration guys collecting our dead, flopping them up into trucks like sacks of potatoes.

We come upon a row of dead Japs slumped over the parapet of a trench dug into the sand at the edge of the beach. They were defending the last few yards of land with their backs to the sea, which would have made them about the last to die. The hot sun has stretched their skin so tight and smooth that they look like wax figures, the kind you see in a museum.

A lot of marines have been shot by "dead" Japs—wounded ones, too. We learned pretty quick not to try to help wounded Japs. Some of them would roll over and let go of a grenade or shoot the marine trying to help them. We shoot the dead Japs to make sure. You leave a live one behind, and it's likely to cost some marine his life.

We look up and down the beach but don't see a moving soul. We figure we're safe enough; other marines are walking in the open across the island. From the water's edge we see patches of coral all over the place but decide, if we're careful, we ought to be able to walk far enough out in the shallow water to bathe.

I pick up a stick on the beach and use it as a third leg to stack my carbine and Sam's rifle, tripod fashion. We strip down, naked as the day we were born, and carefully wade out maybe forty yards to waist-deep water. The fresh breeze keeps the smell of the dead away. The water is cool, clear, and beautiful. We see brightly colored little fish. I feel lightheaded, happy. Maybe we are a little crazy from what all we've seen, or maybe this is how you feel after combat, just plain silly being alive. We start soaping up and joking and laughing. It is so good to feel clean. It is as if we are washing all the killing off of us.

All of a sudden we hear yelling from down the beach to our right. We look up and see two damn Japanese soldiers running like hell straight for us. They aren't more than 150 yards down the beach, screaming like crazy. One has a rifle, the other a bayonet. They're both holding something in their free hands, waving 'em around, banging them on their helmets . . . grenades!

Sam and I are standing naked in waist-deep water forty yards from our weapons on the beach. We're not just scared—we're panicked.

Move!

We struggle back to the beach. We reach knee-deep water and lift our legs high in a crazy galloping run. We stumble wildly on the coral but don't feel a thing.

Run!

That's all I think about. Run!

We get to our weapons, snatch 'em up, and start firing. The two Japs are less than thirty yards away. Even after we hit 'em they come on a few more yards, me shooting the one with the rifle and Sam taking the other.

They fall, and the grenades they're holding tumble toward us as they go down. We hit the sand. The grenades explode twenty yards away, throwing sand and coral all over us. We don't think we're hit. We get up and shoot the hell out of them again, just in case.

Then we see blood on the sand around us! It's our feet. We cut the hell out of them on the coral. We get our clothes on, fast. I pick up the Jap rifle. It's empty. They had no ammunition, only the grenades. I take the rifle, and Sam picks up the bayonet. Souvenirs.*

Our feet hurt now. We limp back across the island.

For less than a square mile of sand the Fourth Division suffered 750 casualties—dead, wounded, or missing. Of the Japanese defenders of Roi-Namur, only 264 surrendered. One of these came out yelling, in English, "Don't shoot! I have a brother in Brooklyn!" Elsewhere on the island, 3,472 Japanese lay dead, many from committing hara-kiri with grenades or by placing the muzzles of their rifles under their chins and pulling the triggers with their toes rather than surrender to the "hated American devils" treading on Imperial Japanese soil.

SAIPAN
June 15, 1944

The marines watch from the decks of troop ships as the naval bombardment pounds Saipan and the smaller island of Tinian. The pep talks they receive during last-minute briefings are not as effective as before. It had been tough enough to wrest less that one square mile of land at Kwajalein Atoll from four thousand Japanese troops. Now they face the Japanese stronghold of the Mariana Islands, nearly seventy square miles of fortified ridges, hills, and fissurelike valleys separated by flat cane fields and defended by low, earthen, camouflaged bunkers

---

*Dee mailed the rifle home. He still has it.

and pillboxes, all of which are overshadowed by fifteen-hundred-foot-high Mount Tapotchau in the center. On shore, the marines are told, are thirty thousand seasoned Japanese troops (seven thousand of them imperial marines) waiting in protected underground bunkers, waiting to take up positions in well-fortified emplacements as soon as the bombardment ends.

The Second and Fourth Marine Divisions will lead the assault, landing on a beach four thousand yards long on the southwest shore of the island. As the marines climb down the cargo nets into bobbing Higgins LCVPs or board growling amphtracks, the memory of Kwajalein Atoll is vivid. This time they know what is waiting for them.

Anxiety grows as H-Hour is delayed. It's nine in the morning before the wave of boats carrying the Twenty-fourth Regiment leave the assembly line four thousand yards offshore. Dee's unit has been assigned to go ashore through a narrow break in the coral reef that had been cut years before to allow access to a sugar mill at the small town of Charan-Kanoa. The town and the sugar mill have been pounded to rubble by naval guns and aircraft. Only a few buildings, the shell of the mill, and its smokestack still stand.

Dee Hamilton

A few hundred yards from shore, mortar and artillery shells start falling around us. The boat on our left is hit, bodies blown into the air. Seconds later our boat hits the submerged shoulder of reef on the edge of the cut and crunches to a stop. The driver tries to back off but can't. We're sitting ducks. There's nothing to do but drop the ramp. We step off into water up to our armpits. We're so loaded down with ammo a couple of guys who fall down nearly drown. We hold our weapons over our heads and wade to the shore seventy-five yards away. Shells are dropping around us. I'm too busy being scared to be afraid.

It's worse ashore. They have the beach zeroed in. We move out to the right and into the ruined town to find a little cover. Not much small-arms fire, but the mortars follow us. Jump down into a shell crater made during the bombardment. Climb out, run for the next crater. Climb out and run for next. Mortar and artillery fire are terrific.

There was nothing like this on Roi-Namur. We're taking casualties and haven't yet seen the enemy. How the hell are they keeping their mortars right on top of us? Keep going.

Word goes out that the Japs must have a spotter in the sugar mill smokestack. The C.O. calls for an air strike. It takes awhile but a navy plane bombs the stack, and we're able to work our way inland out from under the mortar fire. Late in the afternoon we dig in for the night.

I'm all right. So is Sam. Sporadic fighting. Star shells bursting. No sleep. Eat cold rations. Wait for counterattack.

JOE IRBY

They get us up before dawn and loaded into the Higgins boats, but we don't go anywhere. We slop around in the damn boats for hours waiting to hit the beach. God, we're hot, miserable, tired, and many of us are seasick by the time we start for the beach. The boat stinks of sweat, vomit, and fear.

Some of the boats and amphtracks are hit before they reach the beach. We head for a cut in the reef while the amphtracks are going in over the reef on both sides, leaving the cut for the boats. They can crawl over the barrier reef, plunge back into the calm water on the shore side, and make for the beach. At least that is the theory.

We see two of them broach sideways to the reef in the rolling surf and capsize. The guys that aren't crushed or drowned get badly cut up on the razor-sharp coral.

We think we are in the cut, but the boat hits a reef and is stuck. We step off the ramp into chest-deep water and wade for the shore that's fifty yards away—the longest fifty yards you can imagine.

We had been taking artillery and mortar fire on the way in, but it gets worse once we are on the beach. My squad takes cover behind one of our tanks that has been knocked out as soon as it rolled ashore. We aren't receiving much small-arms fire, but mortar and artillery shells pound us. It's horrible to see what these shells do: rounds exploding, shrapnel zinging and whistling all around, sand, coral, and pieces of bodies flying up in the air, people screaming.

The company commander gets everybody moving directly inland off the beach. We don't meet any mass resistance, but once we get into scrub brush and grass we start running into a hail of small-arms fire every few yards. I set up my machine gun. Can't see what I'm shooting at, just spray everything out front to cover the advance of the riflemen. When they get forward, they cover my team while we move the gun up. Then we do it all over again and again, gaining a few yards each time.

The Japs are good at camouflage. We can't see 'em even when they're shooting at us. We have a hell of a time when we run into bunkers they've dug low in the cane fields. Don't see 'em until they let go at us with machine-gun fire. Can't move until we knock them out.

I had gotten a little combat experience at Kwajalein, but machine gunners have a short life expectancy in combat. (Some statistician calculated it to be eleven minutes.) They are the greatest immediate threat to an opposing enemy, and therefore the most critical target. It doesn't take long for an enemy to zero in on them. I learn pretty quick that, if I want to live, I have to fire for a few minutes from one place then quickly pick up and change position.

The first step of the invasion of Saipan was getting the marines on the beaches. Clustered under the scant cover of an LVT, the first wave prepares to move out. Twenty thousand marines landed on the first day.

U.S. MARINES

My company has been able to move inland only about a quarter of a mile when darkness falls. We dig in for the night along a narrow-gauge railroad that had been used to transport sugarcane. I have my team dig two gun emplacements so we can switch back and forth if we get a counterattack. There's been so much killing, I don't think about it anymore. I sit behind my gun and wait. We hear firing off our flank. Star shells light up the sky most of the night. Eat cold rations, get no sleep.

DEE HAMILTON

I came ashore with the Thompson submachine gun I picked up when Colonel Dyess was killed on Namur. I think I'm really loaded for bear, gonna tear 'em up.

The next morning we start across a field of grass, cane stubble, and palm trees. I've never fired a Thompson before. When I pull the trigger, the thing sprays the whole area, kicking up dirt, grass, cane, palm fronds out of trees, giving it hell. Suddenly, it seems to me, the Japs stop firing at everybody else and concentrate on me. I'm too stupid to know why.

Sergeant Grimes shouts at me to get rid of the Tommy gun. I guess everyone in the outfit but me knows that automatic weapons draw fire from an enemy like honey draws bees. I throw that thing down and move out fast.

I'm without a weapon. I take a carbine and ammo from a dead marine. I don't look at his face. Don't want to know.

Grimes probably saved my life. He's a good-looking, tall guy with a black mustache. Looks like Gilbert Roland, and they say he used to date Maria Montez, the movie star. Gets letters from her.

This is a big island. Patrols are sent out to find the enemy and routes of attack. I hate patrol duty. The three scariest words in the English language are "You take point." It's really spooky in the dark.

One night one of our patrols goes missing—the whole patrol. The next day we find them just off a trail toward the center of the island. It's bad. The Japs pulled out their fingernails and burned their faces and arms with cigarettes to make them talk. Then they slit their throats. It's easier to kill Japs now.

JOE IRBY

We fight all afternoon and finally get to dig in at sundown. There are sporadic attacks by small enemy groups throughout the night. We repel them all, but by morning I'm down to my last two belts of ammunition. I get permission to take a guy named O'Donald and two other men back to the beach for more ammo. We are making our way across a burned-out cane field when mortar shells begin landing all around us.

The only cover is a large shell hole a few yards away. The four of us dive headlong into it.

Damn shells falling everywhere. The ground shakes and the sides of the hole cave in every time a shell goes off nearby. The noise of the explosion shatters your ears, and shock waves knock the air out of your lungs. Shrapnel screams past just above our heads. We're being covered with sand, cane stubble, and coral. Red-hot pieces of shrapnel fall on us, burning through our clothes and blistering our skin.

We're all terrified. O'Donald suddenly screams, "We'll all be killed if we stay here!" He jumps out of the hole and takes off running. The other two guys are his buddies; I can't remember their names. The first one darts from the hole with his friend right behind. I know I might die where I am, but I figure it's safer than being out in the open. I stay put.

The mortar fire lifts a few minutes later. I'm shaking so hard I can hardly crawl from the hole. The first thing I see is what's left of O'Donald and his buddies. There isn't much. None of them got more than thirty yards.

I reach the beach and see supplies stacked in between wrecked tanks, amphtracks, 75-millimeter cannon, and piles of dead marines covered with ponchos. Offshore the amphtracks are plowing back and forth from the supply ships in spite of heavy artillery fire picking some of them off. Seabees and shore parties of Negro ordnance personnel unload them as fast as they get to the beach. There's an aid station crowded with wounded.

Another terrific barrage begins. The Japanese are damn determined to stop the invasion, and the beach is the worst place to be. The

U.S. COAST GUARD

A Coast Guard photographer captured this remarkable image of two marines falling under fire as they came ashore at Saipan. American casualties totaled sixteen thousand; by comparison, twenty-nine thousand Japanese died.

nearest cover is a knocked-out amphtrack, and I run like hell for it. Finally I round the corner and run into some guy, knocking him flat on his back. I look down and see he's a damn general!* Binoculars, map case, and all.

Mortar fire or not, I take off around the other side of the LVT and jump into a shallow hole a few yards away. It's not a good place to be. There are a lot of shallow shell craters on the beach, and I sprint from one to another, trying to work my way down the beach and out from under the barrage.

I make it to where a few palm trees are still standing and leap into an abandoned Japanese trench. It's good and deep. A moment later another marine jumps in with me.

We are not alone, however. The body of a dead Japanese soldier lies at our feet. The smell of the decomposing corpse is awful, but the

*The general turned out to be H. M. "Howling Mad" Smith who was in command of the invasion.

bombardment going on all around us is a worse option. We aren't about to leave the trench. We try throwing sand over the body. It doesn't help much.

The marine beside me keeps looking at me. There's something familiar about him, but I can't place him.

Finally he yells over the noise of the shelling, "Are you Joe Irby?"

"Yeah, I'm Irby," I tell him.

"Damn, Joe!" he yelled. "I'm Gene Carr. We were in grammar school together in Orange Grove, Mississippi."

We hadn't seen each other since his family had moved to Idaho when he was ten. War is crazy!

When the shelling stops, I load up with all the ammo I can carry and start back inland. I pass by the pieces of the three men I lost on my way to the beach. I try not to look at them. When I get back to my company, I report their loss. A few minutes later, we start toward our objective, Aslito Airfield, where we are to join up with the army's 165th Infantry.

It's the same old routine now. We can't see the Japs until they start firing. We wipe out a small group, pick up, and move forward until we run into another group and another one.

DEE HAMILTON

Ten days into the battle, Sam and I are still together, still okay. Our platoon is assigned to help protect a company of tanks as they advance across a burned-out cane field toward a ridge.*

We're in the middle of a field when the Japs open up with big guns.† All our tanks turn around and withdraw, leaving us exposed in the open. We've walked into a trap. The Japanese open up on us from camouflaged machine-gun bunkers. A bunch of our guys are immediately hit. The only cover out there are shell craters and foxholes the

---

*Tanks advanced with infantry so that enemy troops could not crawl up to the tanks as they passed and drop grenades into them. More than a few tanks on the island had already been knocked out in this way.

†The marines and tankers could not see them, but the Japanese had their tanks dug-in along the base of the ridge.

Japanese and farmers had dug in the fields for protection from the initial bombardment. I dive into a hole.

Three men on my right are cut down by a machine gun before they can make it to the crater. They lie screaming a few yards from me. Bullets hit all around them. I go a little nuts, leave my hole, get to one of them, and drag him out of the line of fire. I don't know how, but the next thing I know I've gotten the other two in the hole. I didn't plan it, didn't think. I somehow just did it. Plain crazy I guess.

I yell for a corpsman. When I see one coming, I leave the four men in the hole and start for another one. There I find Sam. We start running, firing, going from one hole to another, making our way to a shell crater at the edge of the cane field.

We're still under fire when Sam takes off toward higher terrain. I don't like it, don't know what's up there, but take off after him anyway. We keep moving, take cover where we find it. Finally we jump into a small shallow hole that has straw at the bottom, only it isn't just straw. Someone has hidden a half-dozen straw-wrapped bottles of wine in that hole.

About that time, the marine tanks return with a vengeance and start blasting the ridge and everything in between. Sam and I grab a couple of bottles of wine and move up the rise to the cover of some rocks.

The wine labels are in Japanese except for the word *port*. Neither of us has ever consumed much alcohol, but we drink that dark, sweet, heavy wine while we watch the tanks and some fresh troops take the ridge. When things settle down a little, we start back for the company.

I have a wonderful warm glow on and feel absolutely invulnerable. I stand up and walk perfectly upright the whole way back. Snipers are still in the area; I hear shooting now and then, but that wine and I don't care a whit. Later I wondered why I wasn't killed, walking in the open like that, drunk as a lord.

JOE IRBY

By the fifth day I have burned up three machine-gun barrels and am down to the last spare my platoon has. We're just about out of everything: ammo and food. That night I Company is allowed to fall back and dig in on a small hill to the rear to get a little rest, replenish ammo and supplies, and hopefully get a few replacements. Every squad has lost men.

Everyone is dead tired since we've had hardly any sleep for five days. We are numb, zombies. We are told we are in a rest area cleared of Japs. We dig in and post guards all the way around the perimeter. We feel safe enough to get a little sleep.

In the middle of the night the sky lights up so bright I am blinded when I open my eyes. The next thing I know there are yelling, screaming Japs right in the middle of us, firing rifles and machine guns! They're everywhere, tearing us to pieces. Dead tired or not, we come wide awake fast—confused, scared to death, but wide awake.

There's no time to think about my machine gun. The first thing I see clearly is a Jap standing over the foxhole next to mine and firing into it. I grab my carbine and shoot him.

Somehow a whole platoon of Japs has infiltrated into the middle of us. A guard must have seen something and fired a star shell to light up the place. It's a melee. There's hand-to-hand fighting all around. Everybody's shooting at point-blank range. The harsh white light from flares casts eerie shadows and makes it hard to tell friend from foe. You try to be certain you're not shooting a fellow marine, but the Japs don't care. They open up in the middle of it all with machine guns.

What's going on around us is horrible, but we can't do anything but fight for our lives. Out of the corner of my eye I see a Jap officer come screaming out of the darkness with a Samurai sword and cut a marine's shoulder almost off. The marine stands there in shock, hacked open from collarbone to armpit with his whole shoulder hanging halfway to his waist, blood going everywhere. He collapses. Someone shoots the Jap.

Some guys are holding their rifles by the barrels and swinging them like clubs. Some guys don't even have a weapon. I see our first sergeant grappling with a Jap, but I can't get to him. The sergeant chokes two Japanese attackers to death that night with his bare hands. It's like Custer's last stand: screaming, yelling, close-up killing.

Then, as quickly as it began, things are quiet except for the cries of the wounded. Either all the Japs are down or the ones who were able have left. We learn quick not to go up to a wounded Jap. One who is offered help will shoot you. Another pulls a pin on a hand grenade. After that we go around and kill every Jap twice.

The next morning we count sixty-seven dead Japanese. Among their weapons we find seven light machine guns. The scene around us is bad. We find our gunny sergeant among the dead. He had lost both hands, we think from a blast of machine-gun fire. Without hands he had no way to stop himself from bleeding. He died in the middle of the fighting before anyone knew or could get to him. Our losses are bad enough, but it's a wonder they didn't wipe out our whole company.

After that night of "rest," we are ordered back into the line. We run into pillboxes so well camouflaged we can't see them until they open fire. The only way to knock them out is for our guys to get close enough to toss grenades or satchel charges through their gun ports or turn flamethrowers onto them. My job is to pour machine-gun fire into the emplacements to keep the Japs down while one of our guys works his way in. These Japanese don't surrender, not even when they know a flamethrower is coming at them.

Flamethrowers are terrible weapons. The burning fuel spews out and sticks to everything it touches. When a flamethrower is fired into a pillbox or cave, we can hear the poor bastards inside screaming. It's God-awful. Sometimes one or two will run out with the stuff burning all over their bodies. None get very far. They writhe and collapse in a burning heap. If we can, we shoot them to put them out of their misery. It's better than letting them burn until they die. You never forget the mixed smell of flamethrower fuel and burning flesh.

As horrible as flamethrowers are, without them I don't know how many more men we would lose trying to clear the caves and boxes. We lose enough as it is.

One day it is already dark when we stop for the night. I get out my entrenching tool and start digging a foxhole. The ground is soft, and it goes all right until I get about two feet deep. There the ground feels kind of spongy. I chop down in the hole, but instead of getting a shovel full of dirt, I get a piece of a dead Jap. I'm so tired I just say the hell with it, shove the dirt back in to smother the smell, and sleep in the open next to the grave.

After a week the smell all over the island is that of rotting bodies, Japs and marines. It's only then that grave registration starts to pick up dead marines from the interior of the island. They have to wait until the bodies stink because that's the only way they can find most of them in the tall grass and hills and crags where they fell.

One afternoon while leading a detail back for ammo, we see a large pile of dead marines beside a road. Graves registration troops wearing heavy, black rubber bib aprons, boots, and gloves that go up to their elbows are lifting the bodies up into the back of a truck. After two weeks the bodies are all pretty ripe. As I walk by, one of the grave detail grabs a body by the feet while another tries to grab its arms to swing it up onto the truck. The flesh comes off its arms. They have to make a second try to get the body into the truck. I walk on by and wonder when it will be my turn.

Dee Hamilton

The farther the company moves inland, the harder the fighting. We wipe out one pocket of resistance only to move a few yards to the next. Every tree can conceal a sniper; every rock, hole, rise of terrain can hide a fanatical enemy determined to win victory or die for his emperor-god and the Japanese soldier's code—death before surrender.

We are moving cautiously forward when the guy next to me goes down screaming. A sniper on our flank has shot him. The bullet sliced all the way across his belly, opening it up like a surgeon's knife, spilling his intestines on the ground. I yell for a corpsman and run to him while my squad goes after the sniper. The guy is conscious the whole time I'm gathering up his insides and putting them in a bundle on his open stomach. I tell him not to look, but he does. I keep telling him that he'll be all right. What else can I do? A couple of days later I hear he died at an aid station on the beach before they could evacuate him.

And so it went day after day, field after hill after ridge after pillbox after cave for Dee and Joe and the marines like them. The men hadn't bathed since leaving their ship, hadn't shaved, hadn't brushed their teeth, hadn't changed clothes or underwear, couldn't stand the smell of their own bodies, but they kept their weapons clean. They slept in holes or on the bare ground—if they slept at all—and ate cold rations. They were often dead on their feet, and when things were quiet, they took turns nodding off for five or ten minutes of restless shuteye until it was time to move or the next shot rang out.

Fatigue was an enemy, and fear was a friend. Fatigue could make them careless, get them killed. Fear made them cautious, kept them alive . . . but fear also kept nerves on edge and bodies tense, thereby adding to fatigue. Fear, like fire, could also get out of control, could grow into terror and terror into panic, and panic could get them killed.

They became accustomed to daily acts and sights that would have made noncombatants gasp, puke, maybe cry. Killing was so common that they stopped thinking about it, had to stop thinking about it. If they saw the enemy, they killed him. It was part of every working day.

Dee Hamilton

One day merged into another until I didn't know what day it was and didn't care, but there was one day . . .

My platoon was making its way up a sharply rising slope at the base of a cliff when suddenly we took a hail of rifle fire and grenades from a ledge above. Half a dozen marines fell, and the rest of us were pinned down until a squad from another platoon on our flank worked their way up high enough to see the ledge. They silenced the defenders.

My platoon then climbed up to the ledge and discovered seven dead Japanese riflemen. Behind the ledge was a cave we had been unable to see from below the ledge. We hated caves, feared them, but couldn't ignore them, couldn't move on without clearing out each one. The last thing we wanted was the enemy behind us.

We approached this cave the way we approached them all— cautiously. Several men moved forward and were covered by the rest of us. They met no gunfire; no grenades were tossed out at them. Those of us who worked our way close enough to make the assault took a deep breath and, on signal, rushed the entrance and beyond. We were unprepared for what we found.

At the back of the cave a torch cast flickering light on thirty or forty badly wounded Japanese soldiers scattered about on the floor. Some wore soiled bandages; some had no dressings at all. The odor of rotting wounds and human waste was awful. Those who were conscious stared back at us in silence. The only sounds were occasional involuntary moans from the sea of hopeless, wounded creatures dying hard.

We didn't know what to do and sent word to the commander of A Company. He came up to the cave and wished he hadn't. It's hard, I guess, to understand what happened. He was afraid to send the medics among them. The wounded might have grenades. Wounded Japs had used grenades on our men before. If they had them, they would try to take a marine or two with them.

There was hard fighting going on up and down the cave-pocked ridge. A Company was on the flank. Even if the enemy wounded would accept help, A Company, what was left of it, couldn't spare the thirty or forty men it would take to move them. Nor could the captain leave two or three men behind to guard them. There were Japs all around. Two or three marines left out on the flank by themselves wouldn't stand a chance.

With a dark, terribly grim face, the captain ordered a machine gun set up at the mouth of the cave. Twenty horrible seconds of gun-fire and screaming then silence. It was slaughter, terrible . . . but perhaps merciful. Their suffering was over.*

JOE IRBY

The killing on both sides went on and on for twenty-five days. On July 9, 1944, Saipan was declared secure, but the horror wasn't over. During mopping-up operations, civilians began to come out of hiding. At first they came out at night. For fatigued, edgy marines, it was often startling to see figures moving toward us out of the darkness. Sometimes Japanese soldiers drove civilians in front of them to get close enough to throw grenades or open fire on the marines in a last suicidal act. In the dark some civilians were shot.

Now, with the hard fighting over, large numbers of civilians come out in the daytime, thousands of them. We don't know where they are coming from, where they have been hiding. They are filthy and hungry, especially the children. We offer them food, but some of the

---

*Their suffering may have been over, but as Dee told of the incident, it was apparent that at least one marine who watched that day suffers still.

people are terrified at the sight of us and run away. They gather on a cliff not far from us, and several jump!

We pass the word up to command, and battalion headquarters sends up interpreters with loudspeakers to plead with the islanders to stop, to tell them we won't hurt them, that we have food and medicine for them. The mayor of one of the towns comes to plead with them, but many commit suicide anyway. Jap soldiers among them urge the civilians on and jump themselves. We learn the Japanese have told the people that we would torture them, eat their babies, all kinds of nonsense. We helplessly watch women, clutching their screaming children in their arms, jump off ledges a hundred or more feet high.

One of our guys, a kid named Brenzinski, is with a group trying to move up a ridge to reach the cliff and stop the civilians from jumping. Just above Brenzinski's squad, five or six figures pop out of a rock crevice. One of them throws a grenade. Brenzinski has a BAR* and shoots them all with one burst. It was a reflex action. They were trying to kill him and the marines with him. It turned out that the "enemy" were all little kids.

Brenzinski nearly went crazy over killing those children. His buddies had to forcibly drag him away crying and threatening to commit suicide himself. It broke him. He was never the same after that.

The Fourth Marine Division sustained six thousand casualties on Saipan, more than 27 percent of its strength. Some individual units lost 50 percent. After ten days of rest on Saipan, the Fourth Division loaded up in boats and LVTs to assault Tinian.

TINIAN
July 24, 1944

Tinian, twenty-five square miles smaller in area than Saipan, was separated from the larger island by three miles of water. The enemy was estimated to have nine thousand troops defending the island. The Japanese expected the main invasion force would land on the wide beaches near Tinian Town at the south end of the island, and they reinforced their defenses there.

---

*Browning automatic rifle.

The planners selected an improbable landing site at the north end of the island: two tiny beaches, one only 130 yards wide and the other a mere 65 yards wide, both flanked by coral reefs. Some members of the planning staff thought it impossible to land an entire division there, that even if the enemy were caught by surprise, not enough men could be landed across the tiny beaches in time to defend against the counterattack that would come quickly once the enemy caught on. The plan was adopted on the basis that if some members of the staff thought it impossible, the Japanese would surely think so, too.

The Fourth Marine Division was assigned the task of making the assault landing. The battle of Saipan had left the division at less than 75 percent fighting strength. Men who were physically tired and mentally numb from nearly a month of continuous hard fighting grimly got themselves and their gear together and once more loaded into the boats and amphtracks.

Dee Hamilton

Our amphtracks line up abreast with the first assault wave and head for the little sixty-five-yard-wide beach. We had been told there would be little opposition to the landings, that all the Japanese were down at the south end of the island where a fake landing force was making a feint attack. They were right . . . almost.

It looks easy going in. No artillery shells are landing in the water as we near the shore. There are coral reefs on both sides of the open beach. The amphtracks are supposed to be able to climb the coral to the right and left, effectively widening the landing area by letting the boats land on the beach. We're hunched down low and can't see much. We've learned the hard way not to stick our heads up to look around on the way in.

Our amphtrack hits something hard, and the bow tilts up steeply about thirty degrees, tossing us in a pile at the back. We had run up on a large coral obstruction near the beach that lifted the whole front end high in the air. Engine grinding, tracks spinning, spitting coral and water up over us, we go nowhere. The hull is poised on the obstruction, leaving the tracks dangling on either side of it. The tracks can't get a bite. We're stuck.

There doesn't appear to be much resistance coming from the land in terms of numbers, but it doesn't take much to cover a beach only sixty-five yards long. A single Jap machine gun opens up on us. Over the noise of the engine we hear rounds striking the armor plate in front.

Our amphtrack has a crew of two, a driver low up front behind an armored shield and a machine gunner in a small open turret just behind and to the side of the driver's position. While the driver throws the thing in reverse and tries desperately to free us from the coral, the gunner returns fire. We are all looking up at the gunner's back when his head flies off his shoulders! Blood spurts everywhere, and the head, helmet and all, falls down among us.

Grimes—the guy who had told me to throw away the Thompson submachine gun that day on Saipan, the guy who dates the movie star—climbs up to the machine gun, throws the gunner's headless body down on us, and starts firing. The damn Jap shoots half of Grimes's head away! It just explodes all over us.

A third guy, I've forgotten his name, moves Grimes's body aside and mans the gun. They blow a hole in his head! One machine gun has done all this!

All of this happens within a couple of minutes. The whole time we've been stuck on that piece of coral with our heads down. We don't know where the rest of the landing force is or what is happening to them. Nobody wants to stick his head up to find out. Then mortar shells start falling around us. We know we can't stay there bunched up in the LVT any longer.

We climb over the back of the vehicle into shoulder-deep water, using the amphtrack for cover. To the right I see our company commander, Capt. Buck Schechter, in the water about forty yards away. I don't know how he got there. Maybe his LVT sank. He must have lost his radioman because he is yelling and motioning at our radioman who was holding the platoon radio over his head and out of the water.

He starts for the captain and is about halfway there when a mortar shell drops almost on top of him. He disappears, just gone.

Other amphtracks make it past us to the beach, and marines start laying down covering fire for those of us caught in the water. That same Jap machine gunner directs his fire on them, pinning them down on a beach with almost no cover. It looks like that one damn machine gun is going to wipe out the whole company when it suddenly stops firing. We later learn that a staff sergeant with a shotgun, the first one I heard that we had out here, swam pretty far down the shore, parallel to the beach, worked his way around behind the Jap machine-gun crew, and pumped five loads of buckshot into them.

Mortar fire is going over us and landing in the water as we move out from behind the amphtrack toward thirty or forty marines up on the narrow beach. I get within a few feet of shore when the enemy mortar rounds that had been hitting in the water walk up on shore.

I dive for the beach and land with my feet and legs still in the water. Shells are exploding all around. A big hairy arm with a gold wristwatch clumps on the ground six inches in front of my face. The watch is still running. A guy twenty yards up on shore disappears in an explosion—nothing left but a smoking hole in the ground. I've never seen anything like what's happening—arms, legs, torsos are flying up in the air and coming down all over the beach.

Someone, maybe the captain, must have gotten to a radio, because a bunch of navy planes come in over us and start strafing and bombing inshore. The mortars stop.

The area grows silent except for the moans and screams of our wounded. More amphtracks and Higgins boats make it in. Navy corpsmen start setting up a first aid station on the beach while what is left of my platoon and A Company move out with First Battalion.

Sam is okay; so am I. Several hundred yards inland we set up a defensive perimeter for the night. None of us has to be told to dig in. Division artillery sends up six little 37-millimeter guns to join us in the line. They dig in and break out canister shot. We are damn glad to see them, but we figure their presence means the brass is expecting a pretty good counterattack.

JOE IRBY

We load onto a landing craft right on Saipan and motor straight across to Tinian. It is one of the larger landing craft, an LCM (Landing Craft, Mechanized), large enough to carry two squads and four trucks. We lost so many boats on Saipan that they pack the ones we have left with everything they can carry. The trucks riding with us are loaded with ammunition, flamethrower fuel, explosive charges, TNT. If we are hit while we're going in, we'll all be blown to kingdom come. The beach we land on is only 130 yards wide, but we don't meet much resistance on shore. Our company quickly gets organized and joins the rest of the regiment to move inland a few hundred yards and dig in for the night.

DEE HAMILTON

I don't know what time it is, maybe two or three in the morning when the first attack comes. The Japanese come screaming out of the dark. Someone fires a star shell, and in the eerie light of that parachute flare it looks to me like a thousand men are charging us, officers out front with drawn swords, screaming men behind them, firing rifles and light machine guns.

We open up with everything we have—rifles, carbines, machine guns, mortars, and 37-millimeter cannon firing canister—at point-blank range. We turn back the first wave but hardly have time to catch our breath before a second wave comes at us then another. Wave after wave, they just keep coming.

I fire a magazine, reload, exhaust it, reload again and again as fast as I can. My carbine gets so hot I think it might jam. The barrels of the machine guns turn red hot. The gunners change them and burn up the new ones.

Some parts of the line are overrun. Mixed in with the terrible noise of the firing and screaming, you can hear marines shouting for ammo. We are barely holding but using up ammo faster than it can be brought up from the beach.

Just before dawn, things die down; the shooting stops. All you can hear are the cries of the wounded—theirs and ours. My heart is beating like a kettle drum, and my hands are shaking. We sit there, wild-eyed, waiting for them to come at us again, but they don't.

When dawn brightens the sky, all we can see in front of us are dead Japanese, some as close as three yards. The scene is not one of scattered dead littering the field; we have seen that before. But piles of bodies. A continuous carpet of bodies. An acre of bodies piled three high in some places.

Except for the moans of the wounded, there isn't a sound from anywhere up and down our line. Everyone is peeping awestruck out of their holes. We have seen plenty of dead Japs, but nothing like this.

Down the line I see a marine stand up in his foxhole, I guess so he could see better. The marine has his helmet pushed back on his head, kind of cocky, and I know who wears his like that. I scream, "Get down, Sam. For God's sake, get down!"

From somewhere out front among the Jap bodies a single shot rings out.

I jump out of my hole. Guys reach for me, but I run down the line to him. After all we have been through together, my friend is dead. A bullet in his forehead.

I stand up and open fire on the dead and wounded in front of me. Everyone in the battalion close enough to see what had happened also opens up on the piles of bodies laying in front of us. Machine guns, rifles, carbines, everything we have chews the piles of flesh into hamburger. The firing goes on for five, maybe ten minutes. When we stop there is silence, not a moan from out front, not a word from our lines, just silence.

JOE IRBY

About one in the morning the Japs make a banzai attack. I start shooting, and I don't stop all night except to load new belts of ammo or change barrels. Wave after wave of Japs attack. We don't see how they can keep coming, but they do. Star shells are fired all night so we can see them, hundreds of them, thousands of them.

I am firing a light, air-cooled .30-caliber machine gun, firing it until the barrel turns red hot. We have been scared before, but this night we are terrified. There is barely enough time to issue fresh ammunition after one wave is turned back before another one comes at us. We have to keep shooting at the screaming bastards or they will overrun us.

I have to fire in short bursts to keep my gun from overheating and jamming. Even then I still burn out barrels and have to stop to change them. About fifty or seventy-five yards away, two machine gunners—Daigle and Showers—are holding our left flank with a couple of heavy water-cooled .30s. They can keep firing as long as they have water circulating around the barrel. That's why they're on the flank. They have been firing steady all night. In between my bursts, I can hear them firing. Then, during the last charge, I don't hear them. Worse, we hear firing behind us. The Japs have broken through on our left.

On our right, Japs get into our lines, and hand-to-hand fighting erupts. It is chaos up and down the line. The night is lit up with rifle and machine-gun fire from both sides. Parachute flares and mortar shells. People yelling for ammo, and wounded screaming for corpsmen. The Japs just keep coming.

I am on my fourth and last barrel. I try to preserve it by firing in even shorter bursts, but when the Japanese get close I have to fire for all I am worth. I'm sure the barrel will burn out or the gun will jam at any second, and I'm worried about running out of ammunition. My crew is screaming for ammunition when the fighting tapers down.

Suddenly it is quiet all along the line. We have beaten back another attack, but I'm certain we can't repel another wave. In the lull I send men to the rear to find more spare barrels and fetch ammunition.

Alfred J. Daigle and Orville H. Showers manned .30-caliber water-cooled machine guns much like this one. Note the number of spent cartridges.

We sit, waiting, but no attack comes. I am soaking wet with sweat. I pray it is over and wait some more. Nothing.

There is time now to be scared, and as I sit behind my machine gun, my legs start to shake uncontrollably, knocking my knees together so hard they hurt. I can hear them knocking. I think they might break, and I put my hands between them to soften the blows. I don't know how long I sit there like that, trembling violently.

Finally comes the dawn. We look out on hundreds of Jap bodies, mounds of them. Every wave had to charge over the dead bodies of the wave in front of them, and when they fell, they added to the piles already there. More dead Japs lie in front of us than any of us have seen in all the fighting we have been through.

After we get over our initial shock and there is good light, men are sent out to kill them again, all the ones who might only be wounded and playing dead. We have become so hardened we think nothing of it. We have lost too many men in the past to Japs we thought were dead.

Before we move out, we have to clear paths through the field of corpses so that trucks and amphtracks can get through without bogging down in human flesh.*

Dee Hamilton

I can't remember moving out or fighting the four days it took to reach Tinian Town. I was still stunned by Sam's death, I guess. Maybe numb. I don't know. All of a sudden I realize we are walking into the ruins of a town. It had been well fortified with pillboxes covering every corner, but everything had been pounded into rubble by the navy's guns and planes.

All is quiet. Troops walking around, nothing happening. Maybe some outfit has reached it and cleaned it out ahead of us, I don't know, but I think we better watch out for snipers. A private named Swartz and I are together, making our way through the town. There are concrete cisterns here and there where the town collected rainwater. The tops of most have been blown away.

We are passing one of these when a Jap jumps up from it and attacks Swartz with a long, thin bayonet on the end of a rifle. Swartz is a big, strong man, maybe 250 pounds and no fat. He throws his hand up to protect himself, and the bayonet goes right through the center of it up to the hilt. Swartz raises the hand with the bayonet sticking through it, and in one smooth motion jerks that Jap, still holding the rifle, out of the cistern and slams him down on the ground. I shoot the son of a bitch. Then I wrap a field dressing on Swartz's hand and send him back to find an aid station. I move on through the town with my squad.

Japanese hand grenades are different from ours. They are smaller and smooth on the outside. When they explode, they break into tiny slivers of steel, not squares of shrapnel like ours. On the far edge of the town, a Jap pops up and throws one at us. I am close enough to get a whole bunch of splinters up the front of me. Swartz is still at the aid station when they carry me in.

JOE IRBY

While we are getting reorganized to move out the morning after the banzai attacks, a single Jap artillery piece fires a few rounds directly at us and falls silent. It may be an antitank gun, because it fires directly down at us like a rifle. At first we can't find it. Every time it fires, it slows everything down. Finally, everyone quits what he's doing and takes cover.

For the second time I jump into a ditch and find my childhood schoolmate Gene Carr. This time we don't have a dead Jap for company. We talk of school back home when we were kids. He says his family is moving back to Orange Grove and shows me pictures of them. His sister is all grown up and pretty.*

Finally we find the gun about eight hundred or a thousand yards up on a ridge. The thing fires a few rounds right into the middle of us then stops. An amphibious truck full of Negro ordnance troops arrives to unload ammunition coming up from the beach. That gun hits their truck right in the side and blows those poor fellows all over the place. We can't knock it out, so the C.O. calls in our artillery.

---

*Back home after the war, Irby will marry Carr's sister.

They fire a ton of shells at it, but a little while after they cease fire, the thing fires on us again. We figure the Japs are rolling it out of a cave, firing a few rounds down on us, and rolling it back in. Finally a navy plane comes in and drops what looks like a belly tank right on the ridge. The whole area goes up in great roiling orange flame. We don't know what it is, but it is one terrible weapon and silences that Jap gun.*

We pick up our dead and stack them to one side to await graves registration trucks. It's an awful task. You try not to look at the faces of the dead, the ones who have faces, and you try not to read their dog tags. You've already seen too many dead friends.

We are standing around, waiting to move out, when we notice a naval officer in a clean, pressed khaki uniform step out of a Jeep and walk toward us. We laugh and make snide remarks like, "I bet that navy puke slept in a clean bed last night," and "Yeah, he probably ate steak and ice cream, too."

Then he comes directly up to us and says, sort of with pride, that his brother is a marine with the Twenty-fifth and asks if any of us know him. I don't, but one of the guys looks kind of funny, starts to open his mouth, then stops and points to the pile of dead marines. He had just helped to carry the man's dead brother. I'll never forget the pain in that officer's face. We move out a few minutes later.

After mopping up Tinian, the Fourth Marine Division sails to Hawaii, to Maui to rest and lick its wounds. The respite was short.

SULFUR ISLAND

Iwo Jima (the name means Sulfur Island) is only 758 miles from Tokyo. It is a staging point for Japanese fighters intercepting U.S. bombers flying from Saipan to bomb the Japanese mainland. The island could provide the United States with a bomber base 700 miles closer to Tokyo, close enough to act as a supply point for the final invasion of the Japanese mainland.

---

*This was the first time that Joe and his fellow marines witnessed the use of napalm on the battlefield.

The Japanese are well aware of the island's value. They have spent months implementing an intense construction program designed to make the island impregnable. Assigned to its defense are twenty-three thousand crack troops under the command of veteran Gen. Tadamichi Kuribayashi. Much of their construction is photographed by navy reconnaissance planes. These photographs of concrete blockhouses, pillboxes, and bunkers leave no doubt of the difficult task ahead, but the most formidable defenses on the island go undetected. Hidden from overhead reconnaissance is a vast labyrinth of tiered and linked concrete-reinforced caves . . . caves that will escape damage during the long, intense pre-invasion bombardment.

Iwo is waiting . . . waiting for the men of the Fourth Division to make their fourth amphibious assault in less than thirteen months.

Meanwhile, Joe Irby was nearly court-martialed, threatened with a charge of mutiny.

Iwo Jima was the next-to-last steppingstone to mainland Japan. The last would be Okinawa. Plans called for the Fourth Division to be a part of the Okinawa invasion after Iwo Jima.

To be ready in time, Fourth Division command selected a cadre of officers and men from each regiment to remain on Maui during the Iwo Jima operation and requisition and assemble new equipment, weapons, and supplies, load them, and have it all ready for embarkation when the rest of the Fourth returned from Iwo. The Twenty-fifth Regiment had plenty of machine gunners. What they needed for the logistics job on Maui were clerk-typists. A review of personnel records revealed that Joe had excellent grades in high school and typing ability. Orders were cut accordingly—he was to remain in Hawaii.

Joe, of course, didn't know any of this. It was all top secret. All he knew was that his regiment was en route to another battle somewhere in the Pacific and he was to be held back. Joe couldn't accept that. He belonged with his squad. He was the best machine gunner they had. They were his buddies, and they depended on him. Damn if he wasn't going to go with them wherever the hell they were going.

Irby, with three of his buddies to back him up, marched to their company headquarters to request that he be allowed to remain with his squad for the upcoming operation. It turned into more of a protest than a request. The staff officer they confronted, finally tiring of the argument, informed the four marines that, under the military code of justice, a protest made by more than two men could be considered a mutiny. He called the shore patrol.

Joe was confined to base while his three friends were placed in custody aboard ship pending departure. Joe watched from shore as the Twenty-fifth Combat Regimental Team departed Maui for an unknown destination.

IWO JIMA

Back on Saipan, every night for seventy-two nights straight, mechanics checked out engines, radios, controls, and topped off fuel tanks while armorers loaded bombs and ammunition aboard the planes of the Twenty-first Bomber Command. And every day, for seventy-two consecutive days, flight crews took off from the captured airfields on Saipan and flew across seven hundred miles of ocean to drop their bombs on Iwo Jima. On five occasions they were aided by naval bombardments.

A bleak and uninviting island to begin with, Iwo Jima looked like a moonscape after the longest and heaviest pre-invasion bombardment of the Pacific war up to that point. Postbombardment reconnaissance photos revealed little or no enemy activity. Some wondered if any human beings could still be alive on Iwo. Just to make sure no stone was left unturned, bombers from Saipan and carrier planes and naval guns from the invasion fleet pounded what was left of Iwo's known fortifications for the day and a half preceding the launch of the first wave of assault forces.

During the dark morning hours of February 19, 1945, the troop convoy slipped in to join the warships bombarding the island. When the sun came up, the marines saw Iwo Jima for the first time. The sight was more than grim. The veterans of Roi-Namur, Saipan, and Tinian had been briefed on Iwo en route, but none were prepared for what they saw that morning. The marines looked out at an island like no other they had seen.

There were no palm trees, no cane fields, little vegetation of any kind. There were no white-sand beaches. All they could see through the heavy smoke of the shelling was a desolate, craggy lump of an island with a small bare mountain at one end. Over the reek of spent

The fine black volcanic sand at the landing on Iwo Jima hindered the forward progress of the marines. Twenty-seven Medals of Honor were awarded after the island was captured.

gunpowder from the bombardment, they could smell the sulfurous fumes that oozed from fissures in the island's crust.

For the Japanese troops onshore, the island had already become a seemingly endless nightmare. They had endured the concussions and deafening thunderous roar of bombardment for seventy-two days. Unable to move outside their crowded, hot, sweaty, stifling shelters except briefly at night, some of these men were in shock. Some were deaf. Some wounded. Some dead. Some had gone mad. But the vast majority of the hardened Japanese warriors were there—underground, combat ready, waiting. The heavy bunkers, pillboxes, and fortified caves had done what they had been designed to do: protect the imperial army from the heaviest bombardment any Japanese-held island had ever experienced.

At the appointed hour, the marines climbed somberly into the boats and started for shore. The closer they got, the worse it looked. The beach ahead was dark sand that extended inland in two or three huge steplike terraces, each five to ten feet high and yards across. Beyond the sand terraces lay barren, rocky moonscape. What little vegetation there was looked as if the sulfurous atmosphere was cooking the life out of it. For those headed for shore, Iwo Jima would be what it appeared to be—hell.

There were large numbers of replacement troops in the ranks of the Fourth Division because of the heavy losses incurred by the previous island combat. These men were facing their first combat. They were scared, but they took some comfort in knowing that they were fighting with combat veterans who knew what they were doing. As for those battle-scarred veterans, after three murderous invasions, they had nothing in which to take comfort. They rode the boats toward shore, jaws clamped tight, heads down, weapons ready. Resigned to the fight they knew lay ahead, they grimly choked down their inner terror and waited for the landing ramps to drop.

Dee Hamilton

The Twenty-fourth Regiment was heading for its fourth invasion. I had recovered from my Tinian wounds and was back with my platoon. Most marines are taught that their survival in combat depends on the marine next to them. I was making this landing without the guys I had earlier depended on, trained with, laughed with, fought beside. They had all died on the previous islands. As the boat plowed its white, frothy furrow toward the beach, I gripped my carbine, tasted the salt spray that curled over the Higgins's blunt bow, and breathed the air that smelled of gunpowder, sulfur, sweat, and vomit.

The first step I took on dry sand told me we were in trouble. My foot sank ankle deep in black sand so fine, it was like walking in powder. All I could see were huge banks of sand like giant steps leading inland. The amphtracks that came ashore, and the tanks and trucks that rolled off the LCMs, could get no traction in the powdery sand, much less climb the steep terraces. The more they wallowed around, the deeper they sank.

We could hardly climb the steep slopes on foot. The terraces gave us some cover from Japanese small-arms fire, but not from their artillery. Jap spotters on Mount Suribachi looked down on the entire length of the beach. Furthermore, their artillery and mortars had the beach zeroed in. Shells came down on us like rain and tore marines, trucks, tanks, and amphtracks to pieces. Many of the boats bringing in reinforcements, supplies, and equipment were blown to bits.

You couldn't dig a foxhole in that sand. It was too fine. The more you dug, the more the sides caved in. The best you could do was hollow out a little depression. The fine sand got in your eyes, your mouth, stuck to your sweaty body. You couldn't keep it out of your carbine and feared it would jam.

I had seen dying and wounded men around me before, but nothing like the numbers on that beach. There weren't enough corpsmen to handle the wounded. Those guys were really brave. They risked their lives just getting to the wounded, much less tending to them under fire. On the beach right behind us, a whole aid station was blown away.

We had to get off the beach; we were being slaughtered. But when we finally got to the top of the last sand terrace, we found the barren ground ahead covered by interlocking enemy machine-gun fire. The Japs in the first line of beach defenses had caught hell in the bombardment—maybe they were crazy—but they fought like hell from the rubble of bombed-out pillboxes, shell holes, trenches, and bunkers. And the Jap artillery kept pounding us in spite of our navy's planes and heavy guns giving us support. The noise was God-awful. We yelled back and forth but couldn't hear one another. Hand signals were all we could understand.

We measured advances in yards. We'd move a few feet forward and get pinned down by a pillbox or bunker. We'd fire everything we had to cover a marine with hand grenades or a flamethrower or a satchel charge while he crawled forward to attack it through the gun slit. If he didn't make it, someone else would have to try. Whenever we knocked one out, there was always another one and another one after that.

When the sun went down that first day, we had barely advanced a hundred yards. I looked back toward the beach, and all I could see was wreckage and death, bodies everywhere. I was shaking, scared to death. Anyone else says he wasn't that first night is lying. As soon as the sun mercifully went down, I lay in the sand, in the dark, thinking about tomorrow.*

The second day we worked inland a little farther. There were fissures leaking sulfur gas, and the rocks were so sharp they tore your clothes if you brushed against them. The firmer ground made it easier to move, but there were ravines, draws, and crevices enough to hide a million Japanese. In a whole day we might make a hundred yards, on a good day maybe two hundred. Some days we couldn't move at all. Some days we were driven back.

The Japs had learned something from the fighting on Saipan and Tinian. They didn't come after us in massed banzai charges—they made us come to them. All the other invasions had been hard and terrible enough, but not like this. For the first time the awful thought entered my mind that it was possible to lose a battle.

As we got farther inland, supplies and ammo became scarce. The trucks and amphtracks that were supposed to supply us couldn't get up the sand terraces and were being destroyed by the enemy's accurate artillery fire while they were still on the beach. So supplies and ammo had to be unloaded and moved up by hand. Seabees that came ashore behind us worked under fire to lay steel matting and finally got the vehicles moving to firm ground beyond the terraces. That helped, but the farther inland we advanced, the harder the fighting got.

My company commander, Capt. Buck Schechter, was small and thin; he looked more like a bookkeeper than a combat leader. Although he didn't have the look of a hero, he had a ton of courage. He was maybe the bravest man I've ever known. He had gotten nicked on every island we assaulted,[†] but he never let the medics take him off the line and away from his men. He had been with us all the way, and we had a lot of faith in him. When things got tight, he would wave his pistol in the air and holler, "Let's go!" and we would, but even Captain Schechter was stunned when we ran into the cliffs of Iwo.

Every cliff was a network of connected caves and tunnels. We thought the pillboxes and blockhouses were bad, but they were nothing compared to the reinforced caves we had to clear. It would take forever to clean out even the smallest section of them. We had to absolutely annihilate every Jap in them. They would not surrender.

---

*In terms of American dead and wounded, the first day on Iwo Jima was the costliest D-Day of the Pacific war.

[†]Schechter was awarded five Purple Hearts.

Even lying there dying, they would try to kill you with their last breath. If they knew we had them trapped, and they could kill no more of us, they would kill themselves rather than face the dishonor of our taking them prisoner.

Fighting day after day like that, you lose a little sanity. You can't remember how many days you've been on the island. You get so tired you can't think straight. You catch yourself daydreaming about ordinary things, trying to remember what they were like: a glass of cold milk, a night's sleep in a bed, a hot shower, a clean pair of socks, a hot meal. You think if only you could live to have them again, it would be heaven.

You are a long way from heaven on Iwo. You're in the same sweat-soaked clothes you wore when you came ashore. They're torn and starting to rot. You stink so bad your own body odor sometimes overcomes the stench of bloated bodies decaying in the heat. You don't sleep, don't eat much. A drink of good water is the best treat you get. You figure you are in good shape if all you have is insect bites, diarrhea, and fever.

Marine gunners respond to fire from Japanese guns positioned in caves and fortified pillboxes along the base and northern slope of Mount Suribachi. Despite heavy naval fire, air strikes, and artillery fire from the beach, the island's defenders were only forced out when marine infantry moved in.

U.S. MARINE CORPS

Every day you hear the screams of wounded men dying hard, then again you don't hear them. You shut them out, the screams and guts and body parts and the killing you are doing. The killing like yesterday, when your platoon caught forty Japs down in a ravine with nowhere to hide. They ran in every direction, like rats trying to find cover, while you and your platoon shot them, all of them. You try and shut out those sights and sounds and feelings because if you don't, you're afraid you'll go crazy.

I don't know what day it is, but we come up on some shallow ravines spilling off a ridge. The company splits into small teams. What is left of two squads from my platoon starts down one of them to sweep it, make sure it's clear. With the whole company in the area cleaning out every foot of ground the same as we are doing, we figure our flanks are secure. We're wrong. Japs appear over us on both sides of the little ravine and pin us down. It is just like the other day, only this time we are the rats caught in the ravine and it's the Japs shooting down on us.

There is no place to go. All we can do is return fire at the Japs above us on both sides. We have to get to higher ground. Everybody starts firing cover while a couple of us start up one side of the ravine. I'm halfway up. I turn to get a better footing, and something knocks me down. I don't know what has happened. I'm trying to figure it out when everything, everybody, the whole world just fades away.

To this day I don't know what happened in the ravine after that. I woke up on the beach. I remember being lifted into a boat and the boat rocking. The next time I open my eyes I'm in a bed on a hospital ship. I hurt pretty bad, but the clean sheets feel wonderful.

It turned out that I had been shot through, from one side to the other, and somehow the bullet missed my heart and spine. I figure I'm okay, I have come out of hell alive.

Dee wasn't so okay. It took more than four months in navy hospitals, much of it in intensive care after several operations, to make him whole again.

Joe Irby

I was on the dock to meet my squad when the ship carrying I Company returned from Iwo Jima. Out of the original squad, only two guys are left.*

The trucks, tanks, amphtracks, and supplies regimental logistics had worked so hard to make ready were never loaded aboard ship, never took part in the landings on Okinawa. On Iwo Jima, the Fourth Division had suffered 9,098 men killed or wounded—half the division. There was not enough time to reorganize, train replacements, and attain combat-ready status prior to the departure of the Okinawa invasion force. Instead the Fourth Division and its equipment were scheduled for the invasion of mainland Japan. It never happened.

During the last half of July 1945, after a successful test of an atomic bomb at Alamogordo, New Mexico, the Allies issued a surrender ultimatum to Japan and waited for a response. None came. On August 6, 1945, a B-29 took off from Tinian and dropped a single bomb on the city of Hiroshima. Still the Japanese Supreme War Council did not respond to the Allies' joint declaration. A second bomb was dropped on the city of Nagasaki three days later, August 9. Finally, six days after the second bomb was dropped, August 15, 1945, Japan surrendered.

Joe Irby and Dee Hamilton fought in actions as fierce as any in the history of warfare. The capture of four small islands in the Pacific cost the Fourth Marine Division nearly 75 percent of its original divisional strength. Although their respective battalions were among the most decorated units in U.S. Marine Corps history, neither marine mentions his personal decorations.

Joe and Dee remember vividly their homecoming. They talked of being so happy just to be alive, of seeing their folks, of wonderful things—eating at the kitchen table, walking down familiar streets,

---

*The marines had landed on Iwo Jima on February 19. The island was not secured until March 26. It was the costliest operation in marine history.

meeting girls at the corner drugstore. But they also remember being unable to sit still or relax during the day and waking, covered in sweat, from bad dreams.

Being home didn't seem quite real. People, family, and friends wanted to hear about the war as if it had been some exciting adventure. Like so many other combat veterans, the two marines found it impossible to communicate their experiences and feelings, and so they hardly talked at all. Joe Irby said, "When I returned, I wanted . . . no . . . I needed someone to talk to, but there was no one at home who could possibly understand. Even when I was with a buddy who had been there, neither of us could talk about it. We would just sit there, over a couple of beers, saying nothing. As time went by, I figured no one cared."

Dee Hamilton recently recounted, "A Jap broke my rib just a few months ago." He explained, "I dreamed I was back in combat, on some island fighting this Jap hand to hand. His rifle was leaning against a tree nearby. I had no weapon. No matter how hard I fought, he kept getting closer and closer to his rifle. I must have really been thrashing around, because I woke up on the floor with a broken rib." He laughed, trying to make light of the matter, but it was an indication of how close and deep and vivid the memories of World War II remain with those who fought it.

It's the same with Joe Irby. His wife, the sister of Joe's fellow marine Gene Carr, insists that he not watch any war documentaries on television. This prohibition came after he saw a segment of the television series *World at War* that featured combat footage of the Pacific campaigns. That night he was screaming in his sleep, fighting a war that had been over for fifty-three years.

CHAPTER 14

SAIPAN, 1944

THE DIARY OF
TARAO KAWAGUCHI

AMERICA FACED A DETERMINED, fierce, and fanatical enemy on the islands of the Pacific. This is the story of one among that enemy—Sgt. Tarao Kawaguchi, Homare Unit 11943, 43d Division Hospital Unit—the story of a medic in the imperial army of Japan told in his own words. It is taken from a 1944 carbon-copy "flimsy" of the original rough translation of his diary by a U.S. Army field intelligence unit. It has been edited here only where necessary for clarity.

June 11, 1944

There have been two air raids since we landed on Saipan Island. The bombing was carried out in large patterns. The bombardments were terrific. They came just after noon, and again toward the evening. The bombs fell as we NCOs were cooking our meals, and we didn't have a chance in reaching the cover of the air raid shelters. Although our antiaircraft gunners put up a heavy barrage and our planes intercepted the enemy bombers, it seems the damage they did was considerable. The Charan-Kanoa and Tinian areas are burning.

June 12, 1944

Same as yesterday, the enemy bombers attacked again. Spent the whole day in the air raid shelter. It seems, like so many of us, I have dengue fever.

June 13, 1944

Also today, the enemy bombarded us. Our commander ordered each squad to dig air raid shelters. In the afternoon, the enemy's naval fleet appeared offshore and commenced a furious naval bombardment. It looked like the bombardment was concentrated around Charan-Kanoa and Garapan. Our hospital was hit and caught fire. After dark, Second Company was able to resupply material to the hospital. First Lieutenant Omura and Second Lieutenant Yamaguchi expressed high spirits when we received the new supplies. We received orders to move the patients and supplies to the prepared air raid shelters.

June 14, 1944

Again today we are receiving naval bombardment and aerial bombing. Even so, we transferred the patients to the air raid shelters on the left side of the valley. In the early evening we prepared to return for our medical supplies and tents. We commenced moving at twelve midnight, but it was very far to the old camp and we didn't finish until dawn. On this day the enemy landed on the island. The time has come at last.

June 15, 1944

This evening our unit commander and a large part of the NCOs departed our shelter for the Saipan Shrine to treat patients brought there. During a fierce naval barrage, First Lieutenant Kunieda performed courageously treating the patients there. He should be considered an ideal model for the whole medical section. We administered medical aid for the first time to a casualty of the enemy [ground forces] landed here on Saipan Island. In spite of being under a terrible naval bombardment, an impressive ceremony for our country was carried out at the Saipan Shrine. Tonight we worked to transfer patients up to the Third Company on top of the hill. Shortly after returning to the Saipan Shrine we were ordered to depart for shelters in the cliffs.

June 16, 1944

After so much movement and work of the previous day and night, we were allowed to rest in the air raid shelter. I was very tired.

June 17, 1944

I and other NCOs, plus five enlisted men, were ordered to try and secure new medical supplies. We did so in spite of enemy planes. They were in their glory strafing and bombing at will. Do we have any planes left?

June 18, 1944

Patients arriving in ever increasing numbers. Last night we transported medical supplies to the pharmacists section. Today the strafing by enemy planes was intense.

June 19, 1944

We were given new assignments. I was placed in the pharmacists section commanded by Second Lieutenant Yamaguchi.

June 20, 1944

The enemy strafing is becoming heavier. Naval gunfire forced us to stay in the shelter all day.

June 21, 1944

Strafing, bombing, and artillery fire is getting near our positions. We are endeavoring to dig more shelters into the cliffs.

June 22, 1944

Today the enemy attack was furious. While carrying out our duty below the cliffs, the enemy artillery found its mark and killed seven of us. During the night we worked to transfer our hospital unit to the top of the mountain.

June 23, 1944

Terrific assault by the enemy. We were unable to provide thorough treatment for the patients. The best we could do was obtain water and food for them, which they greatly appreciated.

June 24, 1944

Today the enemy barrage is increasingly terrible. They were mostly overshooting the hospital, but finally one landed ten meters from our dugout and regrettably, we received several casualties.

June 25, 1944

Situation growing worse. We received orders to once again move our unit to the vicinity of Tara-Hoko. During the night we moved all the patients to Tara-Hoko, but it is most regrettable that we had to abandon some supplies.

June 26, 1944

I spent the night below the cliffs with the patients. Conditions are getting increasingly worse. Because of the concentration of artillery, we took cover among the trees. Somehow we had no casualties. During the evening we learned we were going to move to Donnay. The situation is very bad. Some of the patients committed suicide with hand grenades.

June 27, 1944

I slept well because of the sake we were allowed last night. We were awakened early by Captain Warnanbe with orders to depart for

Donnay. Proceeded to Donnay under terrific artillery fire. Received heavy casualties from the concentration of fire by enemy land units and tanks. The hospital commander gave us orders to prepare to attack the enemy with rifles, hand grenades, and with bayonets attached to sticks. I was ordered by Second Lieutenant Yamaguchi to burn our medical supplies. Because of furious fire by our troops, one enemy tank was knocked out and the enemy withdrew. We kept going and finally took refuge on top of the mountain.

It was decided that the severely wounded would be evacuated back to Tara-Hoko by way of the mountain pass. That night we split into small units. On the way we were separated from Lieutenant Yamaguchi and lost our way. We came out near the seacoast.

June 28, 1944

We found the main strength of our company and were relieved to hear that Lieutenant Yamaguchi was safe. Suddenly we received a terrible bombardment as we were resting near the "Y" junction. We immediately hit the ground and were covered by dirt and sand from the explosions. I received a slight wound across my forehead. When the barrage subsided, I could hear cries of pain and calls for help all around the area. We assembled the casualties in the forest and waited for orders. During the night there was another artillery barrage. We quenched our terrible thirst with rain water.

June 29, 1944

We dug in because of the scare of the bombardment last night. In the afternoon we again received a terrific bombardment. When the firing was over we came out of our holes and saw that everything was desolated. We again took up our duty of treating patients and new casualties. After dark we followed orders to leave the area and proceed back to Tara-Hoko. We were hampered by heavy rain squalls. Light from enemy flares sometimes helped us to see the road. There was a feeling of sadness, pity, and anger for all our casualties suffered at the "Y" junction, and we resolved to gain revenge.

June 30, 1944

Near dawn we reached the Tara-Hoko area once again and immediately started the construction of air raid shelters. Before we could finish them we received a rain of bombs from enemy planes. When they were gone, we finished our shelters and stayed in them all afternoon. Toward evening I went back on duty as a medic. That night we ate rice for the first time since the 25th and I regained strength. We felt helpless when on this day the hospital received concentrated fire. I struck the ground with my fist, and tears came to my eyes as many casualties occurred. I received only a slight wound on my left thigh.

We immediately went to work when the firing stopped. It was as if everyone had somehow regained his strength, and upon seeing this, my spirit was greatly lifted. We had to work in the shelters all morning due to continued concentrated fire. When it let up, rice was cooked. The taste of hot rice was indescribably good! After eating, we repaired the dugout shelters and retrieved and inventoried what medical supplies we have left.

July 2, 1944

[There was no diary entry on the 1st of July. It would appear from the following entry that Kawaguchi's unit was engaged in close combat by an American unit on that day.]

At dawn, visited the place where my friend lay dead with a bayonet wound in his head. I covered him with grass and leaves. Upon returning to my unit, ate a meal of hardtack and pickled prunes for breakfast. Suddenly, while eating, heard gunfire. Orders were issued for defense positions. However, no attack was received, so returned to shelter. After dark, attended to medical supplies and repaired shelter.

July 3, 1944

At daybreak the sound of enemy artillery and rifle fire echoed throughout the valley. We immediately took up defense positions. The rifle reports are nearer and more terrific than yesterday, but our situation cannot be comprehended. If the enemy attacks, the whole unit will repulse them with every weapon at hand. Toward the end of the day, took refuge in the dugout with Lieutenant Yamaguchi due to attack and fire by land units. Later, tried to transport rations under command of Lieutenant Yamaguchi but failed due to enemy fire. Today three men in my section were casualties.

July 4, 1944

Different from yesterday. The morning was extremely quiet. Near noon there was a terrific artillery barrage, and then rifle fire came near, so we immediately took up battle positions. Then rifle fire subsided and nothing happened. At 2100 [9 P.M.] we began moving toward top of the mountain but were greatly hampered by enemy flares. I was bothered by my wounded leg. Our commander issued orders to fight to the last in the bivouac area. I dug in with all my might. I was prepared for my foxhole to be my grave, but we heard that the division commander had ordered all men to take part in the last assault. To prepare myself, I went down to a little stream to wash and quench my thirst. Shortly after I returned we suddenly heard rifle fire and took battle positions, but again nothing happened.

July 5, 1944

First Lieutenant Matsumai came to our dugout and said, "As long as I am going to die, I want to die with the pharmacists section." That made us very proud. He joined us and said, "If this is going to be our grave, let's make it clean," so after reveille we attended to cleaning up the area. After breakfast we were waiting in the hole when the enemy commenced a furious assault. The Second Company under the command of Lieutenant Matsumai formed into three squads and took up positions on top of the mountain behind us. We were surrounded but determined to annihilate the enemy when they attacked.

We learned that the enemy was advancing along the road below us. We were given milk and coffee and sake to drink while awaiting orders for battle. The order was issued that each company will carry out night attacks.

Second Lieutenant Yamaguchi went to work with Lieutenant Colonel Takeda. Lieutenant Omura and the pharmacists section bid the final farewell among themselves. Second Lieutenant Yamaguchi came to bid farewell to the pharmacists section too. We all promised to meet at the Uasukumi Shrine after death then awaited the commencement of battle.

Two of our men too severely wounded to fight committed pathetic suicide.

I was honored to be chosen to serve with Second Lieutenant Yamaguchi in the command section. Our section didn't have rifles, but under the command of Captain Watanabe, we commenced night sneak attacks with hand grenades. We lost communication between units.

July 6, 1944

After sunrise we received an artillery barrage and took cover among the rocks. As the rounds approached nearer and nearer, I closed my eyes and waited. Then rifle reports and tanks could be heard approaching. We all took cover within the forest and waited for the enemy to appear.

Soon the voice of the enemy was heard and machine-gun bullets began striking the foliage over our heads. I thought this was the end and stood up to charge out with a hand grenade, but Captain Watanabe ordered me to take cover. I ducked down behind a rock. When I looked from behind it I could see the hateful bearded face of the enemy shining in the sunlight. With a terrific report the rock in front of my eyes exploded, and a sergeant who had joined us last night was killed. Also Corporal Ono received wounds in his left thigh. I tried but could not reach him to treat his wounds. Everybody hugged the ground and kept quiet, waiting for an opening at the enemy. After a while, I stood up to get a rifle from one of our dead. A bullet struck between my legs and I thought I was hit, but glancing down, to my happiness, I saw nothing was wrong. I heard another shot and looked back to see my friend, Corporal Ito, lying on his back with a rifle in his hand. Oh! Corporal Ito, who has been in my section since training days in Nogoya!

We all kept fighting, and after fierce counterfire the enemy was repulsed. I moved to the body of my friend Ito. He had a bullet hole through his left temple. His eyes were half open, and his lips were tightly clenched. I took the rifle that was clenched in his hands even after death and waited beside him for the enemy to attack. I said, "I will take revenge for you, Ito."

Nearby Corporal Yusuhiro lay with terrible wounds to both of his legs. Pathetically he kept asking, "Please kill me." First Lieutenant Matsumai said he would do it and took out his sword. Yusuhiro said only, "Please cut skillfully." The lieutenant nodded his head. He measured carefully with one slow stroke, two slow strokes, and with a flashing third stroke beautifully cut off Yusuhiro's head.

Soon after that, rifle fire roared in our frontal area. I pocketed a scroll written by Corporal Ito as a farewell gift to his family and bid farewell to his spirit. Then I grabbed Corporal Ono's hand in farewell. His wound prevented him from leaving. He stated pathetically that he would commit suicide tomorrow morning at sunrise.

By utilizing the cover of a heavy rain squall, we tried to commence movement to join friendly troops, but the path turned bloody. Because of firm enemy positions, we could not get through to the friendly force we were supposed to meet near Mount [Ta]potchau.

July 7, 1944

Everybody got drenched by a terrific squall. While we were shivering from the wetness, orders to move were issued. Facing the dawn of the north, I bowed reverently to the imperial palace and bid farewell to my parents, aunt, and my wife and pledged to do my utmost. Then, with Sergeant Hasegawa and Corporal Watanabe, I departed from the rocks and came out of the jungle. It is regretful that we somehow became separated from Lieutenant Yamaguchi, because we promised that we would all die in the same place.

We tried to reach the shore but could not. The enemy is approaching us from all directions. Helplessly we took cover back in the jungle. Enemy activity commenced below on the road with vehicles, tanks, and walking soldiers.

At last the end is approaching. We have separated from the unit staff. The remaining members of the Second Company consist of Sergeant Hasegawa, Corporals Watanabe, Narusi, myself, and six patients from the transport unit. Counting the wounded, we have ten men. Even though we want to attack, we have no weapons, although we are determined to die for the emperor.

We pass the time by preparing for our remembrance. I am only twenty-six years old, but looking back, thanks to the emperor, both of my parents, and my aunt, I am deeply gratified to have lived to this day. At the same time, it is deeply regrettable that I have nothing notable to report at this time when my life is fluttering away like a flower petal falling to earth to become part of the soil.

Since their landing, I have fought against the enemy, endeavoring with my utmost power to carry out my duty. Thus I have become a warrior and am very happy. It is only regrettable that we have not fought enough, and that the American devil is stomping on imperial soil.

The spirit of my sacrificed body will become the whitecaps of the Pacific, and I will stay on this island until the friendly forces come to reclaim the soil of the emperor.

Dear Keiko—Please live with courage. My sincerest regards to Mother and Brother.

Dear Brother—Take care of the family and Aunt. Please take my revenge. Sincerest regards to my sister.

Dear Sumiko [his wife]—Even though I am ending on this southern island, your brother is firmly convinced that you will continue in my place.

Dear Aunt and Uncle—Thank you for [your] long hospitality. I regret that I cannot repay you. Please take care of Sumiko.

I am happy that I can die on the seventh anniversary of the Sino-Japanese incident. I firmly believe the enemy will be annihilated and will pray for certain victory for the imperial land.

Good-bye to all.

THE DIARY of Tarao Kawaguchi was removed from his body on July 8, 1944, and turned over to an American intelligence unit, which translated it and reviewed it for military value. Ed Anderson (pp. 23–44) provided a copy for me, and it helped me to interview Joe Irby and Dee Hamilton (pp. 181–222).

CHAPTER 15

JEREMIAH J. O'KEEFE

A LONG WAY TO OKINAWA

I N 1935 A MODEL AIRPLANE CONTEST was announced in the *New Orleans Times-Picayune* newspaper distributed along the Mississippi Gulf Coast. A boy named Jeremiah, living in Ocean Springs, built and entered a model for himself and one for his younger brother. For his efforts, both boys won a prize. To collect it their daddy had to drive them to the newly dedicated Shushan Airport (now Lakefront Airport) in New Orleans. Their prize was a ride on a Ford Tri-motor airliner. The boys walked through the beautiful, new art deco terminal building, at the time the grandest in the nation, and out onto the ramp where the "big" plane with three 420-horsepower radial engines and a capacity of ten passengers was waiting. The thrill of that flight was to lead young Jeremiah J. O'Keefe on an arduous journey to a place in aviation history.

When the Japanese bombed Pearl Harbor in December 1941, Jeremiah, whom the family called Jerry, had just finished his first semester at Soule Business College in New Orleans. Like most Americans, he had never heard of Pearl Harbor, had no idea where it was located. What he did know was that his country was at war. He went directly to a navy recruiting office and tried to enlist. He discovered that anyone under age twenty-one would need his parent's permission to sign up. (That would soon change with the introduction of the wartime draft.) Jerry was eighteen. Disappointed, he took the permission form home. After a long discussion, his father finally decided that his son, "like everyone in the country, wanted to do his part," and signed the form. After Christmas, Jerry took the form back to the navy recruiter in New Orleans, took a bunch of tests, expressed interest in aviation, and was inducted into the navy. His first instruction as a navy recruit was to go home and wait for orders. It was January 1942.

The United States with its isolationist mindset had been caught unprepared. The bureaucracies of government and the armed services became centers of chaos in the massive national effort to prepare for war.

Jerry O'Keefe was one of thousands left dangling as the volume of paperwork overwhelmed every organization. The Navy Department, whose clerks had been handling a trickle of depression-era, out-of-work volunteers at scattered recruiting offices, suddenly had mountains of paperwork from thousands of volunteers signing up to fight for their country.

Jerry, certain orders would arrive any moment, did not sign up for a new college semester. Waiting at home as requested, days turned into months while his navy recruitment form was shuffled along through the system with thousands of others. He overheard his father talking to a business associate say, "I don't want Jerry to get killed or anything, but he wants to do his part, and if they don't call him soon this war will be over before he gets his chance."

At last, a letter arrived from the navy addressed to Jeremiah J. O'Keefe. The communiqué was not in the form of an order. It was more of a "suggestion" that upon filling out more forms he could proceed to a Civilian Pilot Training Program at Nacogdoches Junior College in Louisiana. He would not be paid, but the navy would pay for his travel, room, and board and the cost of ground instruction and eight hours of actual flying time in a 65-horsepower Piper J-3 Cub operating off of a grass field near the junior college.

Jerry packed a small bag and caught a bus to Nacogdoches. He successfully completed eight hours of instruction in the Cub, logging thirty minutes of solo time.

The flying was more fun than anything I had ever done. When the instructor got out and told me to take it by myself, I experienced a different sort of freedom I had never imagined. I guess no pilot ever forgets his first solo flight.

Jerry returned home. He asked if he could help in the family business to earn a little money while he waited for orders. Jerry's great-grandfather, Ned O'Keefe had moved to Ocean Springs just after the Civil War and opened O'Keefe Livery Stable. Because he saw a need in the community, he added a sideline and the business became the O'Keefe Livery and Undertaking Company. Three generations later, Jerry's father owned the O'Keefe Funeral Company. Since Jerry was on standby for orders, he was of little use to the business and was regulated to sweeping, cleaning, grass cutting, and handyman work. The only good thing about the wait at home was that he got to date his sweetheart, Annette Saxon. It was about this time that the family moved across the mouth of Back Bay to Biloxi and opened a business there.

Finally, after months of waiting, I received real orders from the navy. I kissed my girl goodbye, shook my father's hand, and set off by train to the University of Georgia at Athens for Navy Induction and Pre-flight school. We were given uniforms, the enlisted rank of aviation cadet, and quartered at the college. After a battery of written and physical exams, a program of indoctrination began that included a sort of boot camp where we learned all the military stuff from polishing shoes and brass to physical training, marching, saluting, lectures on navy organization, rules and regulations, customs of the service, and leadership. This was followed by classes on aviation including aerodynamics, theory of flight, aircraft controls, instruments and power plant principles and navigation. Oh! And we were paid.

We had a military graduation ceremony. I was all raring to go and rushed to the bulletin board where our new orders were posted. I couldn't believe it. I was once again ordered home to await further orders. I began to believe that Dad was right; the war would be over before I got into it.

On January 1, 1943, a year after Jerry had enlisted in the navy, he received new orders: "Cadet Jeremiah J. O'Keefe is hereby ordered to report to Naval Air Station Dallas for primary flight training."

NAS Dallas was itself officially opened on that very same day at Hensley Field, which had been built by the city of Dallas in 1929 as an army reserve field. The Texas airfield, named after Major William N. Hensley who had been on the first transatlantic dirigible crossing in 1919, suddenly became a very busy place. The army air corps retained its training facilities and established the Army Ferry Command across from the new navy training facility. In addition, North American Aviation transferred its manufacturing of the army AT-6 and navy SNJ advanced training aircraft from California to Hensley Field.

Jerry packed his uniforms, kissed his sweetheart goodbye, and headed for Dallas, Texas, by train. He reported to the base; was issued navy aviation cadet insignia, uniforms, a leather flying helmet, and goggles; and got squared away in the barracks. Next he attended weeks of classroom lectures on more rules and regulations pertaining to the navy and aviation cadets. The cadets, dressed in khaki uniforms, always with neckties, marched to class, chow, and everywhere else they were directed, saluted almost everything that walked, and said "yes, sir" and "no, sir" even in their sleep. Finally, his class began ground school on the plane they would be flying, studying its characteristics, how to preflight it, start it, take off and land it, local flight patterns, and the proper way to wear a parachute and use it if necessary.

When the day came to begin flight training, Jerry reported to the flight line where he saw long rows of Boeing Stearman biplanes better known as "Yellow Perils." They were painted bright yellow—the idea being that planes flown by students should be easily identified and avoided by all other aircraft. The navy designation for the Stearman trainer was N2S. (The army called it the PT-17.)

The big biplane fully loaded weighted almost three thousand pounds. It would make three of the little Cubs O'Keefe had flown. Each N2S had a large number painted on its fuselage. Jerry reported to his assigned plane and was met by an instructor.

"Climb in, Cadet. I've been assigned to give you a check ride."

Jerry, wearing a parachute and flying helmet for the first time, thought it strange he would be given a check ride on his first day, but he said, "Yes, Sir," got in the rear cockpit, and strapped in while the instructor did the same in the front cockpit. A ground crewman, the "cranker," approached the plane, took out a crank, positioned himself in front of the wing and just behind the propeller, and began to wind up the inertia starter.

"You know the routine, Cadet. Let's get this thing started."

Jerry didn't know the routine, had never seen a Stearman before, but he had heard that the navy only wanted the best and would "wash out" anyone they thought didn't measure up. He thought it best not to ask questions and answered, "Yes, Sir." He tried to remember what the ground school had taught, found and turned on the fuel valve, located the engine primer, and gave it a number of pumps. All the while the "cranker" kept winding up the inertia starter, which by now was whining loudly. Jerry remembered the J-3 had to be hand propped, so he waited for the commands from the "cranker."

The ground crewman disengaged the crank and yelled "Brakes and Contact!" Jerry depressed the toe brakes on the rudder pedals, turned the magneto switch to "both" position, and yelled, "Brakes and Contact!" The crewman engaged the inertia starter, and with a high whine it spun the propeller. The engine caught, coughed a coupled of times, burped out a blob of smoke, and settled down to a loud, steady rhythm. The ground crewman stowed the crank in its pocket, removed the wheel chocks, and motioned the plane was clear to taxi. Jerry couldn't see a thing in front so he S-taxied as he had done when flying the Cub solo from the back seat. When he got the plane to the end of the runway, the instructor had a few words for him.

"That was pretty sloppy for a cadet of your experience, Mister. Let's see if you can keep it straight on the takeoff."

Jerry had a grand total of eight hours in a 65-horsepower Cub, only about thirty minutes of which was solo. Very conscious of sitting there in a big, 220-horsepower, open-cockpit biplane, the young and, at the moment, not too bright naval aviation cadet did as he was told without question.

Cadet O'Keefe took a deep breath, taxied onto the runway, lined up the best he could, not being able to see anything in front, held the stick back, and pushed the throttle forward. The radial engine roared, and the plane began to move. Due to aerodynamic factors called torque and "P" factor, the N2S, like a horse taking the bit, started toward the left side of the runway. Even in the 65-horsepower Cub, Jerry had learned to use a little right rudder on takeoff. Evidently the N2S needed more than a little rudder. In his effort to control the beast, Jerry pushed in a little too much right rudder and the plane started to the right. Playing the rudder as he remembered doing in the Cub, he straightened the Stearman out and hung on using his peripheral vision to estimate the center of the runway. Four hundred feet or so down the runway the tail lifted itself, and he could see ahead. Jerry relaxed back pressure on the stick. Immediately, the N2S left mother earth. Once in the air he found the Stearman responded to the controls much like the Cub only it felt heavier. It was heavier by about a ton and a half.

Once in the air he climbed at seventy miles an hour as the book said. The instructor pointed his arm about 45 degrees to the left. Jerry turned that way. He leveled off at three thousand feet as he had been told to do. Soon they were over a grass auxiliary training field. The instructor pointed and told him to go down and land.

"You want *me* to land?"

"What do you think I just said, Mister?"

Cadet O'Keefe thought a lot of things, the most prominent of which was, "Boy! They don't mess around in the navy." He throttled back and started a descent to eight hundred feet and did his best to fly the standard rectangular pattern he remembered from Nacogdoches and the Cub: downwind at eight hundred feet, turn base and let down to four hundred feet, turn final indicating no less than sixty-five, and over the fence ease back on the throttle and stick. *Damn! Too much!* The Stearman sank quickly to strike earth with a jolt and bounce back into the air. Jerry kept the stick back. It bumped again and was back in the air followed by a final thud, and they were down. *Thank you, Jesus!*

The instructor took the controls, taxied downwind to the end of the field, turned into the wind . . . and got out!

He looked up at Jerry. "According to your records I reviewed this morning, you should be doing much better than that, Cadet. That's one of the poorest landings I've seen all day. If you are nervous over your check ride, go ahead and fly it around for about twenty minutes, do some maneuvers, settle down, then come back and pick me up. I want to take a smoke."

Jerry thought, *What records? I didn't bring any records here!* But he said, "Yes, Sir," and took off, doing a little better keeping it straight this time. O'Keefe did not venture too far from the field. He didn't know the lay of the land and didn't want to get lost. He flew S-turns and then eased off the throttle and pulled the stick back to try a stall. The Stearman dropped out from under him like a rock. *Whoa!* He pushed the stick and throttle forward and eased back to level cruise. *Boy! That's sure different from the Cub.* He did a few lazy eights, tried a steep turn or two, and braved a wingover. The force it took to move the stick around was decidedly more than the little Cub, but he was enjoying himself. *God, I love flying.* For the first time that day he relaxed a little and looked around. The countryside beneath and the sky above were beautiful. Making a big circle to try to orient himself, he was able to just make out Hensley Field on the horizon and spotted another yellow plane to the east maybe three miles away. Jerry checked his watch. *Time to pick up the instructor.*

O'Keefe picked out the grass field and established himself on a downwind leg. He could see the instructor standing below watching him. Jerry wiped his sweaty palms on his knees, tried to chase the butterflies out of his stomach, and prepared to make his second landing ever in the Stearman—this time by himself. He turned base and then final. Sailing over the fence he cut the throttle and pulled the stick back. The first bounce was a pretty big one, the second not so bad, and with just two more little ones he found himself proudly rolling along in the grass. It wasn't pretty, but he had managed to get the big biplane down in one piece. Jerry turned around and gingerly taxied back to the end of the field, carefully S-turning, swinging his head from one side to the other to be sure he did not run over the instructor.

The instructor, whose name Jerry didn't know and wasn't about to ask, shook his head. "Forget the aerobatics, Mister. This check ride is over." He climbed in without a word and flew them back to Hensley Field.

Once parked on the ramp, the instructor got out, looked up at Jerry and said, "I don't know what was wrong with you today, Mister, but you better not have another day like this one if you want to keep in the program," and walked off.

Jerry was crushed. He unfastened his harness, got down from the cockpit, and walked away from his first day of flying as a navy cadet, wondering if it would be his last.

That afternoon he was told to report to the base commander.

His heart sank, *Oh Boy! They're gonna wash me out.*

He entered the commander's office and stood at attention before his desk.

"At Ease, Mr. O'Keefe."

The officer looked up at Jerry. "O'Keefe, a terrible mistake was made today." He paused a moment as if searching for words. "Son, we could have killed you."

Expecting a reprimand, Jerry was too stunned to reply.

"Somehow your assigned plane number this morning was wrong. The pilot you flew with thought he was administering a check ride to a Cadet Byrd. Check ride pilots are different from a student's regular instructor. He had never met Cadet Byrd, thought you were him. Somehow he got you instead of Byrd who has thirty hours in the N2S including aerobatics and some cross-country. Based on his record and the performance the instructor witnessed today, he was prepared to kick Byrd out of the program and called him in. That's when he discovered it wasn't Byrd he had flown with but a brand-new student named O'Keefe. We now know you have never been in a Stearman before today. You could have been killed. We're sorry about that, but all in all we think you did pretty well for your first flight, hell, your first solo in the N2S. Keep it up, O'Keefe. You just might make a good navy pilot." The officer smiled. "Dismissed!"

"Yes, Sir. Thank you, Sir." Jerry did a smart turnabout and left headquarters with a big grin on his face.

He finished the program near the top of his class and received orders to proceed to Pensacola Naval Air Station for advanced training in the North American SNJ. On the way he was able to stop at home in Biloxi to see his family and his girl. Then he would be on to Pensacola.

Aviation cadets at Pensacola NAS were under strict military rules of conduct. They had daily uniform inspections and weekly barracks inspections; and woe be unto he who failed to salute an officer, beginning six paces away, or in the case of passing, saying "to your left, Sir," holding the salute until well clear. They were graded on everything from conduct—there was no drinking and no dating—to appearance,to neckties, which were part of their uniform whether in class or flying. They were graded on class instruction and flying. No one wanted a bad mark of any kind on their record, which might eliminate them from the program.

They were there to take advanced flight training in the North American SNJ (the army designated the same plane the AT-6). It was an all-metal, low-wing monoplane with retractable landing gear, flaps, and a 600-horsepower Pratt and Whitney radial engine. It had a maximum takeoff weight of 5,700 pounds and a top speed of 208 miles per hour. It was designed to transition student pilots from the primary training planes they had flown to the navy's heavier, faster combat fighter planes. It was a good teacher. It demanded the student pay attention and fly it properly. If a student got sloppy or acted smart-alecky, the SNJ would likely give him a lesson he would not forget. On the other hand, if flown with coordinated input of throttle, stick, and rudder, it would do anything asked of it. Cadet O'Keefe would find out all the above was true.

Flight training was done at several satellite fields scattered around Pensacola, each with a specific purpose. Primary training in the SNJ was carried out at Whiting Field.

The SNJ was a lot bigger and heavier than the N2S, and was more complicated with flaps, retractable landing gear, and adjustable propeller pitch, but it was an airplane and the controls worked the same. I think we were all a little anxious at first. Once we learned to handle the plane in normal flight we were taught aerobatics and would play around at fighter tactics. The instructors were good but tough. If you did something they didn't like, or they thought was sloppy, especially landings, and you would hear about it. In aerobatics, for instance, if you stalled and fell out of the top of a loop they might sit there and see if you could regain control saying encouraging things like, "You going to get this thing flying again, Cadet, or are you planning on killing us both?" They had a lot of nerve to sit through things like that, but they were there to teach us and they were good.

After basic training, we went to a different field to learn formation flying and another to learn instrument flying. Then we did some night flying. There were accidents, some fatal, but none in my group.

Then one day a marine colonel talked to the class. He said the marines were allowed to pick three pilots out of every one hundred cadets. He said he wanted the best and asked who wanted to be a marine. I was sure that joining the Marine Air Arm would be a fast track to fighters. A bunch volunteered, and I was flattered to be chosen as one of the three to be a marine. Then I found out I would not have to go through carrier qualifications because the marines needed multiengine pilots.

Just before graduation I was given an allowance to go downtown and buy marine officer uniforms. I sure did like that uniform. My family drove the 120 miles from Biloxi to Pensacola for our graduation ceremony in early May of 1943. I was proud to be commissioned a second lieutenant in the U.S. Marine Corps at age nineteen. That same July, I turned twenty.

While my navy classmates were qualifying for carrier duty, I was taking multiengine training in PBY flying boats and C-47 transports. It wasn't the kind of flying I wanted. We were flying the older Consolidated PBY-5 Catalina, which was the last model to be a pure flying boat as opposed to the later amphibious models. This was a big airplane. It had a wingspan of 104 feet, two Pratt and Whitney twin-row Wasp engines of 1,200 horsepower each, a max takeoff weight of over thirty-five thousand pounds and a crew of ten.

One day I nearly racked one up. For training flights we had only a couple of students and an instructor, not a full crew. Two of us second lieutenants were up in the cockpit; I was flying the left seat, and the instructor, bored as we were heading home after a long practice patrol, was asleep in a bunk in the back. I decided we should take turns making a couple of extra water landings on the way home. It would look good in our logbooks. I would take the first and my acting copilot could take the second. We had been taught to judge the wind direction from reading the waves so we could always land into the wind. On this day we had whitecaps on the Gulf below so we knew the wind was blowing fifteen knots or better. Well, looking down from about three thousand feet I misread the waves by 180 degrees and landed the thing downwind! We touched down nicely, but the strong tailwind took a bite on that big, high tail back there and quick as a wink we did an abrupt unplanned maneuver—what I would call a water loop, as opposed to landing a plane doing a ground loop. That is, the PBY, rather violently while throwing up a great deal of spray, swapped ends. From landing downwind, it was suddenly facing upwind. From somewhere in the cavernous hull behind the cockpit we heard some very colorful language coming from the instructor who had been rudely thrown out of his bunk all the way across the fuselage. He thrust his head into the cockpit asking what in the hell just happened and if were we trying to kill him. We tried to pass it all off as a rogue wave, but that did not fly, so to speak. We spent some time crawling around in the bobbing plane to determine what damage may have been done. Not finding any, Consolidated really made those old birds strong, we took off and flew back to base where it was determined that indeed, no harm had been done. The instructor, not wanting it known that he was sleeping on a training flight, and two young marine pilots not wanting it known that they misread the wind direction at sea, quietly filled out the aircraft and pilot logs in normal fashion, logging one landing in route to base, and walked away to fly another day.

After the twin-engine training was done, I was sent to San Diego, California. It turned out I had almost nothing to do. The marines had only a couple of PBY and C-47 aircraft there, so between a bunch of multiengine pilots taking turns, there wasn't much flying for any of us.

Now there was a family I knew from Ocean Springs, the Hortons, who had moved to Long Beach. I made a call on them and discovered that their daughter, Betty, had grown up. I dated her for old time's sake, and in the course of conversation told her that I was not happy flying transport planes and wanted to move into fighters. Betty said, "You need to meet my friend, Marion."

It turned out that Betty's "friend" Marion was Marion Carl who happened to be the first marine ace of the war. He had been one of two pilots in his squadron to survive the Battle of Midway before going on to Guadalcanal and other islands in the Pacific to shoot down a total of eighteen Japanese planes. As a result, he was a very young colonel, returned to a training squadron and dating a very pretty girl named Betty Horton.

Carl was sympathetic to Jerry's plight and may also have been only too glad to get rid of a perceived rival with Betty. In any case, he got Jerry a transfer to the newly opened Marine Corps Air Station El Toro.

Once at El Toro I transitioned to the Grumman F4F Wildcat. It was powered by the same Pratt and Whitney 1,200-horsepower, double-row Wasp engine that powered the PBY.

The F4F was the first-line navy and marine fighter until well into 1943. The Japanese Zero was faster and could outclimb it, and was more maneuverable. But American pilots learned how to hold their own through tactics such as the Thatch Weave, and because it was more rugged in construction and armor it could take more punishment than the Zero. Still, O'Keefe and the other pilots in the squadron were taught not to get into a turning dogfight with the Zero.

There were no two-place Wildcats. For a pilot's first flight he simply got in and flew it, or not. Operating procedure on all navy planes was to leave the cockpit canopy locked in the open position during takeoff and landing to allow a pilot quick egress should he have to ditch or crash land. Failure to do so could result in a bent, jammed canopy trapping the pilot inside. This was good advice especially for the pilots at El Toro. The F4F fighters they were learning to fly had been brought back from the Pacific for use in training. They were old and patched up and tired. Engine failure was not uncommon. No pilots in Jerry's class were killed, but some had close calls crash landing or ditching after losing an engine. One friend who lost an engine made a good forced landing. He had slid back his canopy but not securely locked it in the open position. As he belly-landed the plane he braced himself by putting his left hand up on the windshield frame. On impact the loose canopy slammed forward against the windshield and cut his hand in two.

The F4F was a good flying airplane once in the air, but it had a very narrow landing gear that folded out of the fuselage like its biplane F3F ancestor, and it had to be manually operated. The gear once extended and locked down had a stance of only six feet. Considering the wingspan was thirty-eight feet and the fuselage only twenty-nine feet, the narrow landing gear made for a very squirrelly bird when taking off or landing, especially in a crosswind. Landing a F4F has been compared to touching down on a child's tricycle backward at eighty miles an hour. All it took was a soft spot, a bump in the runway, or a second's distraction and the F4F would be wildly off on an adventure of its own.

Marine Second Lt. Jeremiah J. O'Keefe was to experience such an adventure with just over forty hours' time in the little fighter. He taxied to the end of the landing strip, went through the pretakeoff procedure, and started the takeoff roll. The strip they were using had low earthen berms down the length of both sides of the runway. Somewhere during the roll after the tail had lifted, but before flying speed had been reached, for reasons yet determined, the fighter struck to the left quick as a snake. Jerry stomped on opposite rudder to correct the path, but to no avail. The F4F hit the berm on the side of the runway, tore off its landing gear and flipped heavily tail over nose.

Thank heaven there was no fire because I couldn't get out. My canopy was open, but there wasn't room for me to squeeze out from under the plane. A crash crew was quickly there. Behind them, a truck crane trundled along. I was seeing all this upside down. The rescue chief said, "Stay in the plane, Lieutenant, we're going to lift it off you." Well, thinking about that and either imagining or actually smelling gasoline, I reached down with a gloved hand and felt the dirt. It was damp and soft. I tripped my safety harness, fell on my head, and started to dig with both hands, which wasn't easy while in an upside-down, balled-up position. "Stay in the plane, Lieutenant; we almost got the harness on." I kept at it like a dog digging under a fence and wiggled out from under the thing.

A sailor helped me up. I backed away to watch the operation. They got the plane about four or five feet in the air and dropped it! I think if I had stayed in that thing they might have killed me. Anyway, I was flying another one the next day.

The F4F pilots trained in fighter tactics and then were sent off to get carrier qualified—in the middle of the Mojave Desert. The nearest carrier used for training was in the Gulf of Mexico off Pensacola NAS. All the carriers on the West Coast were either on station in the Pacific or having battle damage repaired. The solution for the El Toro marine pilots was to select a flat, clear, hard dirt site in the Mojave, scrape it off, and use paint or lime powder to mark off the dimensions of a carrier deck including painting six faux arresting wires across the deck and marking off the footprint of the conning island on the starboard side. If an El Toro F4F pilot, following directions from a paddle-wielding landing signal officer (LSO), could spot land and drag his tail hook down the deck within the area of the painted faux arresting wires, and repeat the feat at least eight times, he was written up as being carrier qualified. Some of the group who were not so accurate but who could touch down somewhere within the confines of the marked-off carrier deck were quietly written down as qualified. The marines needed pilots to replace the ones lost in the Pacific.

After "carrier qualifications" it was back to El Toro and more flying—squadron patrol formation, two-plane sections, fighter tactics, and night flying—all through which Jerry kept his little fighter under control. In spite of all the constant training, a few of the pilots, including O'Keefe, were able to pull off a few shenanigans. "Flathatting" was a term used to describe flying down low, sneaking up on agricultural workers in the field, and scaring the devil out of them. Another forbidden hijinks involved attacking Los Angeles at night. The city was paranoid about the Japanese sneaking in and bombing or submarines shelling it. Jerry and his buddies would turn off course at night and fly over the city. Searchlights and sirens all over the city would pop on and frantically sweep the sky searching for the intruders. The fighters would hightail it out of there and get back on course. The El Toro base commander would catch hell from the city fathers and in turn pass it on to all the squadron commanders, but with so many planes in the air day and night they never caught the perpetrators.

It was about this time that Jerry heard about a big new fighter built by Chance Vought, the F4U Corsair. Rumor had it that a new Corsair squadron, VMF 323, had been formed by a marine major at Cherry Point, North Carolina, and that as soon after it arrived at El Centro, California, almost all of its pilots had been transferred out to the Pacific as badly needed replacements. Now the buzz was that the VMF 323 commander, twenty-four-year-old Major George C. Axtell Jr. was looking for pilots to rebuild the squadron. O'Keefe volunteered and became a member of the "Death Rattlers," so named from the capture, stuffing, and mounting of a rattlesnake on the wall of the 323 shack at Cherry Point. Axtell soon moved his squadron from El Centro to a strip at Camp Pendleton to commence training his new pilots.

Jerry had never seen a Corsair up close. In appearance it was decidedly different from all other American fighters. It was designed around a Pratt and Whitney double-row, 18-cylinder, 2,000-horse-power radial engine that swung a three-bladed propeller with a diameter of thirteen feet, four inches. That huge propeller gave the designers a problem. With a straight wing it would take a long and heavy landing gear to clear the propeller above the deck, one too large to retract into the wing that already held six 50-caliber machine guns. The answer was to "bend" the inboard sections of the wing down and the outboard sections up in a sort of V that gave it the appearance of an inverted gull wing. A shorter, lighter landing

F4U Corsairs over Okinawa.

gear could be put at the bottom of the V and be retracted backward into the wing—problem solved.

Jerry walked up to the biggest, meanest-looking single-engine plane he had ever seen. He had moved from a 65-horsepower Cub to the 220-horsepower N2S, the 600-horsepower SNJ, and a 1,200-horsepower F4F. Now he stood before a 2,000-horsepower Corsair, almost twice the horsepower of the fighter he had been flying. The thing had a top speed of well over four hundred miles per hour. At that speed, if a pilot pulled back on the stick too hard and too fast he could immediately black himself out. Pilots had no G-suits in that day.

O'Keefe had studied the book. Now he walked around the dark blue and grey bird.

"Go, Lieutenant," Major Axtell said grinning, "You can handle it."

O'Keefe did.

Starting the big radial was the hard part. Before takeoff he locked the tail wheel, dialed the rudder trim six degrees right and the aileron trim six degrees right wing down to counteract the torque of the big engine and huge propeller and help the pilot keep it straight on takeoff and level in climb out. Unlike the F4F, the Corsair had a wide stance that made it much easier to control on the ground.

Once in the air Jerry thought, *Whoopee! What an airplane!* He took the Corsair to eight thousand feet and tried a stall from cruise speed. He had been warned that it had a rather abrupt and wicked stall characteristic. He pulled the nose up and let the speed bleed off. Most aircraft will give warning, a vibration to signal a stall is imminent—not the Corsair. With no warning, at eighty-five knots, the left wing dropped like a rock and the bird tried to roll over. With opposite aileron, forward stick, and smooth throttle, Jerry caught the roll just past ninety degrees, leveled the wings, and got the bird flying. He had been warned never to stall a Corsair below a thousand feet. Now he knew why. He climbed three thousand feet a minute to ten thousand feet to try a stall in the landing configuration—gear and flaps down, power back. With hardly a ripple, the left wing dropped and the bird tried to enter an incipient spin. *I don't much like that either*. Spins were not advised in a Corsair; the bent wing tended to interfere with rudder effectiveness. It was said that after two turns in a spin, the parachute was the only means of survival a pilot had.

With that in mind, it was time to try a few loops, rolls, Immelmann turns, and hammerhead turns, always conscious of altitude and book-recommended entry speeds. *No trouble there*. Jerry did a few tight turns as if in a dogfight. On one he got a little slow and stalled out rather violently into an incipient spin that he quickly caught. *Whoa!* The experience confirmed the advice he had been given. "Don't get in a slow-turning dogfight with a more maneuverable adversary like a Zero. Use your superior power to get yourself out of there."

It was time for his first landing. Once in the pattern on downwind, O'Keefe kept in mind the warning every pilot of a high-powered fighter had to remember on landing: never ram the throttle forward when low and slow, as for a go-around on a balked landing. To do so would result in the torque of the powerful engine and propeller rolling the plane onto its back. Smooth handling of the throttle was the key. As Jerry turned on final approach it was easy for him to see why the Corsair had given the navy trouble with carrier landings and why they turned the big fighter over to land-based marines. The beast had a big, fourteen-foot nose sticking out in front of the pilot. When Jerry flared to a three-point attitude on landing, not only the runway, but also the whole airfield disappeared behind that big nose. On the other hand, with its huge barn door flaps, wide landing gear, and relative low landing speed, O'Keefe set the Corsair down with no trouble. Jerry loved his new mount but kept in mind its reputation. It had garnered names like Bent Wing Bastard, Ensign Eliminator, and Widow Maker. It would kill a pilot quick if mishandled.

Axtell, at twenty-four, was one of the youngest majors in the corps. He compensated for being so close in age to his pilots by being tough, a little distant, and impersonal. He was their commander, not their buddy. In his sudden need to replace the original VMF 323 squadron pilots that had been taken from him, he wound up with a bunch of dive-bomber, scout, patrol plane, and a few F4F pilots. Among the more colorful of them were Texan Capt. Jo Jo MacPhail; Lt. Mindy Muse of Massachusetts; Harold Tonnessen from Brooklyn; Smoky Tover of Arkansas, who looked about sixteen; Dewey Durnford of Ohio; Moose Martin of Washington; Big Ed Keeley from California; Jeff Dorah from Oregon; the squadron ops officer known as the "Whip"; Wild Bill Hood of Michigan; Bucko Wade of Pennsylvania; Gruesome Ruhsam of Minnesota; Hots Terrill of Washington; Joe Dillard of Texas; and "tall, quick-smiling, slow-talking" Jerry O'Keefe from Biloxi Mississippi. The Ax, as his men grew to call him, but not to his face, was as good a precision pilot as the Marine Corps had. He was determined that every one of his pilots would be as good. He trained them long and hard, sometimes from seven in the morning until ten at night. He emphasized tactics and gunnery. He worked them on navigation with long, butt-wearying cross-country flights, both day and night, and drilled them in instrument flying, taking them on long flights in soupy weather.

It turned out that the pilots did have some time off to relax. They must have had, for somehow Jerry O'Keefe managed to talk his girl, Annette Saxon, into coming out to the West Coast to marry him. Not unlike most men, and especially pilots, he forgot a few essentials. One of them was arranging for a place for the couple to live. Base housing as well as town housing was already overflowing with military couples. In desperation, he took a walk—up and down the beachfront knocking on doors to ask if there was a room available he and his bride could rent.

One owner who answered his knock and opened the door, a young woman, said, "My husband is a pilot too. He's overseas. Bring your bride here; I have plenty of room." That was a good thing for the newlyweds. Time together at Pendleton was limited.

Tragedy struck in March when Lt. Bartlett suffered a fatal accident and again in May when Lt. Freshour was killed in a landing accident. It was a reminder that training accidents were not uncommon. In the forty-five months of participation in the war, the United States suffered 52,651 aircraft accidents, nearly forty a day, involving 6,039 fatalities.

It was time for VMF 323 to head to war. O'Keefe kissed a tearful Annette goodbye at the train station. She, like a lot of young wives, was bound for a long trip home. All the squadron's aircraft were lifted onto the escort carrier USS *Long Island*, CVE-1, a converted steam trawler built in 1939. It had a flight deck only 439 feet long and a maximum speed of sixteen knots. Needless to say, with twenty-four Corsairs tied down on her deck, there was no room for flight operations. When *Long Island* reached Oahu, Hawaii, the aircraft were unloaded by crane at Ford Island. Once on Oahu, Axtell gave the men precious little time for a Hawaiian vacation. There was more training, a lot more, but the major eased off a bit on the pilots. He had molded them into a squadron. Now he would mold that squadron into a lethal fighting team.

As a reminder that danger was always present, tragedy struck again. Lt. Glen Smith crashed into the sea and was killed.

On September 7, the men and their planes were loaded onto another escort carrier, this time the USS *Brenton* CVE 23, converted from a C-3 merchant vessel. It had a 512-foot deck, one catapult, and a maximum speed of nineteen knots. Eleven days later, September 18, they reached their destination: the island of Emirau in the Bismarck Archipelago.

This time the only way to get the Death Rattlers' Corsairs off *Brenton* was to fly them off. It would be the first time for all but a few of the pilots. Major Axtell, his cockpit canopy open, was lined up first. With *Brenton* struggling to make nineteen knots into the wind, Axtell set his trim tabs, dropped thirty degrees of flaps, brought his engine up to forty-five inches of manifold pressure and twenty-seven RPM, braced his hand on the throttle, nodded to the deck chief, and put his head firmly back against the headrest. The catapult fired and off he went! Axtell turned slightly to port, so in case he ditched the ship wouldn't run over him. Gaining sufficient speed, he eased back the stick and climbed away, careful to "milk" the flaps up.

Lt. Gerald Baker, Axtell's wingman, was second in line just in front of Jerry. O'Keefe watched as Baker taxied into position; the catapult bridle that led to the catapult was hooked to the F4U belly. Baker revved his engine to takeoff power. The catapult fired. No one knows what went wrong, but O'Keefe watched in alarm as Baker, turning to port, disappeared.

Jerry, following signals, taxied into position. His plane was hooked to the catapult. Then all plane launches were put on hold. There were no escort vessels near *Brenton* to perform rescue. The ship's skipper turned *Brenton* about to look for Baker. For nearly an hour O'Keefe sat sweating in his open cockpit—sweating partly from the warm sunlight and partly from thinking about Baker and what might have gone wrong. Did the catapult malfunction? Did Baker have engine trouble, or did he try to climb too soon before he had sufficient speed and stall the aircraft into the sea? It didn't help knowing his plane was hooked to the catapult.

Baker was never found. *Brenton* swung back into the wind to recommence launching. A chief climbed up on O'Keefe's wing and yelled into his ear, "We're praying for you, Lieutenant."

"Thanks. I'm praying for me, too." The chief's gesture, meant to comfort the pilot who had been waiting an hour for his turn to launch, only added to Jerry's anxiety.

If the chief of the flight deck thought the crew needed to pray for me, what did they know about the catapult that they weren't telling me? I was scared. I had had plenty of time to double and triple check that everything was correctly set for the catapult shot. The launch captain called for full power. I checked the gauges, all normal, nodded, braced, and was shot off the carrier. I was careful to monitor my airspeed before I started to climb. I didn't want to stall. My Corsair flew as it should, and I was shortly down on Emirau field.

Axtell continued working us, this time with emphasis on close air support (CAS) and navigation. When you make long over-water flights in the Pacific you don't have any landmarks to check your position. A few degrees off and you could miss an island completely.

We put our navigation skills to the test. The VMF 323 Corsairs departed Emirau in small groups for Guadalcanal in the Solomon Islands, the first leg of our flight. There we refueled and continued on to our destination, Luganville Field at Espiritu Santo in the New Hebrides. We already had hard points to hang bombs and napalm, but at Espiritu our planes were fitted with four air-to-ground rocket launchers under each wing. The Corsair proved it was not only a formidable fighter but an attack bomber as well. Out of Espiritu Santo we again practiced close air support, not only dropping bombs but practicing firing rockets.

On March 26, the planes of 323 Squadron were hoisted aboard USS *White Plains*, CVE 66. They were headed for war, triumph, and tragedy. As England was the staging ground for the Allied invasion of Europe, so Okinawa was to be for the invasion of Japan. On April 1, 1945, supported by the largest fleet ever assembled in the Pacific, divisions of both U.S. Marines and U.S. Army landed ashore on the most southern prefecture of Japan, the island of Okinawa, just 340 miles from Kyushu at the southern tip of Japan proper.

On April 9, just after Kadena Airfield had been secured, Marine Squadron 323 flew off *White Plains* to enter the costliest battle of the

Pacific. Joining them to intercept Japanese air attacks from Kyushu were Marine Squadrons 312, 322, and navy carrier-based squadrons. To the west, a British carrier task force, equipped with Supermarine Seafires, was stationed to block Japanese aerial attacks launched from Formosa and the Sakishima Islands.

When we landed at Kadena, a crushed coral strip, we found our luxury quarters waiting: six-man tents with dirt floors. The management did provide cots and mosquito nets as added amenities. Our mess officer, an older marine named Sol Mayer from Bunkie, Louisiana, did a little better. His mess tent had a wooden floor.

VMF 323 was assigned to protect the outer ring of radar destroyers that in turn were protecting the fleet. The Japanese wanted them knocked out. The monsoon season usually runs from May to June, but clouds and rain were already beginning to drift in. On our first day the weather was poor when we took off to fly our initial combat air patrol. On the way back we were flying on instruments in really thick soup. It may have been vertigo, but for whatever reason, Lt. James Brown dropped off on a wing and was lost at sea.

The next day, April 11, Lt. Al Wells made the squadron's first confirmed aerial kill. On April 12, Lieutenants Spangler, Davis, Durnford, Bestwick, and Gruesome Ruhsam each shot down one plane apiece while Capt. Jo Jo MacPhail and Bucko Wade got two each. You would think the Death Rattlers would have celebrated upon their return, but there was no celebration. On the takeoff that morning, a pilot crashed into four other F4Us. Four men were killed, and in the resulting fire a total of eight aircraft were destroyed.

Three days later, on April 15, the Japs threw 185 kamikazes at the U.S. fleet. Bestwick and Ruhsam each added another kill to their score while Bucko Wade added two to his. Lt. Zehring chased an enemy plane into a mountain but was too close and too fast to pull up before slamming into the same mountain.

On the 16th, pilots of the 323 knocked down two Hamps and two Jacks. Lt. Dewey Durnford attacked a Lilly bomber. As it began smoking, the bomber dropped a small, stubby-winged plane from its belly. Dewey, for lack of words to describe what he saw, shouted out, "That thing was carrying a papoose!" The small plane fired up a rocket engine and disappeared in a streak. It was a Japanese secret weapon, a Yokosuka MXY-7 Ohka, otherwise known as the baka-bomb suicide rocket plane. After landing that day, Dewey had to go through a long debriefing on what he had seen while the other pilots got their postflight jigger of whisky.

The Japanese, increasingly desperate, were launching large numbers of kamikazes from Kyushu. Their prized targets were the aircraft carriers and the radar picket destroyers that they knew were giving the fleet early warning. In addition, to harass the Kadena squadrons, Japanese artillery at the island's south end shelled the field intermittently during the day, though rarely interrupting flight operations. At night, to deprive the pilots of sleep, one or two Japanese twin-engine bombers flew across from Kyushu, Japan, and dropped bombs on the field. As a result, the men of the Death Rat-tlers were getting a little rattled themselves, enough so that every tent sported a deep slit trench just outside. It's a good thing. Several empty tents were blown away while their occupants were either flying or had taken shelter in the slit trenches.

It's funny what scares different men. Mindy Muse was terrified of having a bomb land on his head. When bombs began to fall, Mindy would be the first out of his tent and into the slit trench, steel helmet already in place. On the other hand, he went where others feared to go. If Mindy was pursuing a kamikaze headed down for a ship, he would chase him right into the flak coming up from navy gunners—anything to keep a Jap from scoring on a U.S. vessel.

Onshore the Japanese had fortified every ridge, every hill, every mountain, and every cave. For the first time they were fighting on Japanese soil and were fanatically determined to die rather than give up an inch of it. As a result, marine and army troops were paying a terrible price in blood for every foot they advanced over the difficult terrain.

Although the primary mission of the three marine Corsair squadrons flying off Okinawa was to establish and maintain air superiority, they also rotated missions of close air support.

Combat air patrols can pump your adrenaline up, but close air support really gets your attention. Our Corsairs could be loaded with five-inch rockets, bombs, and napalm. We had to struggle to take off with over two thousand pounds of munitions hung under our wings, giving us a gross weight of 14,600 pounds or more. The Corsair could do it, although you didn't do any fancy flying with that kind of load. Troops in a spot would call in air strikes. They marked their lines with cloth panels spread out on the ground or colored smoke, or sometimes just talked us in. The last thing you want to do is hit friendly forces, so you come in low to see friendlies and to hit designated targets, so low you know you can be hit even with rifles. With bombs you have to be careful you are not so low your own bombs take you out. You try to hit the target on the first pass. If you have to come back they'll be ready for you. You could stand off a little to fire rockets. Flying close air support will make a Christian out of any fighter pilot.

The Corsairs must have done the job, for American troops called them the Angels of Okinawa. The Japanese had another name, Whistling Death, because of the sound air made moving at high speed through the oil coolers and air intakes set in the leading edge of the wings.

Flying combat air patrol, the Death Rattlers learned early that not all aircraft on kamikaze raids were unarmed suicide planes. Some had guns, and there were fighters among them to provide protection in the hope of breaking up navy and marine interceptors long enough to allow the kamikazes to get through to hit the ships. They could and did take some American planes out. There came a most memorable day when one such fighter took on Lt. O'Keefe in an unconventional way and came so very close, literally, to knocking him down.

On April 22, 1945, a flight of eight Corsairs led by Major Axtell received word from one of the radar picket destroyers that a large number of bogeys were approaching from the north. The Death Rattlers changed course to intercept what turned out to be eighty kamikazes headed for the U.S. fleet. When VMF 323 made visual contact they were flying a few thousand feet higher than the Japanese formation. Axtell led his pilots in a descending turn calculated to bring them in just above and behind the enemy. In the melee that followed there were planes all over the sky. Just avoiding a midair collision took vigilance, skill, and maybe luck.

There were so many you just picked out one and went for it. In a shallow dive I nearly overshot the first one but managed to hit him. He flamed and went into the sea. I exploded the next one so close that I had to pull up to avoid hitting debris. Pulling up and over I flamed another one. I had excess speed so I zoomed up, rolled over, and was able to get on one from above. He exploded. I had overshot the pack and turned back. That's when I met one that had guns. We exchanged fire in a head-on pass. On the first pass I thought I made some hits. I turned hard trying not to lose him. The Jap pilot was good and fast. He had already turned around and was closer than I thought he would be. He was trailing smoke so I knew I had hit him. He must have thought he was through because it suddenly became coldly clear to me that he intended to end it by ramming me. I mean, no matter that I fired at him, he just kept coming and fast. I reckon our closing speed must have been close to six hundred miles an hour. He was there in my face so fast that I was sure he had me. I pulled back on the stick as hard as I could and nearly blacked out. I don't know how he missed me. I turned hard again, afraid he was coming back, but saw he was headed for the ocean. I thought he was trying for a ship so I followed him down, got close, fired a burst, and he exploded. I was suddenly tired and wringing wet. When I looked around everyone was gone, not a plane in the sky. My guys, until they ran out of ammunition, had chased after the pack of remaining kamikazes. There had been too many for us to get them all.

Jerry landed with three rounds left in one gun and eight in another. The other four guns were empty. The Corsair carried 385 to 400 rounds per gun, about thirty seconds' worth of ammunition.

VMF 323 set a record that day. The Death Rattlers had shot down twenty-four Japanese planes in thirty minutes and come home with three new aces, the Skipper, the XO, and Lt. O'Keefe.

That night Sol Mayer, our mess officer, came out with steaks, which we had not seen since we arrived and which he probably stole from the navy, and beer. April 22 belonged to the Death Rattlers and we had one fine celebration.

Speaking of Sol, he was a character. One day I was walking back from the flight line when he came roaring up in a jeep and told me to get in. I did before I noticed he had a carbine and his forty-five on his belt, all unusual for Sol. He tore off down a road I had never been on. "Where we going, Sol?" He told me how bad he felt being just a mess officer, that he wanted to get in a shot at the Japs and that he had just heard that a bunch of them had landed on Moon Beach and we were going to help take them out. "Why me, Sol," I asked him. "Well you got a pistol and I didn't want to go alone." I was young and stupid, and I liked Sol, so I rode around all over that side of the island like Sancho Panza with Don Quixote. We never found any Japs. Dejectedly, Sol drove back to the squadron. That evening he found out there had been no Jap landing. It was all a rumor.

April 28, I was one of a flight of twelve Corsairs led by Axtell. We were tasked with protecting the hundreds of ships unloading supplies off Okinawa. I was leader of the first section with Bill Hood flying my wing. It was a sunny day, and we had turned east at about twelve thousand feet. Constantly looking up, down, and all around, I spotted five dots in formation several thousand feet below us, called them out to the skipper, and told him I thought they must be bogeys because we never flew a five-plane formation—two, four, eight, but not five. Axtell said he didn't see anything down there. I had very good eyesight back then and was sure of what I saw. I asked the skipper to allow my section to investigate. He gave the OK. With Hood on my wing, I began a wide, descending turn to the north to place us slightly above and behind the five planes heading south. As we got closer and identified them as Japanese, I called it in to Axtell. Hood and I armed our guns. I positioned myself at their five o'clock and Hood at their seven o'clock. The bandits were older, fixed-gear Ki-27 Nates headed for our fleet. They seemed unaware of us and made no move to evade. I was in a shallow dive and a little fast. I nearly overshot my first target, opened fire at three hundred yards, and the Nate exploded. I pulled up and around to the right, planning to make another run when I saw a single plane had broken away and was diving for the ocean. I used my speed to get on his tail and exploded him. I was again alone. I climbed back up, found and joined our patrol. I learned that Hood had downed two and Axtell one. That accounted for all five of the Nates.

Lt. Jeremiah J. O'Keefe, with seven kills, was top gun at VMF 323. The month of April 1945 clearly belonged to the Death Rattlers. They had shot down fifty-four Japanese planes. The pilots of VMF 323 had vindicated the hard and thorough training Major Axtell had put them through.

The news was never all good. On May 5, Major Arthur Turner's plane was hit while flying close air support. He pulled up and bailed out of his flaming Corsair only to land too close to Japanese lines. They killed him. On May 13, First Lieutenant Murray was killed during another close air support mission. On May 16, Second Lieutenant Reynolds was killed making a forced landing after his engine was shot out.

Despite such losses, the Death Rattlers set another record for the month of May by shooting down fifty-two enemy planes. The squadron now had twelve aces. Sol Mayer hung a sign over the entrance of the Death Rattlers chow tent that read, "Mayer's Mess Where Aces Meet to Eat."

The Death Rattlers moved to Awase Air Field. Kadena was being improved to handle army air force bombers. A group of army air force P-47 Thunderbolts, flown off a carrier, had already moved in, all in preparation for attacks on mainland Japan.

By mid-June the eighty-two-day battle of Okinawa was won. VMF 323 Death Rattlers were credited with 124 enemy planes shot down. At the top of the list of its aces stood the name of twenty-one-year-old Marine First Lieutenant Jeremiah J. O'Keefe from Biloxi, Mississippi.

The Death Rattlers was the highest-scoring squadron in the Okinawa campaign and was awarded both a Presidential Unit Citation and a Navy Unit Commendation. The squadron paid a price. They had lost sixteen pilots to combat, not counting several to operational accidents.

With Okinawa secured, VMF 323 began flying eight-hundred-mile round-trip missions out of Awase to attack Japan proper at Kyushu. About that same time three replacement pilots arrived. This created three slots for rotation home to be chosen from among the remaining original squadron members. Their names were placed in a hat, and three lucky winners emerged from the drawing. O'Keefe's was one of them.

I thought about going on one more mission with the squadron to hit Japan, but good sense prevailed. I had a wife at home and a daughter I had never seen.

Jerry's travel orders home stated "space available" on military aircraft. Such space was scarce. His journey across the Pacific entailed hitching a ride aboard one C-47 transport after another whenever he could find space available to the next island waypoint.

The Golden Gate Bridge was a beautiful sight. Like all sensible men returning from the Pacific, I put on my best uniform and went to the Top of the Mark in San Francisco to celebrate a little—okay, a lot, before heading home. Home! What a wonderful word.

If you ask Jerry O'Keefe if he was scared he will answer, "You bet I was. We all were." O'Keefe refuses to allow the word "hero" to be used in reference to his military service. "We did our duty as it was given to us, did our bit for our country like everyone else."

JERRY O'KEEFE CAME HOME to Biloxi with a pocket full of medals including the Navy Cross and the Distinguished Flying Cross. His bride, Annette, and their baby daughter were thrilled to have him return home safely. Jerry laughs and said Annette was not always thrilled to have him home. You see, she wound up giving him thirteen children. With such a large family as an inspiration, Jerry went on to expand the family business across several states and created an insurance company, but business success could not absorb all of his

energy. Jerry became a state congressman and later took a turn as mayor of Biloxi. Today he quietly and philanthropically supports his community. At this writing, Jerry had just celebrated his ninetieth birthday and is going strong.

AFTERMATH OF THE
BATTLE OF OKINAWA

U.S. LOSSES

The American casualties during the eighty-two-day battle for a sixty-mile-long island were appalling.

- U.S. Army and Marine combined troop casualties: 62,000 (756 a day) of which 12,500 were killed (152 a day). Many more would later die of their wounds.
- U.S. vessel losses: 36 sunk and 368 damaged.
- U.S. Navy losses: 9,844 casualties (120 a day) of which over half, 4,970 (60 a day), were killed; the highest death toll of any navy engagement and nearly equal to that of the army or marines.
- U.S. aircraft loses: 458 aircraft to combat; 310 to operational accidents.

JAPANESE LOSSES

- One hundred thousand soldiers fought to the death. Ten thousand surrendered, the largest number of the war.
- An equal number of civilians, one third of the population, were killed or committed suicide.

The tremendous casualties inflicted on U.S. forces by the uncompromising ferocity of the Japanese defense of Okinawa led U.S. leaders to desperately search for a way to end the war without ordering an invasion of Japan proper. President Harry Truman said in effect that he did not want to see the Battle of Okinawa repeated along the entire shore of the nation of Japan. Using the hard evidence gathered from the battles of Okinawa, Iwo Jima, and Saipan, studies estimated that the invasion of Japan could result in half a million U.S. deaths and many more casualties, and an estimated four or more million Japanese casualties. Many believe these estimates led to the decision to use the atomic bomb, which ended the war with Japan on August 14, 1945.

CHAPTER 16

THE HOME FRONT

CHILDHOOD MEMORIES ARE NEVER filed neatly away. They lie in piles of singular outstanding moments thrown like abandoned toys into some distant corner. Like the child we were that hides somewhere in the adult we become, such moments, pleasant or painful, return at odd moments, triggered by something we see or read, by some event, sound, or odor. The fiftieth anniversary of World War II was such a trigger for those of us who were children then. For a moment, the child in me looked back on those dark, distant, hard, exciting, glorious, and frightening years. The words below are those of that child.

SUNDAY, DECEMBER 7, 1941
Tuscaloosa, Alabama—Granddaddy's House

My grandmother sat with me on the living-room carpet and read the funny papers spread out before us. I was five years old. In front of us was the centerpiece of the room: the grand mahogany console radio. Its huge, round, glowing dial was tuned to a local station. Suddenly Grandmother stopped reading, got to her feet, and turned up the volume on the radio. Granddaddy put down his paper, told everyone to hush.

I had never seen adults so unsmiling and quiet—and something else. They were fearful. Children instinctively recognize fear in adults. The words "WAR!" and "Oh, God!" were uttered by the grownups standing over me, standing on the funny papers in front of the radio.

Tom Beauchamp was my uncle. He was tall and kind and good-looking and some said as wild as a March hare, but I didn't know what that meant. He disappeared after that Sunday. Then, one day, I was told that Peter White, Tom's best friend, was going to take me somewhere special and that I was to mind him. That did not seem unusual to me. When visiting Granddaddy, Tom and Peter often took me places with them, sometimes to get ice cream at a drugstore soda fountain or to a playground. I think they talked to girls while I ate ice cream and played.

What was unusual is that, when Peter picked me up, he was wearing a uniform. He drove me out to Vandergraff Field where I saw rows of tents and trucks and cannon and lots of soldiers marching everywhere, with dust rising over everything. I didn't know big words like "disorganized" or "confused" at the time, but that's the way I remember that field of men suddenly called to war.

Peter took me to one of the tents. Tom was in uniform there with other soldiers. They had real guns. When Peter said we had to go, I thought Tom would come with us, but he didn't. I didn't know the difference, but Peter was an officer and Tom was an enlisted man. Tom picked me up and told me to behave myself while he was gone. I didn't understand.

Peter led me by the hand across the field to the white two-story airport terminal building, up some stairs, and into a room where a group of older men, dressed in uniforms like Peter's, were sitting at a long table. I didn't know then (but I know now) that this day was Peter's and Tom's way of telling me good-bye. Peter had somehow arranged for me to be a guest at the officers mess of a unit of the Alabama National Guard on its way to hell.

It was a very exciting day for a five-year-old. Yes sir! I was going to be a soldier, too! And so I was, so were we all, the children in my neighborhood.

Concepts of time, of years, are beyond comprehension to children. War was the long, long year during which we grew up. Bombs never reached us, but the war did.

Suddenly everyone had a father, brother, uncle, or granddaddy in the war. I remember my father's leaving several times on "special trips." Mama cried when he left and cried when he came home. I later learned that he kept trying to enlist but was turned down repeatedly, the last time by the marines. I later learned that the navy doctor there told him, "Any man who is thirty-one, totally blind in one eye, with a wife and child, should stop acting like a fool and go home."

Along the Gulf Coast every window was fitted with a blackout curtain. Streetlights were painted black on the seaward side. Automobile headlights were covered half over with black tape or paint, and when a car turned down a street toward the shoreline the driver had to turn off the headlights altogether.

All of this was not for practice, nor was it "playing war." It was done for real and desperate reasons. German submarines prowled the Gulf offshore at night. Any ship silhouetted against lights on shore made an easy target for an enemy sub. My father was a volunteer Civil Defense warden. Late one night he woke me and took me down to the sea wall. A handful of other people were gathered there and looking out across the darkness at a faint orange glow far out to sea. Dad told me that it was one of our ships burning, that a German submarine had torpedoed it. (Military secrets like that were hard to keep in coastal-port towns.) There were murmurs of "those poor men burning at sea." It scared me, but I didn't say so. I knew I had seen a real piece of the war, and it was just over the horizon.

The idea of air raids on Gulfport seems silly now. It wasn't then, not to the children. If there were no real air raids, there were plenty of practice ones. They were frightening enough. Just up the street from our house an air-raid siren was installed on the roof of the neighborhood grocery. It sounded like the ones in London we heard on the radio, and in the newsreels at the movies. When that thing went off at night, its mournful wailing sent chills down everyone's spine, child or adult. Blackout curtains were pulled down or the lights turned off. Streetlights went out. Cars pulled to the side of the road and switched off their headlights.

Neighborhood air-raid wardens with their white World War I steel helmets went out in the darkness and patrolled the streets to make sure everyone was following blackout procedures. (No one worried about crime or looting during blackouts; there was none.) Sometimes small airplanes with loudspeakers would fly just over the treetops and shout down things like "Cut off that light!" and "Put out that cigarette down there!" Some of the adults may have laughed, but the children didn't. We had seen newsreels of the London blitz. We knew that children got bombed.

You could walk down the street of any neighborhood in town and see small banners, each with a star in the middle, hanging with pride (and heartfelt fear) in the front windows of homes. Each star represented a loved one in uniform. There were other stars, too, the gold ones that were put on the pictures and by the names of the boys who would not come home again.

A day came early in the war when our neighborhood learned its first boy had been killed. Everyone walked down the street to the boy's home. The little crowd stood quietly in the front yard. I held my mother's hand. The family came out on the front porch, and some of the people walked up and touched them and said things softly. All had come to show they cared. The same scene was being repeated all over the country, but this was our neighborhood. The real war had come to our street.

If the war was real to the adults on the home front, it was surreal to the children. We played nothing but war, had no toys but toy soldiers, planes, boats, and guns. We dug trenches and foxholes and built bunkers covered with logs and dirt in the surrounding woods. We built tanks and planes and boats. They were only paper boxes and wooden crates, but they were real to us. We acted out the war movies we saw on Saturday afternoons, took turns fighting bravely as Americans or dying dramatically as the enemy. We were good children who never thought of hurting anyone nice, just killing the enemy. We learned to sing "Praise the Lord and Pass the Ammunition" and pulled our little wagons around to collect aluminum pots and pans, iron scrap, bundles of old newspapers and magazines. In our kitchens at home we cut the bottoms out of empty tin cans and stomped them flat, rolled tin toothpaste tubes into tight balls, saved bacon grease in jars, and took all of this to the grocery stores, which had collection barrels for such items. I don't know if it really helped the war effort, but it helped us; we were doing something for our country. We were helping.

Once a month we brought things to school—toothbrushes, toothpaste, washcloths, soap, candy bars, basic little necessities—and packed them into small white boxes with red crosses on them to send to American boys who were in prison camps and to children in war-torn countries.

Years later I was told by older folks that the Gulf Coast was a rough place during the war. The army built two airfields, Keesler Field and Gulfport Field; a merchant marine school was established at Henderson Point, and the Coast Guard was expanded. Merchant seamen were in town from the ships that moved in and out of the port. Ingalls Shipyard was bursting at the seams. And there was a new branch of the navy, the Seabees, that built a base in Gulfport. The coast provided recreation for all of them. Officially, there were church suppers and USO dances. Unofficially, along the Biloxi strip, there were nightclubs and bars. There were also pretty girls to fight over, about one for every five hundred boys in uniform.

The Seabees were altogether a different breed of volunteers. They weren't young kids like in the rest of the services, not the first ones. They were construction workers, many in their late thirties and forties, and a lot of them older than that. They already knew how to build roads, buildings, and airfields, and they knew how to drink, cuss, and brawl, as younger men who called them things like "Pop" and "Old-Timer" quickly found out. They were sent to Gulfport to learn a little military discipline (for which they didn't care a whit) and for combat training before shipping out to the Pacific.

I was too young to know about any of that. My dad had a café in downtown Gulfport. It smelled of strong coffee and hamburgers and was always crowded with men in uniform. The big jukebox played "Boogie Woogie," "Swing," "Jitterbug," or a sad song sung by some lady with a pretty voice.

Every week hundreds of men shipped out and new ones arrived to take their place. All felt they might not be coming back. Sometimes when I was downtown to see my dad, a soldier or sailor or an older Seabee would come up to me and say he had a little boy just like me at home, that he was going overseas tomorrow, then he would try to hand me money and tell me to buy a toy with it. I was taught to be very polite and say I couldn't take the money. Mother explained that they were just sad that they were leaving their little boys behind to go far away to war. I knew they were sad because some of them had tears in their eyes when they bent down to give me money. It was hard for me, too. I didn't know soldiers cried. I was suddenly glad they wouldn't let my daddy go to war.

The small-craft harbor was off-limits to civilians. All the yachts went to war. They were painted navy gray and assigned submarine picket duty offshore. Many of their owners were commissioned into the Coast Guard and commanded their own boats. I got to see them and to visit the airfields because Dad always knew someone who would take me to see such places.

An air-sea rescue squadron of fast patrol boats was set up at the Coast Guard air station at Point Cadet in Biloxi. They were needed. My father took me to see a bomber that had ditched in the Gulf, not far off the sea wall, and another time to see one that had crash-landed in the bayou behind Handsboro.

Homes were not air-conditioned. During hot summer evenings, neighbors would bring their lawn chairs and gather in one front yard or another to chat (sometimes have a little bourbon in their Coca-Colas) while the children played or sat on the ground and listened to the grownups talk. Our street was within the traffic pattern of the bombers that constantly flew training missions and submarine patrols out of Gulfport Field. At night, returning from the Gulf, their brilliant landing lights would suddenly blaze out of the darkness as they entered the landing pattern. It was a beautiful and exciting sight. One night a bomber flew low overhead with one engine engulfed in a huge ball of fire—flames trailing far behind the wing, bits of burning fuel, oil, and molten metal falling away.

"Bless those boys!"

"They'll make it, honey."

"That engine is going to drop right off and start a fire down here."

"Don't you say things like that in front of these children!"

"Before it's over, we'll be lucky if one of them doesn't crash right on the street."

We children listened and looked wide-eyed at the flaming plane streak across the night sky. It was exciting and frightening and somehow glorious. It was the war right there in the night sky over us.

Everything was rationed. Mother had one coin purse for money and another for ration stamps and tokens. It took both to buy things like coffee, meat, sugar, and shoes for home and family or gasoline and tires for automobiles. I don't remember going without anything, except Dubble Bubble Gum (which I think went to war with the soldiers). It seemed that everyone had a little chicken pen and a victory garden in the back yard. There was always plenty of food for the children at East Ward Grammar School, but we had to eat everything on our plates before we were allowed to go out to play at noon recess. The teachers reminded us at every meal that there were little children starving all over the world. (I am very careful of how much I put on my plate to this day, for I cannot leave food on my plate without feeling guilty over starving children somewhere in the world.)

Buses ran every half-hour on most streets. They were always crowded. Even those who owned cars rode them, because gasoline rationing allowed only three gallons a week for each private automobile. On Saturday afternoons one of the older children would take a string of us downtown on the bus to one of the three movie

No other wartime measure impacted as many Americans at home as much as rationing. Each month the Office of Price Administration released new figures, and families received an allotment of ration books: blue for canned goods and red for meat, poultry, and fish. Individuals were allocated forty-eight blue points and sixty-four red points monthly.

theaters. Most of us got a twenty-five-cent allowance. The movie cost fifteen cents for which, in addition to the film, we also got to see a newsreel, an adventure serial, and a cartoon. We had three choices of how to spend the dime we had left. We could buy a box of popcorn or candy at the theater, a comic book at the newsstand after the movie, or we could help win the war.

The movies always played a short appeal to buy war bonds, which were sold in the lobby. Children never had enough money to buy a twenty-five-dollar bond, but we were given little books of cartoons superimposed with stamp-sized squares. The cartoons made fun of Hitler, Tojo, and Mussolini. A stamp cost ten cents, and when you had enough stamps to "wipe out" all the cartoons of the enemy, you could trade the book in for a bond. If we saw a cowboy movie, usually the popcorn or the funny book won out, but if we saw a war movie, pasting a stamp over Hitler's or Tojo's kisser won. (It took me almost the entire war to fill out a book and proudly trade it in for a twenty-five-dollar war bond.)

Parents weren't concerned about their children riding buses to town or playing outside on summer nights or going into the woods to play. The thought never entered their minds that anyone would hurt a child in those days, and no one did. Nor were parents concerned about what we saw at the movies. Hollywood had a code of decency in those days. People got killed in war movies, and there was a little blood (I'm told chocolate syrup was used when filming in black and white), but there was no depiction of guts and body parts blown all over the screen in slow motion and close-up detail as is the norm today. As for sex on the silver screen—adults must have been considered a lot more intelligent back then. They were actually given credit for having enough imagination to figure out what went on when sweethearts were kissing and the camera panned up to the stars above.

Letters were written on paper as thin as tissue so as many letters per pound as possible could be transported to and from the men overseas. It was called V-Mail; the V stood for "victory." Occasionally letters arrived from Uncle Tom. They always said he was "fine and not to worry" and "Tell Tommy hello." That last part was big stuff! I always wanted to write and ask how many Germans he had killed, but of course, I wasn't allowed to ask such a terrible question. He killed many, it turned out, and he saw many of his men fall around him. He never quite got over it.

He started in Belgium as a sergeant, quickly received a battlefield commission, fought all the way into Germany to the end of the war, and came home a much-decorated captain. He commanded his unit from an armored half-track in an armored infantry outfit that suffered heavy casualties. He never talked about the war. Still kind and handsome, the boy who had gone to war came home a man who could never quite fit into a steady civilian routine. He had a quiet, desperately hard time, I think. Tom is dead now, but he is still my hero. He kept the enemy out of Gulfport, and he did it for me. They all did, for all the children at home, and for new generations that don't seem to know or perhaps care much about it. Maybe that's reason enough to tell this now.

The Western Union bicycle delivery boy was a dreaded visitor in those times. Everyone took note when he stopped in the neighborhood. "We" got a telegram. It was addressed to Mrs. James, a widow whose two sons were in uniform. It was our telegram, I reckoned, because we all lived under the same roof. There was a housing shortage, and we rented an apartment in the back of Mrs. James's home.

The little teletype strips glued on thin yellow paper said that her son Jiggs's plane had been shot down over Germany and he was missing in action. It was better than the telegrams that began, "We regret to inform you . . . ," but it was terrible enough. Jiggs was "my pilot," smiling out at us from the picture sitting on his mama's mantle. He had sent me letters, and like Uncle Tom, he was my hero. Those "dirty Germans" had shot him down! My friends and I talked for days about how we were going to grow up real fast so we could fight the Germans and Japs to make them leave America alone.

Word finally came from the Red Cross that Jiggs was alive and a prisoner in Germany. He received good care in a German hospital before being interned in a prison camp where he found a high school friend from Gulfport. Happily, they both came home.

I find it hard to believe that I was only nine years old when the war ended. Admittedly much of my understanding of the war's causes and effects have come from postwar study and from informed observation of the political and economic events that were and continue to be influenced by World War II. Still, the real feelings and insight I possess of that intense period of history come from the depth and vividness and honesty of a child's memory.

Talking with my peers, I find that my experience is not unique. How could children have such accurate and clear memories of that war? Certainly part of the answer is that unlike the Korean and Vietnam conflicts, the whole country was involved daily, not just as observers of news programs, but as participants. It was not business as usual. It was not guns *and* butter for America. The cause was larger than politics, larger than self-interest, and demanded something of every man, woman, and child in the country. Everyone played a part, made a contribution, sacrificed something, shared in a common cause if ever there was one. And they knew it. All wars are started for political reasons, and politicians and generals have often been wasteful of other people's sons, but for the Allies, World War II was as it was perceived to be by the people: a desperate and terrible struggle against unquestioned blind obedience to the leadership of dictators whose dreams were evil.

Whether it was rolling bandages, knitting sweaters, packing Red Cross boxes, buying war bonds, working in factories and shipyards, standing in line for ration stamps, collecting scrap, putting blackout curtains over the windows, or praying for loved ones and peace, people on the American home front, including the children, were reminded there was a war on and that "their" boys were in harm's way, fighting a war that had to be won no matter what.

If children on the American home front did not suffer bombings and were spared some of the visual horror of war due to the discretion of the news media and Hollywood and the absence of television, they were certainly aware of the courage and sacrifice of the men who were fighting. They placed their hands over their hearts and pledged allegiance to the Stars and Stripes every morning at school, and they knew what the words meant. They sang "God Bless America" and grew up believing the most beautiful flag in the world does indeed, by the grace of God and the personal sacrifices of good men and women, fly over the land of the free and the home of the brave. Corny? Perhaps. Outdated? Let's hope not. Still proudly held in the hearts and childhood memories of those who grew up on the home front? You bet.

Epilogue

THE SENSE OF DUTY, perseverance, and sacrifice of but a few young men are recounted in this work, but their stories vividly illustrate how an entire generation of Americans somehow found within themselves the courage and determination to overcome their natural fears, put aside their personal desires and the good times of youth to fight a war not of their making. Why? Why did America, safe behind two great oceans, send its young men to fight a war at so great a cost?

The reason cannot be better illustrated than by the words of the leader of Nazi Germany in revealing a goal that can only be described as evil: "We do not intend to abolish the inequality of man. . . . There will be a great hierarchy of [Nazi] party members. They will be the new middle class. And there will be a great mass of the anonymous and serving collective, the eternally disenfranchised. Beneath them there will be the class of subject alien races—we need not hesitate to call them the northern slave class."

The goals of the Axis power of the Far East, the Supreme War Council of Japan, dominated by Gen. Hideki Tojo (war minister and later premier), were no different. As evidenced by the cruelty exhibited by the Imperial Japanese armed forces toward the defeated peoples of Asia and the Pacific and toward Allied prisoners of war, there is little doubt that rule of the Pacific Rim by the Japanese militarists would have resulted in a society similar to that envisioned by Hitler.

The Axis powers—Germany, Italy, and Japan—came frighteningly close to achieving their goals. By November 1941, while America remained neutral, Germany and Italy occupied nearly all of Europe, the Baltic States, Greece, the Balkans, North Africa, Norway, and much of Russia. Only the British Isles held on. Desperate for food, fuel, arms, and materiel, the only hope of the British was aid from the United States. By May 1942, Japan, having nearly destroyed the U.S.

Pacific Fleet at Pearl Harbor as part of a plan to conquer the Pacific Rim, occupied Manchuria, much of China, Burma, Korea, French Indochina (Vietnam, Laos, Cambodia, Thailand), Malayasia, Singapore, Hong Kong, the Netherlands East Indies, much of New Guinea, the Philippines, and the smaller islands of the Pacific Ocean from Kiska in the Aleutian Islands to the north to the Solomon Islands in the south. The light of freedom was flickering dimly like a candle in the wind with darkness descending.

If England had been allowed to fall, there would have been no Allied invasion of Europe, no western front. Germany could have concentrated all her military might toward conquering Russia, North Africa, and the Near East. In the Far East there was no one left with the ability to wage war against Japan. Both Germany and Japan would have been glad to negotiate a treaty with the United States, the last and only remaining threat to their respective new empires, glad to isolate the last great democracy, which they knew was, at the time, woefully unprepared to wage war at all, much less on two fronts. The Axis powers would have been glad to lay the United States aside for a later day. Germany would have been free to conquer Russia and, with Italy, rule all of Europe, the whole of North Africa, and the oil fields of the Arab nations. Japan would have been free to add India and China to her conquests. Such a scenario was possible unless the United States made a full, unconditional commitment to join the Allies in the defense of freedom.

The American people, even though shocked, shaken, and fearful, could not and did not stand by to watch freedom disappear from the world around them. Almost too late, they joined the Allies in war at a time when the outcome was in doubt.

Without diminishing the valiant effort expended at a terrible cost by all Allied forces, it was, in the end, American industry, agriculture, blood, tears, and dogged determination at home and abroad that slowly, painfully changed the odds to bring about the Allied victory over the Axis powers.

The cost was horribly high. World War II saw more than seventy million men in uniform, nearly fourteen million of whom were American. The number of soldiers killed, both Allied and Axis, totaled at least fifteen million. At least three times that number were wounded, many of them crippled and maimed for life. The numbers are even higher for noncombatants. More than thirteen million civilians are estimated to have died directly from bombing, shelling, crossfire, and starvation, and this figure does not include the uncountable millions of civilian deaths in China and eastern Asia, nor civilian deaths from deliberate massacre. More than fifteen million men, women, and children died in concentration camps, including six million Jews. It is estimated that, in addition, as many as sixteen million Poles and Russians were massacred during the Axis occupation of those countries.

America's armed contribution to victory was won by the perseverance and sacrifice of young (their average age when they went to war was twenty) men like Bruce Creekmur, Ed Anderson, Mitt Evans, Jac Smith, Mike Kelly, Ferd Moyse, Fred Koval, Knox White, Harry Bell, Amos Pollard, Owen Palmer, Dee Hamilton, Joe Irby, Oscar Russell, Jeremiah O'Keefe, and nearly fourteen million more young Americans like them, many of whom never returned or returned shattered, sick, and broken.

Old men now, the surviving veterans of World War II are dying at a rate of more than three hundred thousand a year. Let us not forget what they did, how hard it was for them daily—the physical discomfort, fear, pain, and mortal danger—and that they somehow found the strength and courage to prevail in the face of it all. Every American, regardless of age or station in life, and each generation that follows has an obligation, individually and collectively, to make certain that the leadership of America, however imperfect in this imperfect world, nonetheless maintains our nation's strength, moral character, courage, and determination to remain a free republic founded upon individual liberty. We owe nothing less to that quietly departing generation as we ride the freedom they preserved for us into the twenty-first century.

THOMAS E. SIMMONS grew up in Mississippi and attended Marion Military Institute, the U.S. Naval Academy, the University of Southern Mississippi, and the University of Alabama. He has been a pilot since he was sixteen. When he was stationed in Korea in the late 1950s, he was an artillery officer. Simmons is the author of two other books, *The Brown Condor* and *Escape from Archangel*.